What they say about this book

D1476016

Larry Telles told me a few years ago he wanted to document the lives of two all but forgotten stars of the silent screen – Helen Holmes and Helen Gibson. Since they both got their starts as serial stars in "The Hazards of Helen," he wasn't sure if each should have a separate book to document their careers or one book that would include both. Larry made the right choice. Helen Gibson's life as one of the early luminaries of the silent screen and who made movies her life for about 50 years deserved a book – and what a book it is. Larry's telling of this star's exploits, daring, professional success, admiration by her fans and durability will amaze the reader. In the days when trick photography wasn't an option and stars did their own stunts, Helen Gibson ranked with the best of the "stunters," male or female – brushing off injuries as a hazard of the trade and moving on to the next more daring, more spectacular feat on the screen. Her days as a rodeo star and subsequent rise to stardom in "The Hazards of Helen" provide engrossing reading. Moving on to starring feature roles in the twenties, she didn't let sound slow her down as she continued doing stunt work and bit parts. "Helen Gibson: Silent Serial Queen" is a deserved tribute to one of the silent cinema's most interesting and brightest stars, and kudos to Larry Telles for bringing us her story in such an enjoyable and well-researched read.

Tim Lussier, SilentsareGolden.com

Reading the lifestory of Helen Gibson is equivalent to a journey back in time, in which Telles brings to life the dawn of the Hollywood movie industry, focusing specifically on westerns. That the story highlights an intriguing woman determined to succeed in a male-dominated industry elevates this author's work to a historical gem.

The vehicle that transports the reader on this fascinating trip is the commendable research that flows through in the author's clear writing style; we are privy to this ambitious young woman's hopes and dreams, successes and drawbacks. Each movie theme is condensed into its basic premise and sets the stage for Helen's daring stunts. The sheer number of personal and professional pictures, on their own not only reveal Helen's story, they also leave an unforgettable image of this fascinating woman.

In the Preface, Larry Telles states that the lifestory of Helen Gibson came to him by divine intervention, and after reading *Helen Gibson, Silent Serial Queen,* I concur!

Patti Dickinson, Author of Hollywood the Hard Way

With the publication of HELEN GIBSON, SILENT SERIAL QUEEN, Larry Telles has produced a delightfully candid, thoroughly researched and detailed account of a remarkable woman whose multi-faceted career included the rodeo, the wild west show, silent film, the circus, vaudeville, sound film, and perhaps most importantly, the professional stunt work that extended throughout her career, a career spanning more than fifty years.

The Author has brought together in one volume a vast array of extremely rare photographs and documents, many loaned by Helen Gibson's own family members that shed a revealing light on an otherwise quite enigmatic figure. In addition, the Author has conducted an exhaustive search among a wide variety of other resources: genealogical records; court house documents; film trade periodicals; newspapers and popular magazines; brochures and advertisements; even wild west show and circus route books!

Last but definitely not least, Larry Telles has made his subject come to life in a most entertaining fashion—all flesh and blood and bruises. He has succeeded in presenting for us an authoritative and illuminating account of this complex, fascinating and immensely talented woman who, one can easily believe, if she were alive today, would be very pleased with this book and proud of the story it tells at long last, *her story: the story of Helen Gibson, rodeo star, stunt woman, screen actress and serial queen.*

Sam Gill, Film Historian, Niles Essanay Silent Film Museum

Author Larry Telles brings a glorious new biography of silent film star Helen Gibson to bookstores in "Helen Gibson: Silent Serial Queen Who Became Hollywood's first professional Stunt Woman." Helen Gibson entered show business as a stunt rider in the 101 Ranch Real Wild West Show. As she worked the Wild West show and participated in various rodeos, her talents would soon be beckoned by the emerging business of silent pictures. Telles delightfully threads stories of Helen's career, personal life with details about her work in her films and the film industry as a whole. The book contains a plethora of artwork (movie posters, fliers, etc.), portrait photography and movie still images that bring to life all of Helen's incredible life. Bringing all of these aspects together, Telles offers up a compelling biography that will have you mesmerized by this talented woman that was ahead of her time.

Helen is one of many silent film actresses that contributed more to film than just their pretty demeanor and acting abilities. For Helen, her talent for performing risky, yet entertaining stunts gave her a long career in the new business of filmmaking. Telles' biography of Helen Gibson proves that the many stars of the early days of the movie industry have been overlooked for their contributions and this true story of this amazing actress and stunt woman will forever cement Helen Gibson as a true movie pioneer.

Kay Shackleton, Silenthollywood.com

It is so important that these remarkable but neglected stars, who contributed so much to the industry, be brought out of the shadows. You have done proud by Helen Gibson.

Kevin Brownlow, Film Historian

OTHER BOOKS FROM BITTERROOT MOUNTAIN PUBLISHING

Bitterroot Mountain Authors, Phantasma 1, 2013, ISBN 978-1-940025-06-3, Kindle

Neil Bricco, Wisdom of the Wound, 2013, ISBN 978-1-940025-00-1, Kindle
Neil Bricco, Wisdom of the Wound, 2013, ISBN 978-1-940025-01-8, Trade Paperback

Dr. Mark William Cochran, Oby's Wisdom, 2012, ISBN 978-0-9852784-0-3, Kindle
Dr. Mark William Cochran, Oby's Wisdom, 2010, ISBN 978-0-9817874-6-6, Trade Paperback

Patti Dickinson, Hollywood the Hard Way, 2012, ISBN 978-0-9852784-2-7, Kindle
Patti Dickinson, Indian's Daughter, 2011, ISBN 978-0-9817874-7-3, Trade Paperback
Patti Dickinson, Indian's Daughter, 2011, ISBN 978-0-9817874-9-7, Kindle

Ana Parker Goodwin , Forbidden Justice, 2012, ISBN 978-0-9852784-1-0, Kindle

Darla Isackson, Finding Hope While Grieving Suicide, 2013, ISBN 978-1-940025-5, Kindle
Darla Isackson, Finding Hope While Grieving Suicide, 2013, ISBN 978-1-940025-03-2, Trade Paperback

Dottie Malley, Downey Parke, 2013, ISBN 978-1-940025-04-9, Kindle
Dottie Malley, Downey Parke, 2013, ISBN 978-1-940025-05-6, Trade Paperback

Bobby Wilhelm, Bobby Convict, 2012, ISBN 978-0-9852784-8-9, Trade Paperback
Bobby Wilhelm, Bobby Convict, 2012, ISBN 978-0-9852784-7-2, Hardcover
Bobby Wilhelm, Bobby Convict, 2012, ISBN 978-0-9852784-4-1, Nook
Bobby Wilhelm, Bobby Convict, 2012, ISBN 978-0-9852784-3-4, Kindle

HELEN GIBSON
SILENT SERIAL QUEEN

WHO BECAME HOLLYWOOD'S
FIRST PROFESSIONAL STUNT WOMAN

Bitterroot Mountain
PUBLISHING, LLC.

HELEN
GIBSON
SILENT SERIAL QUEEN

WHO BECAME HOLLYWOOD'S
FIRST PROFESSIONAL STUNT WOMAN

By Larry Telles
Foreword by Robert S. Birchard

Bitterroot Mountain
PUBLISHING, LLC.

HELEN GIBSON SILENT SERIAL QUEEN: Who Became Hollywood's First Profesional Stunt Woman
Copyright © 2013 Larry Telles.
Published by **Bitterroot Mountain LLC** - **9030 N. Hess Street, Suite 331, Hayden, ID 83835**
Visit our Web site at www.BitterrootMountainLLC.com
First edition: 2013

Front, and back covers and interior design by Larry Telles
Image on the cover taken from a 1919 Universal Studio movie poster of *The Dead Shot*.

Photographs: All images indicate the source. Those without a source are from the author's collection.

Bitterroot Mountain books are available at special quantity discounts to use as premiums and sales promotions, book club selections, or for use in corporate training or incentive programs. For more information, please contact Bitterroot Mountain Publishing at editor@BitterrootMountainLLC.com

ISBN 978-0-9852784-6-5
Library of Congress Control Number: 2012924401

Printed in the United States of America.

20 19 18 17 16 15 14 13 12 11 10 9 8 7 6 5 4 3 2

1. Helen Gibson Film Star -- non-fiction. 2. Silent movie actress -- non-fiction. 3. Rodeo champion -- non-fiction. 4. Vaudeville performer -- non-fiction. 5. Mrs. Hoot Gibson -- non-fiction. 6. Silent film history -- non-fiction. 7. First professional Hollywood stunt woman -- non-fiction. 8. Silent film serials -- non-fiction. 9. Kalem Film Studio -- non-fiction. 10. Silent film railroad dramas -- non-fiction.

This book is dedicated
to Robert A. Peterson
who got me started on this project.
To Gayla and John Craig Johnson
for their wealth of verbal
and written material.
and
To all the young girls out in
this world who have a dream.

BOOKS FROM THIS AUTHOR

A Brief History of the Silent Screen and the World at that Time,
2008, ISBN 978-0-9817874-0-4

Helen Gibson, Silent Serial Queen, 2012, ISBN 978-0-9852784-9-6, DVD

Helen Gibson, Silent Serial Queen, 2013, ISBN 978-0-9852784-6-5, Paperback

"Miss Gibson is an honest-to-goodness cowgirl.
She can ride high and fancy; bucking bronchos
are her matutdinal pastime and she can bulldog a
steer as good as any man that ever flung a rope."

Newspaper article from Helen Gibson Scrapbook,
August 30, 1921

Contents

FOREWORD

Not so long ago I was in the Academy of Motion Picture Arts and Sciences, Margaret Herrick Library in Beverly Hills and overheard a young researcher ask to see the biography file for nickelodeon era star Octavia Handworth. Miss Handworth made her last starring film in 1916, and made a one-picture comeback as a supporting player in 1921, and it is unlikely the researcher had ever seen an Octavia Handworth movie. Still, I was impressed that this long-forgotten film player still cast some sort of spell—if only for a limited audience with little or no knowledge of her work.

When I first became curious about silent films in the early 1960s, it was still possible to forge some links with those who created the art of the screen. Today, only a handful of people remain who had any direct connection to the silent era—either as filmmakers, or for that matter even as filmgoers.

But if it is no longer possible to speak directly with movie pioneers, technology has made it possible to more easily consult the next best thing.

Today, many historical newspapers and trade magazines from the silent era are available on line and in searchable form, making it possible for historical investigators to re-live the era as average folks did back in the day. Video has made it possible to easily see films that for many years were hidden in vaults. And print-on-demand equipment has made it economically feasible to package one's meanderings in the past in an economical fashion that can make publishing for niche audiences rewarding.

Larry Telles has taken advantage of these new technologies to research the life and film career of Rose August Wenger—known to her fans as Helen Gibson. Although not the first actress to portray railroad telegrapher "Helen" in the Kalem Company's famed movie series, *The Hazards of Helen* (that honor went to Helen Holmes), she was the most prolific endurer of those weekly hazards, and became synonymous with the sort of daring exploits that would serve as role fantasies for young women who were just setting off into the working world and striving for full citizenship by gaining the right to vote.

Larry has managed to recover a great deal about Helen Gibson and her film career and has been able to bring it to those who are interested both as a bio-filmography and as a representative DVD collection of some of Gibson's better surviving films.

His work is a labor of long-distance love, for though he sports an "old-timer's" grey beard, not even Larry is old enough to have seen any of Helen Gibson's prime work when it first illuminated theater screens nearly a century ago. But Helen Gibson has cast her spell on Larry, and who's to say that she may not have guided his hand from that place where the stars of yesterday still shine, however dimly, for latter-day fans who may rediscover them in their own place and time?

Robert S. Birchard
Author and Film Historian
www.rsbirchard.com

PREFACE

Why write about Helen Gibson? Well, why not. The life story of this woman who you probably have never heard of is intriguing. I believe this story came to me as divine intervention.

In the middle of June, 2009, I was sitting in a small book store in No-Where, Idaho (Rathdrum) signing copies of my first book. While signing the books I visualized my next book project as five short biographies of silent film female daredevils. Those would include: Pearl White, Helen Holmes, Helen Gibson, Ruth Roland and Grace Cunard. That vision changed drastically when Bob Peterson walked through the door.

Bob walked past me on his way to the counter, returning with coffee in hand. He asked if I liked silent films after getting a quick glance at my book cover. Without looking up I told Bob that I had been interested in silent film since I was fifteen years old. He commented that his great aunt was in silent film and she married a silent film cowboy. His name was Hoot Gibson.

His off the cuff response sent a chill up my spine. My tongue turned to stone and I could only gesture for him to sit down. By way of conversation he mentioned that one of his relatives had Helen Gibson's personal scrap book. When I recovered from the shock, I knew that this would be my next book.

In less than a week Bob emailed me the address of his cousin in Vancouver, Washington who had the scrapbook. In between emails Gayla Johnson sent me a CD containing about a dozen photographs from Helen's collection, which were beautiful. We set up Saturday, August 29, 2009 as a day I could interview her and also scan the scrapbook into my laptop. Her younger brother John Craig Johnson was there to help Gayla with details. After nearly eight hours I had an hour interview on my digital recorder, scans of Helen's movie stills and her complete scrap book on my hard drive. Without that material this book would have been missing many pieces of valuable information.

After a month of Internet research on Helen's background, I found that each site I visited had more incorrect information than the site before it. I needed a professional genealogist, but I had no idea where to find a competent one. I found my answer in Idaho Falls at the Idaho Writers League State Conference in September, 2009. One of the conference speakers, Juvanne Martin, a certified genealogist from Nampa, Idaho, gave a talk on research. I hired her to find Helen and Hoot's marriage certificate. Most all film historians who have written about Helen insisted that the couple were not husband and wife. The reason was obvious. In Hoot's autobiography he never mentioned her name. That was taken literally as no marriage. That idea has been falsely repeated online and in print books since September, 1913.

Shortly after the conference Juvanne and her husband were driving over to central Washington from their home and made a short stop in Pendleton, Oregon. She obtained a copy of the Gibson's marriage certificate and a doctor's letter saying they were both healthy enough to get married. With documents in hand Juvanne went across the street to the newspaper office. She found a front page story announcing that Hoot Gibson, Champion of the 1912 Pendleton Roundup was getting married. Hoohaw!

My next challenge was the incorrect dates on her films or missing films. Her scrapbook had films listed that could not be found on the Internet. In my research I did find a complete print collection of *The Moving Picture World* Magazine archived at the Seattle Public Library. The Library advised me that my local Library was part of the lending-library system and that I could be loaned the actual print books. By now I was delirious with the joy of the results.

My final challenge was photographs. Since eBay was sporadic, I began to contact libraries and historical societies. I found that librarians were and are a writer's best friends. They bent over backward to help me. Even if they didn't have anything I needed they provided leads to others who might.

With Helen's scrapbook categorized, pages of *Moving Picture World* copied I began writing. Since Helen's introduction to silent films early in 1912, she lived through the growth and expansion of that art form. From the information I had gathered I developed the following strategy. I wanted the book to cover three areas surrounding her life.

- information from those readers who knew of her.

- those who were curious about a fearless woman daredevil in early film.

- And finally, develop a detailed reference book about early silent film, with Helen as the center piece.

Nearly four years after Bob walked into my life, you are about to read the finished product, the life story of a talented and resilient lady whose life is an inspiring example, of someone who against great odds succeeded. I truly believe that this book is 98.5% accurate. Nothing is perfect.
.

INTRODUCTION

This book about Helen Gibson's life is taken from 95% of primary source material. The 95% content is from a weekly movie trade magazine, "Moving Picture World." It was published each week and contained information for the theater industry. Each issue had a section for the theater owner or manager, projectionist and for current film releases. A section of upcoming films was complete with cast, running time and scenario. All the film releases were divided into three sub-sections, or columns. A "Comment" article consisted of a brief film description in one short paragraph. A "Story" article covered the film in one, two or three paragraphs, and the "Review" article could be up to five paragraphs.

Two more types of material make up the 95%. Articles from old newspapers and theater ads were taken from online newspaper archives. Only the theater ads required more than one source for its content. All indented text in this book is taken from those three sections.

So I have created stories within a story. Helen's regular life is intertwined with the make believe world of film, her rodeo work, time in vaudeville, the circus and as a stunt double in Hollywood. I found no connection to Helen on radio as some historians have indicated.

The remaining 5% of the material is from Helen's only living relatives who provided a bird's eye view of this fearless daredevil.

PROLOGUE

Many western movie and rodeo stars such as: Tom Mix, Buck Jones, Neal Hart, Helen and Hoot Gibson got their starts at the Millers Brothers' 101 Ranch, Ponca City, Oklahoma. Also Mabel Normand, a non-rodeo star. All were stars of the silent silver screen, but none as interesting as "Daredevil Helen" as she was known. It was in Oklahoma where the seed was planted for her career with horses, movies, and stunt women that lasted fifty-one years.

The Miller Brothers 101 Ranch Wild West Show was founded in the 1890s, known around the world as great entertainment. There was plenty of action for the entire family. Colonel George W. Miller, father of the three Miller brothers started the ranch in Kansas. During that time he met Chief White Eagle of the Ponca Indians which wasn't under the best circumstances. The entire tribe was sick and disgusted since being removed from their homeland near Omaha, Nebraska, in 1871. When Colonel Miller met them they were waiting for a new assignment of living quarters from Washington, D.C. During this agonizing wait the Colonel gave the tribe food and medicine. This Ponca Indian tribe consisted of nearly 900, since about one-third of them had died. The Colonel hearing of Chief White Eagles decision to go to Washington and reject the land offer, stepped in and offered him land known as the Cherokee Strip. Chief White Eagle accepted the offer, moved his tribe near the present location of Ponca City, Oklahoma in 1879. At the time the 101 Ranch spread over 110,000 acres of land in the Ponca Indian country of north central Oklahoma.

With the death of Colonel George W. Miller in 1903, the ranch's management was transferred to his three sons, Joe, Zack, and George. Between that year and 1914 this Wild West show produced annual revenues of $500,000. Most of those years the 101 Ranch was in competition with the big traveling circuses: Barnum and Bailey, Sells Floto, and others. Many attempts were made by the Millers to buy and merge the competition into the 101 Ranch which would expand the 101's public appeal. The Miller show consisted of three categories of entertainment mixed into one: The Wild West, the Circus, and the Roundup. It became an extraordinary empire that involved and employed thousands of people for many years.

The 1929 Wall Street crash ended the 101's operation, but during its heyday it featured Bill Pickett, the Negro inventor of bulldogging, and many rodeo cowboys and cowgirls. Shortly after the stock market crash the ranch went into receivership. This was after Al Capone attempted to change the Miller ranch land into a settlement for Italian families. But, that failed and in 1943 it went on the auction block.

CHAPTER 1

Those Early Years 1891 – 1910

No one in the grandstands knew who Rose Wenger was; neither did the newspaper reporters who wrote about the Miller Brothers 101 Ranch Wild West Show. This would all change with the drop of a handkerchief.

A short figure with a red nose and funny hat scampered across the oval arena after leaving a small white handkerchief on the ground. Wham! A horse and rider bolted out of the north gate kicking up moist dirt from the shower earlier in the day. The gray overcast sky diminished any harsh shadows. Atop the stead sat a teenager, Rose Wenger, dressed in a divided skirt, cowboy boots and a broad brimmed grey Stetson pulled down snuggly above her ears.[1] By mid-arena the horse had reached a full gallop. Like the grace of a swan Rose leaned her body toward the ground on the left of her steed. In a few strides she plucked up the small object.

The horse's forward progress was brought to a halt. The crowd cheered and Rose responded by swinging her Stetson hat in a wide circle over her head. This was her debut as a trick rider.

This handkerchief trick was not openly accepted by most of the veteran trick riders at the Wild West Show and back in Ponca City, Oklahoma. Rose was strongly warned that she could get kicked

GALA OPENING **TO-DAY**

FIRST PERFORMANCE AT 2 P. M.
EIGHT DAYS' ENGAGEMENT.

Laclede and Vandeventer Aves.

101 RANCH REAL **WILD WEST**

Two Positive Daily Performances.
STREET PARADE TO-DAY
If Skies Are Clear.
Admission to all 50c. Children 25c. Reserved and grand-stand chairs 75c and $1.00. Tickets on sale continuously at the grounds and at
Bollman Bros., 1120 Olive Street.

St. Louis Republic, April 16, 1910

1

in the head at a fast gallop and not see her nineteenth birthday. Rose replied, "Such things might happen to others but could never happen to me." [2]

During the finale all the performers entered the vast arena, which included Rose. Her next appearance was completely different. She rode through the wooden gate on a Texas Longhorn steer. After polishing her riding skills at the training grounds in Ponca City, Oklahoma, Rose turned her attention to mastering the art of riding a full grown steer. Until the tour reached winter camp, Rose rode her horse and the steer in every show. [3] Members of the crew and fellow riders looked upon Rose as a daredevil with a sense of humor.

1911

COWGIRL
RIDING
LONG-HORN
STEER.

Newspaper clipping from Helen Gibson's scrapbook

Rose was not born on a horse, nor near horses. There were no horses in her early childhood. She learned the basics of riding during the past year. Rose was a long way from her home town, but with each passing day she felt more at home on this horse.

Rose August Wenger was born in Cleveland, Cuyahoga County, Ohio on August 27, 1891. At that time, the family consisted of two older sisters, Lena (b. 1887) and Frieda (b. 1889). Rose was the middle daughter, with two younger sisters, Annie (b. 1893) and Perlina (b. 1903). According to the 1900 census, the Wenger family had five children, with only four living. * Rose's father Gottfried, was born in Switzerland in July 1862 and her mother, Augueste Ruttenberg, in Germany, May 1865. Fred and Annie immigrated to the United States in 1883. After so many girls coming into the family, Fred desperately wanted a son. Rose took on the job with very little encouragement. Being a tomboy for Rose came naturally.[4] The records show that Rose was performing in Trenton New Jersey on April 21, 1921. That's the day her father, Fred, died. A small mystery surrounded Fred, his life and death. Rose never spoke of him in any interviews, articles or family gatherings even decades later. It was as if he never existed.

The Wenger family lived on W. 28th Street when Rose attended Orchard Street school and among her recollections is that of having a Miss Weinhardt as her teacher. When she was twelve years old the family moved to 1160 E. 78th Street. While living there Rose attended high school, but "for the life of me," she says, "I cannot at this moment recall its name." [5] She might have forgotten the name Central High School, because she wasn't a good student. Rose didn't like to study much, but preferred physical activities such as sports. These outdoor activities combined with her father's coaching taught her how to be fearless at a young age. When Rose's oldest sister, Lena graduated high school she got a job as a floor-lady at a local cigar factory in Cleveland. When Rose graduated in 1908 Lena got her a job at the same factory.

During the summer of 1909, a real "Wild West" show came to Luna Park in Cleveland. Rose went to the show and took her girl friend Suzie Ferris, with her. She also worked at the cigar factory and was one year older than Rose. The two young girls were enthralled with all the cowboys, Indians, bronc riding, bull dogging and girl trick riders. After the performance, they went down to the stable area. Rose found one of the cowboys and asked how they could get a job with the Wild West Show. The cowboy told them if they were real serious, they should get a copy of *Billboard* magazine. The back pages were full of want ads. Early next morning the girls bought a copy

and found just the ad they were looking for. The Miller Brothers 101 Ranch Wild West Show was looking for young girls who were willing to learn to ride horses. Rose immediately wrote a letter to the address in the ad and mailed it the same day. In less than ten days she got an answer. The letter told the girl's if they wanted a tryout to report to Ponca City, Oklahoma the following spring. From that day on both Rose and Suzie saved every penny they earned over the winter and into the spring of 1910. This Wild West Show opened the door to Helen's fifty-one year career.

"When I became of age I was allowed to go to Bliss, Oklahoma, and was taught plain riding. When I was well acquainted with horses, I went on the road with Miller Brothers Wild West Show and was with them for two seasons" It was never documented whether Rose had her parents blessing, or if this endeavor

* Appendix A - Birth Record, page 232

was known only to her and the girl friend. Rose took to her basic training as if she was raised on a horse. Management of the 101 Real Wild West Show signed her on as a show performer. But, Rose's girl friend Suzie Ferris, didn't qualify for the job and returned to Cleveland. The enthusiasm surrounding Rose's training became very apparent when she won the Women's Relay Race and Trick Riding competition at the 101 Ranch contest just before leaving on tour. Rose was ready and eager. [6]

Western Heritage Museum and Cowboy Hall of Fame
Rose Wenger in Ponca City, Oklahoma 1910, just before leaving on her first tour.

The opening show April 16, 1910 in St. Louis, Missouri had an eight day run.[7] Rose and the show crew of nearly 1,000 members moved next through Pennsylvania like clockwork.[8] Rose continued to thrill the crowd with her horse and steer act. Crowds were large with both young and old. One city had one hundred boys and girls in attendance from the School for the Blind, and another city had 1,200 from the Hospital for Crippled Children watching. Rose thrilled them all. [9]

The show crisscrossed the eastern part of the United States and performed every day except Sunday. Large crowds saw Rose ride at the Great Minnesota State Fair. In addition to the Miller Brother's show,

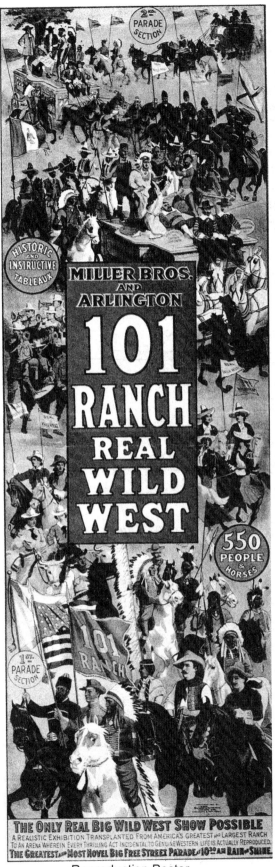

Reproduction Poster

Austin, (MN) Daily Herald, August 25-1910

daily flights of the Wright Brothers and Curtiss Aeroplanes were available. [10] The grueling schedule* had no negative affect on Rose. It had just the opposite effect. For Rose and her love of riding and performing, the season ended all too soon. Waiting in the November winter quarters was agonizing to a nineteen year old who had a love affair with horses and the cheering rodeo crowds echoing in her head.

In the spring, the city of Boston would open the 1911 season. [11]

* Appendix B - 1910 Miller Brothers Schedule, page 242-244

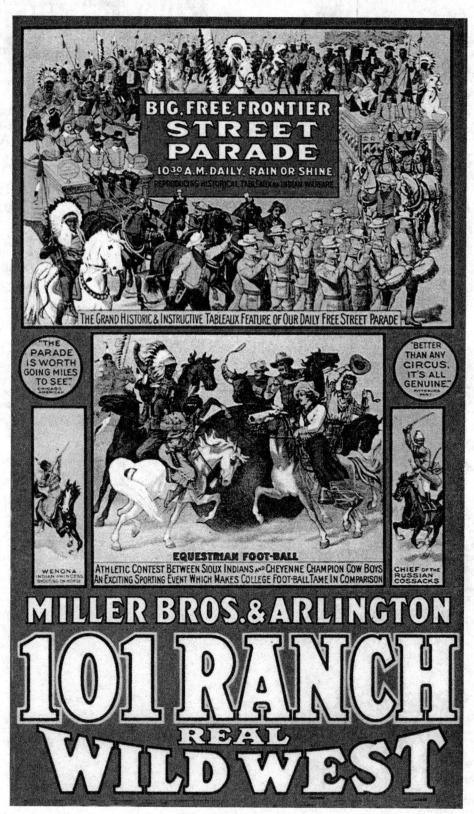

Reproduction Poster

CHAPTER 2

Rose Meets Richard 1911 – 1913

Eight-hundred fifty horses, sixty-eight head of cattle, a herd of buffalo, and four hundred fifty people were loaded onto twenty-three railroad cars in the afternoon rain. Rose starting into her second season was in her glory because the 1911 Wild West Show season had begun. [1]

Upon leaving winter quarters in April, the Miller Brothers 101 Ranch Wild West show performed before a handful of small midwest towns. On June 26, 1911, three months before Rose's 20th birthday, the show arrived in Cleveland, Ohio, Rose's home town. Rose rode her horse and Texas steer in the morning and afternoon shows. It was the first time friends and family had seen her in the show. [2]

After the two day run in Cleveland, the show loaded the wagons and they continued to crisscross the United States. In October the show reached Amarillo, Texas.

> While in Amarillo, the five cowgirls proved that they could do more than just ride horses and do tricks. They were staying in a private boarding house in town. The girls spent some of their non-rodeo time in preparing a meal of chicken and other good things to eat. Rose pitched in, but didn't get any time at the cook stove. The cowboys and crew found out very quickly that these cowgirls knew how to cook as well as ride bucking broncos. Early next morning off came the aprons and on went their cowgirl outfits. [3]

Rose dreaded November since it meant the end of the season and winter quarters. The 101 Ranch Wild West Show had another good season and closed in Venice, California. This closing was much different than in previous years. A soon-to-be pioneer film maker Thomas Harper Ince (1882 – 1924) entered the picture.[4] He hired the Miller Brothers 101 Ranch Wild West Show, including many cowboys, horses, cattle, and a whole Sioux Indian tribe, who set up their teepees in the Santa Monica hills. Rose was also included. The Miller Brothers were extremely interested in motion-picture cameras and how they could record every minute of ranch and rodeo life. [5]

Thomas H. Ince

Ince hired the entire circus for the winter at $2500 a week which meant that each performer was paid $8 a week and lodged in Venice where the horses were stabled. Rose and the other performers would ride their horses to Topanga Canyon each morning, a distance of about five to six miles. It was the location that Ince set up to shoot his films. Filming continued with Ince in the Canyon near the beginning of April of 1912. Pat C. Hartigan, (1881-1951) a six foot actor-director with the Kalem Film Company approached Rose to be test-photographed, which would be called a screen test today. She accepted and was hired at $15 a week, which at the time was considered a big salary for a beginner. It was nearly double what Ince was paying. [6]

Was the lure of moving picture films the reason Rose quit her job with the 101 Ranch Wild West Show? Could it have been the rigorous show schedule over the past two years? Did Rose see a future in motion pictures? Whichever the reason, she pulled out of the show before it left the California winter quarters for the 1912 season. Rose might have seen an opportunity to do something different than doing the same tricks each day and riding a steer. Rose was aware that this young film industry might or might not be steady employment. Not knowing how many films she would be making, Rose got a non-movie job managing concessions at Venice Pier. [7] She loved her new freedom since this gave her the opportunity to attend rodeos between making films and her job at the pier. Rose had the best of both worlds with film and rodeos as it involved her love of horses. [8]

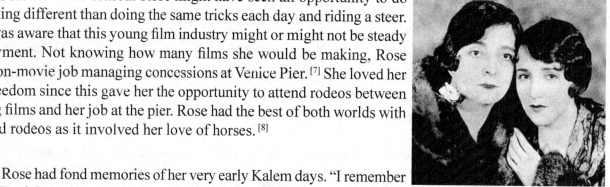
Phyllis and Daughter Bebe

Rose had fond memories of her very early Kalem days. "I remember Phyllis Daniels, Bebe's mother, was then in charge of the Kalem Company's office in Pacific Palisades. She also played mother-roles in several pictures I was in." [9]

Rose's first Kalem film, a one-reeler, *Ranch Girls on a Rampage*, was released on May 15, 1912. It was a western comedy about girls on an Idaho ranch. She played Ruth Roland's sister. The film was made at the streetcar station in Santa Monica.[10] Between pictures, Rose took advantage of her new situation and rode in several rodeos. One of those rodeos was in Los Angeles, California in mid-January, 1913. Rose was featured in one of the exhibition races called "Standing Woman Race." She had a wonderful performance which overwhelmed one of the rodeo investors, Barney Sherry. At the conclusion of the show Sherry offered to finance a tour of rodeos for her, paying all expenses, and splitting the winnings fifty-fifty. It didn't take long for Rose to make a decision.

Sherry's horse ranch was located outside the city limits of Pendleton, Oregon where Rose planned to go after riding in the February 8th through 16th rodeo in Los Angeles, California.[11] Rose also made another film, a western drama, *The Girl of the Range*.[12] At the L.A. Rodeo Rose had a chance to reunite with Art Acord, a cowboy she met in Ponca City, Oklahoma.

8

At Sherry's Pendleton ranch, Rose was where she wanted to be, working with the horses daily which she didn't consider a job. She spent several hours a day learning a set of new tricks and riding techniques. Unknown to Rose, Sherry had called his friend, Edmund Richard Gibson, offering him the same deal he offered Rose. Within a few weeks, Gibson arrived at the Sherry ranch.[13] Her life was about to change.

Gibson was in Australia when contacted by Sherry. He was performing with the Bud Atkinson Wild West Show. He won nearly every contest he entered. They played in Sydney, New South Wales, Victoria, and finally, Melbourne where the show folded. Most of the cowboys including Gibson had spent all the money they had earned over the four month long tour. He eventually got some cash together that allowed him to make the twenty-one day voyage back to the States. Most of the trip he spent washing dishes and peeling potatoes.[14]

Hoot Gibson

Born Edmund Richard Gibson in Tekamah, Nebraska, August 6, 1892, he was the youngest of three children. At age two and a half, he got his first pony and became quite skillful at riding. When Gibson was seven years old, his mother decided to move the family to California because of her failing health.

The young Gibson recalls, "First job I got was on the Postal Telegraph. I was then 15. I rode that for about three months and liked it fairly well. I got a job at the Owl Drug Company, delivering drugs and packages to the different homes throughout southern California or that part of Los Angeles. That is where I got the nickname Hoot. It came from Owl and later the boys started calling me Hoot Owl, then it got down to Hoot and Hoot has stuck with me ever since."

In 1910, Hoot's experience opened the door to the motion picture industry. He had ridden bucking broncos for the Dick Stanley Congress of Rough Riders and worked as a horse wrangler. Hoot's first film was with the Selig Polyscope Company doing stunts and doubling for several Selig stars.

At the 1912 Pendleton Round-up Hoot won the all-around championship. He also won the World Championship Fancy Roper at the Calgary Stampede that year. For the next year or so, Gibson and Art Acord competed in rodeo events during the summer, returning to Hollywood in the winter to double and perform stunts for stars. [15]

Upon his arrival at the ranch, Rose and Hoot began working together preparing for the Pendleton Round-up, and several other rodeos. First Rose and Hoot traveled as a team to Salt Lake City for a rodeo at the Utah State Fairgrounds.

"He and I won everything. The relay race, the standing woman race, trick riding, and Hoot won the Pony Express race. But the promoter of the rodeo skipped town and we didn't get a cent of the prize money." [16] [17]

Would that losing the money was the only problem. This was further complicated with the goring of Art Acord by a mad bull during his turn at bulldogging. The Texas longhorn pierced his right torso and the calf of his right leg. However, the story has a happy ending. When Acord got out of the hospital, he married his sweetheart, Edythe Kessinger. Her stage name was Edythe Sterling, a motion picture actress. [18]

Art Acord

Hoot Gibson and Rose Wenger pooled what money they had left, which was enough to get them to Winnipeg, Manitoba, Canada, for the August 19th Round-up at the Stampede. On the first day, Rose came in third in the Cowgirl's Relay Race. She didn't finish her second try. When she mounted her horse in the second lap of the race, it threw her off. In the process, the horse kicked Rose on the side of the face and on her knee.

The Ambulance Corps got her to the hospital tent where she was attended by two Victorian Order nurses. She wasn't seriously injured.[19] For the second time in a week Rose and Hoot put their money together and had enough to get them to Idaho and the Boise City Rodeo on September 18th. [20] Rose came in third in the half-mile race for cowgirls. She placed second in the cowgirls' two-mile relay race. Four saddle changes had to be made at each relief point. The time of the entire race was four minutes, fifty-six seconds. On the third day, Rose finished third in the cowgirl's half-mile pony race, and first in the trick riding contest. Hoot came in first in the cowboys' relay race, and the Pony Express race. [21] [22]

Pendleton Round-up arena postcard taken in the early 1950s

Hoot and Rose left Idaho and headed for Pendleton, Oregon, arriving a few days before the Round-up began. Rose and Hoot were married on September 6, 1913* by Justice of the Peace, Joe Parkes. [23] "It's strange how marriages occur! Hoot and I had become good friends but had not thought of marriage. However, when we arrived in Pendleton, rooms were almost impossible to obtain – people were sleeping in hallways, even on porch benches. When we learned that married couples were given preference, we decided to get married. The result: A landlady gave us her room." [24]

Photo of Original Button

Copy of Original Program Cover

* Appendix A - Marriage Certificate, page 233-236

CUPID ROPES ED "HOOT" GIBSON

Fewer cowboys are more expert with the lariat than Edmund Richard Gibson, known all over the west as "Hoot" Gibson, but Saturday he became a victim of an expert as great as himself, for Cupid, aided by Judge Joe Parkes, tied him by the holy bonds of wedlock to Miss Rose Wenger, relay rider and cowgirl, with scores of victories to her credit won in wild west shows all over the western half of the United States.

The wedding ceremony was performed in the office of Justice of the Peace J. H. Parkes and was witnessed by only a few of the friends of the young couple, some of them being T. D. Taylor, president of the Round-up association and sheriff of Umatilla county, Directors S. R. Thompson and Mark Moorhouse of the Round-up association, and Deputy Sheriff George Strand. They were immediately taken for a ride in an automobile decorated with a placard stating that the occupants of the machine were newly wedded and upon their appearance at the park where the bucking tryouts were being held became the butts of many good-humored jokes.

The groom last year won the all around cowboy championship gold mounted belt offered by the Police Gazette by virtue of winning the highest number of points in a series of contests. He has participated in nearly every large wild west affair held in the west and has won money in most of them.

Mrs. Gibson has been in the employ of Barney Sherry and has ridden his string of relay ponies. She met "Hoot" at several different contests and a friendship once formed at length culminated in the pleasant affair of Saturday evening.

East Oregonia September 8, 1913, Page 1

ROSE
IN
1913

Helen Gibson Scrapbook Page 7
Rose Gibson at Pendleton Roundup

Helen Gibson Scrapbook Page 19
Rose Wenger at Los Angeles Rodeo, January 1913

Helen Gibson Scrapbook Page 17
Rose Riding in Boise, Idaho Rodeo

CHAPTER 3

Rose Becomes Helen 1913 – 1915

The local newspaper, East Oregonian, accounts of the 1913 Pendleton Round-up were vague. Rose was on a long list of contestants as participating in the stagecoach race. There was no mention of how much she or Hoot won at all the Round-up events. Rose and Hoot Gibson must have had some success, because they used their combined prize money again to look for work in Los Angeles, California. [1]

On October 9, 1913, before heading for Southern California, Rose and Hoot (accompanied by other performers from the Pendleton Roundup) decided to try their luck at "The Dalles", Oregon's Wasco County Fair and Rodeo. [2] They planned to take part in the frontier portion of the opening day program. Rose expressed interest in an exhibition of bucking broncos from local horses procured for the occasion. [3]

Hoot and Rose left "The Dalles", Oregon, and arrived in the Golden State jobless. Hoot immediately landed a job at Selig Studio in Edendale, as a cowboy extra and stunt double for Tom Mix. Rose found a few jobs there as an extra, and occasionally got extra work at the Kalem Studio. The studio was just down the road in Glendale. According to Rose, most of the time she was made up to look like an Indian.

"I didn't regard it as work, although I was paid," she recalled. "Being allowed to ride their horses was a pleasure." [4]

While working at Selig, Hoot was reunited with his rodeo pal, Art Acord, when they both got riding jobs in a Tom Mix one-reeler. Acord and Gibson were fierce competitors off and on the rodeo arena, but remained the very best of friends. [5]

In the latter part of 1914, Hoot began stunting for Helen Holmes (1893-1950) in a new Kalem Studio railroad series, *The Hazards of Helen.*

While performing as an extra Rose was waiting for Kalem to put her on the payroll. In between her extra work Rose traveled to Los Angeles to enter the rodeo and there won several main prizes. This was yet another milestone for Rose, who would hold honors as the Los Angeles Rodeo Woman Rider for the next two years. [6]

Tom Mix   Art Acord

The competition at these rodeo events was a challenge. One of the L.A. rodeo opponents was Jack Hoxie's wife, Hazel. She was a trick rider like Rose, but decided to enter the cowgirl's relay race at this event. An article in the January 1965 issue of *The Western Horseman* told of this event.

> Roy Raley, who had much to do with the start and growth of the Pendleton Round-Up, put on the 1915 Los Angeles Rodeo. Raley lent Rose Gibson the Round-Up's celebrated string of running horses for use in the relay race. Hoot's wife had been a bronc rider and all-around cowgirl with Millers' 101 Ranch Show. She was a classy hand, and mounted on horses of that caliber, she figured to be an easy shoo-in winner.

> Jason and Doc Stanley, however, were also on hand, and also equally determined to win the big race with Hazel Hoxie. For the event, Doc Stanley had the use of a Pasadena racehorse owner's string. These running horses of proven worth but they had never worked in rodeo track events. Jason, a sharp racing event rider, taught Hazel how to nimbly vault into the saddle and thereby shave off a second or two at each horse-changing station.

> There were nine entries in the girls' relay race at that nine-day rodeo in Los Angeles. The ultimate winner was Hazel Hoxie. She remembers that race today as clearly as if it had taken place last summer instead of 49 summers ago.

> During the running of one of those daily relay races, Hazel, in the lead, was coming up to the finish line just as another girl rider was leaving her horse-changing-station for the final run around the track. In real closeup – those girls always rode like charging Indians – the legs of the two horses got entangled and Hazel and her mount went down in a heap across the finish line. Cowboy Art Acord, who was helping handle the Gibson Round-Up string, leaped in and pulled the dazed but victorious cowgirl jockey off the track and away from in front of the other fast finishing horses.

> That was, for sure, winning a race the hard way. [7]

In May 1915, Rose attended a Selig Studio-sponsored-rodeo in Los Angeles. She came in first in the cowgirl's relay event, beating Bertha Stadler and Iola Marks with her time of two minutes and fifty seconds. Rose rode her own horse, Zenobia, in the trick riding program, where her only rival was Vera McGinnis. Rose however, was not so lucky in the cowgirl's pony race. Her mount, the notorious Red Boy, balked when they dropped the flag. The other participants galloped away, leaving Red Boy and rider standing in the middle of the track. [8] Tom Mix also didn't have a good day. The two four-horse chuck wagon teams collided almost head-on. Both Mix and Curley Eagles, an Indian cowboy, were thrown from their seats under the hooves of the teams of horses.

The Cowgirl Hall of Fame
Vera McGinnis

14

They got both men out from under the tangled mass of chuck wagons and frightened horses. Mix had a fractured leg, a crushed chest, a broken jaw, and internal injuries. Eagles was reported to be seriously injured. Rose only had her pride hurt. [9]

A representative of the competition studio, Kalem Company, saw Rose's riding ability at the Selig rodeo. He passed that information on to Kalem Director, James Wesley Horne (1881-1942). Helen Holmes, who worked for Kalem, had been taken ill with pneumonia and a temporary replacement was needed. Rose was hired in April 1915 to do some stunt work on the new *Hazards of Helen* railroad series, for "possibly two pictures," at $35 a week.

The "Hazards" railroad series was being written by E.W. Matlack, a longtime railroader himself. In order to distinguish this railroad series from other similar films, the McGowan-Matlack-Holmes team coined the phrase "The Hazards of Helen." [10]

Helen Holmes signed with Kalem, where J.P. (Jack) McGowan had worked since 1908. Both had personal connections to railroads, which gave a sense of realism and accuracy to their films. For her part, Holmes had learned to drive an engine at an early age. Jack was born in a railroad junction town in South Australia. His father worked at a locomotive factory in Sydney. The first episode of *The Hazards of Helen* was released on November 14, 1914. Each episode was one reel in length, or about 11 to 15 minutes (depending how fast the projectionist cranked). It is listed as a serial, but each episode was a completely self-contained melodrama with a railroad setting. It did not have a cliffhanger ending, nor was the plot too difficult to figure out. It was defined by Helen's character. She was a telegraph operator at Lone Point who had a deep sense of justice; she was quick-thinking and took risks. Helen rescued people in every weekly episode. [11]

Closer Productions
J.P. McGowan   Helen Holmes.

TRUE
BOARDMAN
AS STINGAREE

Moving Picture World - Nov. 1915

The Margaret Herrick Library
Marin Sais

15

While Rose was now stunting for Holmes, Hoot was out of a job. With help from James Horne, he got a part in the *Stingaree* series with True Boardman and Marin Sais. It was a twelve-episode serial released on November 15, 1915, with Horne as director.

Rose stunted for Helen Holmes in a couple of episodes, and rode horses in two episodes as an extra: *A Girl's Grit* #45, *A Matter of Seconds* #46, *The Runaway Boxcar* #47 and *The Water Tank Plot* #48. When the New York Kalem Studio management saw Rose Gibson in action, they directed the Glendale unit to keep her on the payroll. The New York office knew that *Hazard* star, Helen Holmes, and its creator-director, J.P. McGowan, would one day soon marry, leave Kalem and form their own company, Signal Film Corporation. The Kalem front office made only one demand on Rose if she wanted the Hazards job. She would have to change her first name from Rose to Helen. [12]

The British Film Institute
Rose stunting for Helen Holmes drives off the pier and into the cold water below.

The transition between Helen Holmes and Helen Gibson was seamless. Both women were five feet six inches tall, had black hair, and had similar builds. Since the films were in black and white, audiences were not able to see their hazel eyes. Different episode hats hid their somewhat individual hair styles. [13] Most moviegoers didn't notice the change, which began with episode #49, *A Test of Courage*, released October 16, 1915. [14]

Confronting Helen at the Lone Point Switch Tower, Denning and his pal imprison the girl in a clothes closet and then steal everything of value. In making their getaway, the crooks accidentally upset a lantern and set the tower afire. Helen, by picking the lock in the door with a hairpin, barely escapes death in the flames. Denning and Orkanz board a freight and escape. Helen emerges from the burning building just as a local passes. A desperate run enables the girl to swing aboard the last car. Hastening forward the girl informs the engine crew of what has taken place and induces them to overhaul the freight, now on a siding.

Helen Gibson Scrapbook
Episode #49 - A Test of Courage.

Realizing their danger, the crooks hold up the freight engineer, compel him to cut his engine loose and speed away. Helen meets this strategy by having the local's engine crew sidetrack the cars and then drive their locomotive in pursuit. In danger of capture, the yeggs desert their engine and flee. The engine crew follow. Orkanz and his pal circle back, climb aboard the freight engine and open the throttle. Helen runs after the locomotive and just succeeds in swinging aboard it. A hurled wrench lays Orkanz low, while the girl's pistol holds Denning up. Helen assumes charge of the engine and is running it back when Denning turns the tables upon her. By this time, however, the engine has reached the spot where its crew is waiting and Denning suddenly finds himself in the grasp of the railroad men. [15]

On the third Saturday of October, Kalem released Helen's second episode, *A Mile a Minute* #50, which lived up to its title.

Hume and Frintz, while riding in a boxcar, see a trunk in the unguarded baggage car of a passenger train. By a daring leap from the freight to the passenger, Hume steals the trunk, throws it into one of the box cars, and then leaps back. The trunk is missing and the loss reported from Helen's station. Deering, a railroad detective, is sent to investigate. Later, when the box car containing the looted trunk is set out at Helen's station, the girl discovers its contents and makes a report to Deering.

The detective discovers the hiding place of the crooks, but in attempting to capture them is knocked unconscious and placed upon the tracks. Helen discovers the man's predicament barely in time to save his life. Later, the girl sees Frintz and his pal boarding an outgoing freight. Pursuing them, she just manages to swing aboard the last car. After telling her story to the train crew, Helen climbs to the top of the cars and runs forward. A battle between the yeggs and the brakemen ensues. The latter are defeated, and to prevent pursuit the yeggmen cut the train in two. By a desperate leap, the girl telegrapher manages to make the front section.

Film Flashes - Dec. 25, 1915 Page 8
Episode #50 - A Mile a Minute.

The crooks then hold up the engine crew and throw the men off the train. Helen, however, turns the tables on the thieves and runs the broken section back to where the rest of the train has been abandoned. Frintz tries to overpower Helen, but the girl easily frustrates the man who, with his pal, are shortly afterward made prisoners. [16]

Film Flashes - Dec. 25, 1915 Page 8
Episode #50 - A Mile a Minute.

After these two episodes, the newspapers had begun to recognize the new *Hazards of Helen* star: "Helen Gibson is admirably suited for the role because of her absolute lack of fear and her seeming delight in performing hazardous feats. Her protean ability has caused her to be added to Kalem's galaxy of stars." [17]

The *Rescue of the Brakeman's Children* #51 also includes two children who follow the girl telegrapher in the screen stunts. [18]

Discharged for drinking, Coleman attempts to get even by releasing the brakes on an empty boxcar, to which is coupled a flatcar, allowing them to run wild down the main line on which he knows the President's Special is coming. Coleman does not know that his children, Helen and Paul, are playing on the flat car. Mrs. Coleman misses them and, filled with anxiety, approaches the track just in time to see the children on the wild cars that flash by. Frantic, the woman informs Helen of the children's peril.

Knowing that the special is due shortly, Helen commandeers a freight engine held on a siding. Accompanied by Mrs. Coleman, the girl sends the locomotive speeding down the parallel track and overtakes the runaways. Throwing the throttle, Helen lets the engine coast at the speed traveling by the cars and then stations the frightened mother at the air lever. Mrs. Coleman faints, however. Cutting the bell rope free, the telegrapher fastens one end to the air lever, holds on to the other [end] and then jumps from the engine to the flat car. Thus she can stop the locomotive from the latter. This she proceeds to do, after she turns her attention to setting the brakes on the two cars.

By this time, the special comes into sight. The engineer sees the cars and sets his brakes. Thanks to Helen's work, the runaways are halted in time. Coleman, learning what has occurred, vows never to touch liquor again. At Helen's request, the man is not prosecuted. [19]

18

In keeping with Kalem's policy of creating one episode of *Hazards* a week, the first Saturday in November began with *Danger Ahead* #52. Helen is once again in pursuit, but this time it's *two* crooks on the rails. [20]

After a trail trip over the road, to familiarize those taking part in the scene with the action, Director James Davis gave the word for the picture to be made. Miss Gibson first perched alongside of the driver of the auto and then as the racing train and car drew together leaped nimbly to the tonneau of the car, climbed to the top of the cushions and balanced perilously waiting for the train and car to draw together. She gathered herself and as the car flashed by, jumped high and far out. As she struck the flat car, her momentum was so great that it looked as if she would be carried over the side and directly under the wheels, but the young woman pluckily held on and the train was brought to a stop.

An interesting question as to how fast Miss Gibson was traveling through the air when she made the leap has arisen among those who witnessed the picture before it was released. The train and automobile were speeding at thirty-five miles an hour at the time of the jump. [21]

University of Wisconsin at Madison Collection

Episode #52 - Danger Ahead.

The plot for the next November offering, *The Girl and the Special* #53, involves yet another leap, a speeding train, and other daring deeds. It was all in a day's work. [22]

Disguised as baggage men, Burgess and Whelan board the train to which is coupled the special carrying Nina Mallotte and her theatrical troupe. The thieves plan to steal the actress' gems. Uncoupling the special from the train, Whelan and his pal hurl to the ground the brakeman who attempts to interfere, and enter Nina's drawing room. The brakeman is picked up and his story causes word to be flashed ahead. Helen, at the next station, sees the uncoupled car traveling downgrade towards Lone Point. Rushing towards a bridge under which the car must pass, Helen waits until the latter is underneath when she leaps down upon the roof.

The brave girl next slides down the side of the speeding car and enters the actress' compartment via the window. By this time, the thieves have secured the gems. Seeing Helen approach, they leap to the ground. The special has been missed and the train is backed to the spot where the uncoupled car has been brought to a halt. The engine crew attempt to capture the desperadoes but the latter, fighting viciously, lay the fireman low and beat the engineer severely. Helen attacks Burgess and knocks him unconscious with a wrench. Trainmen overpower Whelan. The engineer, stunned, is carried aboard the train. Helen thereupon climbs into the locomotive and, grasping the throttle, runs the train to Harding, where a relief crew awaits. [23]

Episode #52 - Danger Ahead. Helen standing on the stirup reaches out to snag one of the crooks.

A milestone came with the release of *The Girl and the Special* #53. The Kalem Studio claimed the record for longevity in the movie serial business. This railroad series had been running for an entire year, with a release every week. [24] Kalem officials wanted to continue the series indefinitely as they planned for an unusual group of releases to mark the first anniversary of the series. It was felt that the success of the series would depend on E.W. Matlack, the man responsible for the stories, and Helen to continue to perform feats more startling than in the past. Helen smiled when she heard the news, and promised to contribute her share to the celebration. [25]

The Girl on the Bridge #54, released on November 20, 1915, once again finds Helen battling wits with jailbirds, a holdup, and a drawbridge. Just another day at the Lone Point Station. [26]

Episode #54 - The Girl on the Bridge.

Communicating with his pals outside, Daly informs them as to the date upon which he is to be taken from the jail to State's prison. Kling, the head of the gang, arranges to hold up the train carrying Daly and effect the man's rescue. On the day the holdup is to be staged, Kling and his pals abandon their original plan when they see a railroad clerk carrying a moneybag. Knocking the man unconscious, the bandits steal the money. Kling sends his men to raise the Ewing drawbridge and thus hold up the train, while he, approaching the clerk's handcar, carries the loot to their rendezvous.

Helen, however, learns what has occurred. Derailing Kling's car, the girl seizes the moneybag as it drops to the ground, places the car upon the track and then speeds away before Kling, half-stunned, can pursue her. Traveling at full speed, the girl telegrapher is within thirty feet of the drawbridge when it commences to rise. There is no time to halt the handcar, Helen therefore throws the moneybag aside and leaps for the rising structure just as the car hurtles into the river below. The crooks on the opposite side of the stream see what has taken place and, when Helen climbs down the bridge, attempt to capture her. By this time, the train on which Daly is being taken to prison, approaches. Helen's plight is seen and a number of men go to her rescue. Daly attempts to escape but is speedily subdued. Later, the moneybag is recovered and Kling and his entire band captured. [27]

Helen Gibson was quickly being noticed for doing more than the "ordinary" things in her railroad series, as seen in *The Girl on the Bridge* episode. She shared her feelings with a journalist.

"Life is just cluttered up with perils," she said thoughtfully. "But I think the one which made me think I was nearest to eternity was the time I had to go over an open drawbridge on a handcar into a river thirty feet below. I came at a terrible speed down the hill just before reaching the bridge, and for a moment, as I looked across the yawning space into which the car was to be hurtled, I felt a wish that I had remained a sedentary telegraph operator, without aspirations for a career of fame on the screen. It's weird, all the things that you can think of in a few seconds of danger like that. But above all other things I could hear dozens of my friends saying dolefully, 'I told you so.' You see my friends were never enthusiastic over the career I had chosen."

"There wasn't anything left for me to do but to hang on, though, and keep pumping at the handles of the handcar. Then suddenly I reached the edge of the river; the next second the water seemed to rise up to meet me. I know that I was frightened, for I had presence of mind enough to jump clear of the handcar. To carry out the action of the story I had to swim hurriedly ashore and rush to the switch to prevent a box car from taking the same disastrous flier into the river." [28]

Helen did have a few bad days where everything didn't go according to plan. She did suffer a few bruises while filming *The Dynamite Train #55*. It occurred as she leaped from a boxcar loaded with explosives. [29]

The shifting of the dynamite contained in a boxcar causes the latter to be cut from the freight and set out as unsafe. While this is being done, the Jones gang waylays Emerick, a cattleman who has just sold a herd of stock. Detectives are sent after the thieves. The latter make their getaway by climbing atop the dynamite car and loosening the brakes. The boxcar speeds downhill. One of the crooks discovers the contents and, as a result, he and his pals leap to the ground. Helen, who has seen the theft of the car, takes up pursuit in an electric speeder.

As the speeder approaches, the girl leaps from it to the runaway. Half-a-mile ahead, a freight train has come to a halt because of a hot box. One of the trainmen sees Helen atop the dynamite car and gets her signal to sidetrack the runaway. Throwing the switch over, the trainman sends the car down the spur. Helen leaps from the runaway just in time to escape death when it is derailed and blown up. Hastening back to Lone Point, Helen sees the sleuths overhaul some of the crooks and gives them battle. This takes place in the dry river bed under the Ewing bridge. By this time, other yeggmen see Helen and attempt to capture her.

Followed by the crooks, Helen climbs down to the river bed from the top of the bridge. Then she goes to the assistance of the detectives. Trainmen who arrive, help the girl and the sleuths. The criminals are subdued and placed under arrest. [30]

Life was just one bruise after another as Helen moved to the next episode. This time she sustained a sprained ankle while filming *The Tramp Telegrapher #56*. [31]

Beaten by Dun and Corson, Trent is hurled unconscious to the tracks. Helen, who witnesses the attack, drags Trent from the rails just in time to save him from death beneath the wheels of an oncoming train. When the tramp revives, he accompanies his rescuer back to the station. Helen allows Trent to sleep in the baggage room. Later, believing him to be one of a pair of crooks wanted by the railroad detectives, Helen turns the key in the lock. Dun and Corson, the real fugitives, enter the station shortly afterward. After overpowering Helen, they bind and gag the girl. This done, the crooks rifle the safe.

The struggle awakens Trent and after a considerable effort he succeeds in breaking out of the baggage room. The yeggmen have by this time made a dash toward a train which is about to pull out. Helen is released by Trent and together the two hasten after the desperadoes.

Helen and Trent see the yeggmen boarding the Pullman. A minute later the train pulls out. The pursuers barely manage to land on the rods of the last car. Determined to catch Dun and Corson before they can make their getaway at the next station, Trent braces his legs against the rods so that his body projects at a right angle to the side of the car. Helen climbs out upon his form and slowly raises herself to the window above. The brave girl succeeds in crawling through the window and gives the alarm. Cornered, the crooks put up a desperate fight, but are subdued and captured. [32]

Episode #57 -Crossed Wires. Helen hangs onto the crooks arm as he clings to the box car ladder.

Less than a week after finishing the last episode, *The Tramp Telegrapher*, Helen sprained her ankle once again in *Crossed Wires* #57. This happened two weeks before Christmas. [33]

Crossed telephone wires enable Helen to overhear a plot between Joe and Bill, escaped convicts, to join a number of Chinese who are being smuggled into the country in a freight train. The girl telegrapher notifies the railroad detectives and when the car in which the Chinese, cooped up in barrels are hiding, crosses the Mexican border, the detectives surprise the Celestials. After a desperate fight, the Chinamen are subdued, the detectives take their place in the barrels.

Bill and Joe board the freight a few miles from the border. Helen, who has been following them in an auto, leaps from the speeding machine to the side ladder of the racing train. Over the roofs of the cars, the brave girl pursues the fugitives. Joe and Bill turn upon the girl and attempt to hurl her to the ground. Leveling a pistol, Helen subdues the convicts and compels them to leap into the auto which, driven by Conrad, one of the detectives, has been keeping pace with the freight. Later, Helen accompanies the officials when the latter raid the rendezvous of the smugglers and assist in capturing the entire band. [34]

The engagement of Helen hanging on the side ladder fighting off the crooks on the top of the car was an action-packed sequence. However, it was not filmed the way it was originally written. Helen had a knack for adding just a little something to certain scenes. Most of the time the cameraman kept cranking to get it all.

The scenario called for her to leap to the handrail of the freight, a feat perilous enough in itself, and then climb to the top, forcing the convict at the point of a revolver to jump into the auto. But Helen insisted that a plain leap to the handrail was nothing out of the ordinary, so it was arranged that she should struggle with the convict who sought to keep her from coming aboard. Thus for many trying minutes, when a slight swerve of the auto might have tossed her to her death, Helen, standing in the car, and the convict, holding one hand on the handrail of the freight, engage in a fight. Finally the convict climbs to the top of the car, and Helen makes her leap, going on with the story as originally arranged. Had either the auto or the train varied its speed the slightest during her struggle with the convict the result is easy to imagine. [35]

The day after the release of *Crossed Wires*, Helen was given a day off. She decided to go shopping, but this came to an early ending. She sprained an ankle while stepping from a Los Angeles trolley car. "That's what I get for trying to be careful like other people," she wailed. [36]

Helen found out that all people are not treated equally. Back in early November, Helen had applied for a large insurance policy. Just before Christmas she received the formal reply and had been rejected. It was because of her current occupation as an "extra hazardous pursuit," which made her "an unsound risk." Helen's friends and co-workers believed that a member of the insurance company had come to the studio and watched her work without identifying himself. [37]

Insurance or no insurance, her daring actions continued in episode #58, *The Wrong Train Order*. It's another runaway train, and Helen is on it. [38]

Word that his son Jerry has been injured so upsets Torney that he delivers the wrong train orders to the engineer of the freight. Helen, having missed the Limited, accepts the invitation issued by the conductor of the freight and climbs aboard the caboose. Airbrake trouble develops while the train is speeding westward. In their effort to get at the seat of the trouble, both engineer and fireman are hurled to the ground. In the meantime, Torney has discovered his error, phoning ahead, he frantically orders the operator at Arling station to flag the freight. The runaway dashes past Arling, however, and Helen, seeing the operator vainly signaling, senses something amiss. Unable to operate the brake, the girl climbs to the roof of the train and fights her way forward atop the lurching cars. The Melius drawbridge is raised as the runaway approaches, but the tender, taking in the situation, lowers the structure barely in time to save the freight from plunging into the stream. Crossing the bridge, the runaway bears down upon a freight standing on the track ahead. As Helen climbs out on the pilot, a trackwalker throws open a siding switch, and thus averts a wreck. By this time, Helen has reached the emergency [brake]. Applying the air, the girl brings the runaway to a halt. [39]

Episode #58 -The Wrong Train Order. Helen on the pilot hangs on so she can release the air valve to bring the engine to a crawl.

The last episode to be released in 1915, *A Boy at the Throttle #59*, made its debut in theaters on Christmas Day. [40]

Helen is seen as the girl telegraph at Lone Point. One day while a freight train is standing at a station down the road, Bobbie, the son of an engineer, climbs into the cab when no one is looking and accidentally pulls the throttle open. The alarm goes out, and Helen, stationed at Lone Point, is ordered to derail the runaway and thus prevent it from running head-on into the approaching passenger train.

Fearing for his son's life, Layson, the engineer, phones Helen and implores her not to send the engine into the ditch. A small truck outside the station suggests a way out of her dilemma. Putting the truck on the rails, Helen speeds down the grade to the end of the siding, where she opens the switch and flags the passenger. Her warning causes the engineer to sidetrack the train. This done, Helen speeds to the Melius bridge and reaches it before the runaway train. Climbing to the topmost girder, she then hangs suspended by a rope, and as the onrushing train roars across the bridge she drops to the top of the freight car, and in a few seconds the runaway is brought to a stop.

Episode #58 -The Wrong Train Order. True Boardman Jr. receives a package while Helen looks on.

Episode #59 -The Boy at the Throttle. True Boardman Jr. with outstretched arms waiting for Helen to drop to the tender.

Though receiving a slight shock from the impact of landing on the racing train, it is remarkable to note that Helen performed this feat without serious injury. [41]

The Kalem front office gave Helen a chauffeur which they felt was a safe way to travel from her home to the studio each day. Helen got involved by insisting that the chauffeur drive no faster than ten miles an hour. "You see," she explained, "I get enough joy riding on railroad trains in the 'Hazards of Helen,' and it's the greatest pleasure I possess to be able to go as slow as I please in my own car." [42]

A 1915 photograph of Kalem's new Hazards of Helen star.

CHAPTER 4

The Hazards of Helen - January - April 1916

With the start of a New Year, the fast-paced energy on the *Hazards* set never skipped a beat. *At the Risk of Her Life* #60, came on the first day of January. As did the others, this episode title fit the actions of the Lone Point telegrapher.

> Tony, a half-breed Mexican is kicked from pillar to post, but he grasps a chance for revenge on society when he peers through the station window and sees Helen, the operator at Lone Point, opening the express company bag containing a valuable shipment to a local rancher. Tony overpowers Helen and makes away with the package.
>
> He runs down the track and comes to a train standing unguarded and climbs aboard. In a second, he is tearing away at a great speed. Cowboys aroused by Helen's cries come to her rescue and she is released from her bonds. Helen, knowing of a short-cut, jumps on a horse and starts cross-country on a reckless ride. She reaches a stretch of track before the engine bearing the Mexican and climbs aboard a freight train on a parallel track. When the Mexican passes she jumps to the engine, grabs the bag, and leaps to the ground. The engine is going at a great speed but it is soon brought to a stop and the Mexican starts on foot for her. [1]

The next thriller episode could be summed up in three words, *When Seconds Count #61.* Her on-screen activity displays the notion that she will not be stumped. [2] To this day the scenario for this episode is a mystery. No newspaper, nor movie magazine, including *The Moving Picture World*, has anything beyond the title and release date.

However, the next episode, *The Haunted Station #62*, was the film that a possible insurance investigator was also watching being filmed. It was released in mid-January. [3]

If this is so, then the decision of the company seems only natural. Miss Gibson was working that period on "The Haunted Station," a coming release in which the climax of the action shows a drawbridge being elevated to allow a ship to pass. She is escaping from a demented telegrapher who climbs the rope after her and while the pair sway in midair a struggle follows that must have sent the insurance investigator back to his office with a few gray hairs as a memento of the occasion. [4]

Episode #60 - At the Risk of her Life.

It was difficult to understand why several of the Kalem directors just learned that Helen had once been a bareback circus rider before joining the Kalem Studio. Now that they knew this, they arranged with the writers to add a few daring horseback stunts in some of her future episodes. [5]

It appears that after the release of fourteen *Hazards of Helen* episodes that Helen Gibson herself would have encountered critics and criticism among the movie-going public, and possibly even some of her contemporaries. Helen put out a challenge to any actress to perform any one of the stunts in any upcoming *Hazards* episodes. Gibson made it a requirement that the challenger must duplicate the stunt themselves and not use any camera trickery or substitution. [6]

Episode #61 - When Seconds Count.

The following Saturday was the release date for *The Open Track, #63*, in the continuing series, *The Hazards of Helen*.

> Helen's cleverness exposes a band of counterfeiters who later succeed in turning the tables on the railroad detectives and tying the two men to a cowcatcher of a train which they then start off down the grade. Helen pursues the train on a motorcycle and boards it by a leap to the handrail of a freight. The engine is soon brought to a stop and the detectives released. Helen also lends her assistance later to the capture of the counterfeiters. [7]

There was more to episode #63 than the Hazards fan realized. An additional cost was added to the overall production price tag.

> Two hundred and fifty dollars for a scene that takes about half a minute to show on the screen is the cost of one incident in *The Open Track*, an episode in Kalem's *Hazards of Helen* series. The scene occurs when Helen Gibson leaps to a train from a motorcycle, the latter being entirely demolished by falling beneath the wheels of the train. [8]

Episode #62 -The Haunted Station.

In an interview with the *Ogden Standard* newspaper, Helen revealed that once a day, six times a week, over 300 times a year she grits her teeth, and whispers an involuntary "do or die". Then for several long minutes she stands on the brink of death, just so her fans will have the sensation that she craves. Helen described herself as "a specialist in thrills," with railroad hazards her particular specialty.

This reporter described Helen as slim, pretty and a trifle bashful. Helen admitted that she is the type of girl that would climb atop a six-foot bookcase if an innocent little mouse poked its nose out of a hole in the corner. Helen did acknowledge that if the scenario said, "stand unflinchingly," that's what she would do. [9]

During the time of this interview, Helen acquired a new automobile. Her friends suggested that the body of the car should be shaped like a locomotive engine to make Helen feel more at home behind the wheel. There was no response from Helen. [10]

In the course of her interview, Helen admitted she was superstitious. She indicated that she would refuse to do anything that the official dream book said would bring bad luck. [11]

Helen declares that her greatest pleasure is watching herself on the screen in picture theaters and hearing her neighbors say, "That girl will kill herself one day. But I certainly do get angry," adds *The Hazards of Helen* star, "when I hear someone say, I bet she didn't do that herself." [12]

The Moving Picture World ran an article in its late January issue about a forthcoming announcement from the Kalem Pacific Coast Studio. With over a year of success as a one-reel series, it was considering making it a two-reel episode each week. But, could Hazards keep up the pace and devise more stunts for each film?

In explaining the decision to increase the length of the railroad pictures a Kalem official said that it was made after serious discussion with exhibitors in all parts of the country and because of a desire to do the railroad pictures full justice. "A number of exhibitors," says the official, "have written us declaring that they find the 'Hazards' among the most popular offering on their programmes, and that while they feature them strongly now, the series would offer even greater advertising possibilities if produced in two reels. This has had considerable to do with our decision to make the change. [13]

That was the first and last time the idea of a two-reeler was discussed as far as newspapers were concerned.

Tapped Wires #64 is another episode where a band of crooks makes Helen the Lone Point Telegraph Operator move rapidly, this time using an automobile.

After binding Helen to prevent her from stopping the express train to have it await an armed guard, crooks board the train, disable the messenger and dynamite the safe. Helen later takes a shortcut in an auto and overtakes the train, but the crooks leap from the speeding train into her car before she can alert the engineer and train crew. At the point of a gun, the chauffeur is made to follow the crooks' orders, but at the right moment Helen leaps from the speeding auto, the chauffeur turns the car to the edge of the cliff and then jumps for safety himself. The car somersaults down the forty-foot cliff burying its occupants beneath it. [14]

Just as in the previous episode, the spectacular ending increased the total cost of that thousand feet of film by a few dollars.

A seven passenger automobile hurled over a 40-foot cliff is one incident in *Tapped Wires*, an episode of *Hazards of Helen*, by Kalem. The scene requires less than a minute to show and cost the tidy sum of $1,500. [15]

In Helen's next episode, *The Broken Wire #65*, there are no motorcycle or automobiles destroyed. However, a far more serious incident occurs involving "fearless Helen".

When the Limited is forced to stop because of an obstruction on the tracks, the passengers alight for a stroll. In the excitement of boarding again one of the passengers loses a handbag containing her jewels and money. Two crooks aboard the train hear of this and at Helen's station, they alight.

When the trackwalker finds the bag and turns it over to Helen they wait until she has passed on and then attempt to hold the plucky operator up. She flees down the track, and when caught between two fires by an approaching train takes refuge on a telegraph pole. The crooks climb after her, and when the messenger wire on which she crawled out snaps because of her weight she is swung across the track barely brushing in safety the onrushing train. On the rebound, she is thrown in a huddled heap on a flat car. The train is soon brought to a stop and the crew captures the thieves. [16]

It was apparent that it was again Helen's turn to make the newspapers. It happened while the Lone Point telegraph girl was working on episode 65.

In *The Broken Wire*, a railroad picture in the *Hazards of Helen* series produced by the Kalem Company, an accident that recently happened to Helen Gibson, the courageous heroine of the railroad series, is clearly shown and it provides a thrill for the spectator that the producers had not counted on when the picture was planned. Helen was laid up for several days following the unfortunate occurrence, which might easily have resulted more seriously. [17]

The Marc Wanamaker Collection

Episode #65 -The Broken Wire.

The following week another episode, *The Perils of the Rails* #66, was released where Helen had an opportunity to display her wits and nerve which the audiences had come to expect.

Apparent carelessness caused Conductor Lawton and his train crew to be laid off for thirty days. A gang of car thieves pursued by police, jumped aboard a freight, and after a stiff combat, succeed in throwing the crew off the speeding train to the ground. The engine is then allowed to run wild, the thieves not knowing that a passenger train is approaching on the same track. Helen is warned of the danger, and she runs to the camp of the suspended men and asks for their aid. As the train passes, the men succeed in boarding it and engage in battle with the thieves. Before they gain control, the passenger train appears around the bend and a collision seems certain. Her plucky exhibition in the face of danger completes one of the most thrilling episodes in this railroad series. [18]

Episode #66 -The Peril of the Rails.

The Perilous Swing #67, was released by Kalem. The advertised title of this *Hazard* episode is a dead give-a-way. Helen will be swinging around a train at some point in the episode. The theater audiences were not disappointed. [19]

Helen is enjoying a ride on her horse, "Hazard," after her day's work, when news comes that "Red" Purdy and his aides are escaping after making a big haul. When the automobile in which they are escaping breaks down, they take to a handcar. Helen pursues them down the track while the sheriff and his posse set out to head them off on a shortcut. The gang reaches the drawbridge and after crossing, bind the bridge tender and raise the bridge to prevent Helen from following.

Momentarily baffled, she suddenly bethinks herself of her lariat. Tossing a noose around the end of a bridge girder, she spurs the horse from under her and then swings out through space to the opposite bank of the river. The crooks have taken to their handcar again, but Helen reaches the bank in time to board the express and continue the pursuit. Needless to say, "Red" Purdy and his aides are finally brought to justice. [20]

With each episode it appears that things happen behind the scenes. That would be a correct assumption. *The Perilous Swing* is yet another example. The final scene of this episode ended up a mystery on the set.

Helen Gibson, the dauntless "Hazard of Helen" girl, has a mathematical problem that will defy the oldest inhabitant. During *The Perilous Swing*, a recent "Hazard," she was obliged to swing suspended from a bridge on a rope 180 feet long leaving from one bank of the river and landing on the opposite side. To get the proper length a log of wood was first tied to the rope and swung across. It was found that the rope barely dipped into the water. The rope was then shortened 25 feet and a length of it passed around Miss Gibson's waist. The camera was started and Miss Gibson performed her hair-raising feat, and lo and behold she was almost submerged by the water. Now Miss Gibson is not very heavy and the wood was so what became of the extra 25 feet of rope? Did someone move the bridge? [21]

Hazards of Helen Director, James Davis, took advantage of an act of God occurring in Southern California area. Against the advice of veteran railroad personnel, Davis began filming in the flood district of Los Angeles where current storms had created high flood water. These flood scenes were to be used in *The Switchman's Story #68*. The particular scene being filmed has Helen driving an engine across a wooden trestle and then she leaps into the water. That's when the bridge was supposed to fall.

The trouble started when Miss Gibson found herself overpowered by the swift current of the stream over flooded by the storm. When the players gathered on the bank saw her perilous position, Robyn Adair leaped into the water and succeeded in bringing the plucky girl ashore after a thrilling struggle which the camera caught, but which also called for a sudden change in the scenario.

The attention of the company was then called to getting the engine off the trestle. Hardly was this accomplished when the crashing of timber was heard, the bridge toppled and was carried away downstream. While the players were thanking their stars for having averted the catastrophe by a few minutes, the camera man never forgot his duty and continued grinding away. The result is a number of scenes containing thrills that could never possibly be staged by a director. [22]

On the first Saturday of March, Kalem released *A Girl Telegrapher's Nerve #69*. This episode had a background story.

Steve Nelson, a clever crook, arrives at the little station where Helen is operator. He lives quietly at the village's little boarding house preparing for a coup when Helen receives instructions that lead her to suspect Steve. By a clever ruse, she succeeds in exposing him and making him prisoner in the station. He escapes and flees on a stolen engine. Helen follows on another locomotive and after a thrilling chase overhauls him, couples the two engines together, and then crawls on the swaying coupling to the other locomotive to bring Nelson to bay. [23]

Episode #69 was a remake of an earlier episode while Helen Holmes was playing the lead as telegraph operator of Lone Point. It was in 1915 while Helen Holmes was ill and unable to start a new episode. Kalem re-issued a one-reel railroad adventure starring Anna Q. Nilsson released in 1912. It was called, *The Grit of the Girl Telegrapher*. The two plots were very similar, except the telegraph operator was Betty at a railway station in the small town of Oreland. The crook was a gent named "Smoke Up Smith", and the final scene was a little less creative in the 1912 version. [24]

Anna Q. Nilsson

James Davis, director of the *Hazards of Helen* railroad series, appeared to have a lot more left of the flood footage that he didn't use in episode 68, *The Switchman's Story*. He cleverly utilized what was left in this episode 70, *A Race for a Life*, released in mid-March. [25]

A college boy's prank imperils the life of the railroad president's son who has worked his way up to engineer in his course that starts "from the bottom." Tied to the engine, the son is speeding on a runaway engine toward the Flicker Creek bridge which has been swept away by the floods. Helen and her friend, Steve, take a short cut on horseback that enables them to overtake the engine. She swings to the other horse, then climbs to Steve's shoulders, and standing in this perilous position on the racing horse, leaps to the engine which is brought to a stop on the brink of the river bank. [26]

The horse in this episode was carefully picked by Helen herself.

The Gayla Johnson Collection

Episode #70 -A Race for Life. Left to right: Helen Gibson, George Williams, True Boardman Jr. and Percy Penbroke.

The problem of finding the right horse to use in the "Hazards" in which Helen Gibson will be seen in both railroad and equestrian feats was a difficult one because of the necessity of finding an animal who would not become uncontrollable when brought too close to speeding railroad trains. Many had been tried unsuccessfully when Helen Gibson learned that "Black Beauty," who had been her mount when she was the daring star of the Miller Brothers 101 Ranch Show, was wintering with Robinson Brothers Show in California. Negotiations were quickly completed, though it is said that "Black Beauty's" purchase price would make a satisfactory one-year contract for many a famous screen star. [27]

Episode #70 -A Race for Life.

Episode #70 -A Race for Life. Helen (far right) places her foot on the coupler while trying to get to the engineer standing on the pilot.

Episode #70 -A Race for Life. Helen grabs the passenger car hand hold while making a horse to train transfer.

The following episode would be Helen Gibson's twenty-third after taking over for Helen Holmes. Shortly after Kalem hired her for this part, Helen was eager to try her hand at writing a scenario for this fifteen-minute 1000 foot action railroad series episode called *The Girl Who Dared.*

"After making several more pictures I wrote a story for a 1-reeler that I built around a risky stunt. From a wagon standing at a railroad station, I detached a team of horses and rode them 'standing woman,' in order to catch a runaway train, which was effected by catching a rope dangling from a bridge and using it to swing myself from the horses onto the train as it came under the bridge. Kalem rewarded me for this by raising my salary to $50 a week. Marin Sais, who was working on the *Stingaree* series, heard about this and demanded a raise to $50, and got it." [28]

The smugglers seem in a fair way to escape on a stolen engine when Helen, unhitching a team from a nearby wagon, races down the road towards the railroad bridge from which a rope is hanging directly over the track. Standing astride the two speeding horses Helen leaps to the rope and, swaying in mid-air makes a perilous drop to the stolen engine as it dashes past. [29]

39

A slight accident occurring to Helen, which might easily have been serious, is shown clearly on the screen in "The Girl Who Dared." Helen, swaying in mid-air from a temporary railroad scaffolding, is called upon to drop to a speeding engine manned by a gang of crooks. Helen's skirt caught in the rope as she was about to drop and instead of landing on the tender of the engine as intended, she was struck a glancing blow by the top of the engineer's cab and thrown to the floor. It is a tense moment to the person watching the picture and able to see clearly the girl's danger. [30]

"A week in the infirmary," was the sentence passed on Helen Gibson by the studio physician after she completed the thrill scene for *The Girl Who Dared*, in which she accidentally was struck by the hood of the engine cab. [31]

Episode #71 -The Girl Who Dared.

The Gayla Johnson Collection

It isn't know if recent episodes were the cause of the United Kingdom movie fans giving Helen Gibson a nickname. They call her "the nervy flapper." The term "Flapper" is the English slang for "chicken." [32]

Helen didn't get any challenges from the dare she announced a few months ago.But, the Kalem Company received a scenario [script] from an amateur writer from Canton, Ohio. In his scenario, the writer called for Helen to leap over a locomotive. This was to be done on horseback, and when the engine was moving at a fast speed.

"That's great," said Helen, "when do you want me to make the jump over the train?"

"Neither now, nor this year, nor the next," replied the official. "In the first place, we could never find a horse capable of the feat, and in the second place, we are not going to look for any, because there are limits even, for a girl like you, who does not seem to know that there is such a word as fear. No, I'm afraid our poor author will get his scenario back. And I hope it induces him to change the brand he is smoking." [33]

Episode #71 -The Girl Who Dared.

Helen saw the amateur screen writer's scenario while making *The Detective's Peril* #72 that was released near the end of March. It's another one of her stunts that puts Helen in those perilous positions. Taking chances and desperate ones is the main feature of this episode. [34]

Hanging from a rope over the track, the detective seems certain to plunge to death when the oncoming train splits the knot of the rope which has been tied to a rail and slung over the bridge girder. Helen's presence of mind and nerve in swinging out over the waters of the river on the other end of the rope and thus balancing the detective until the train has passed prevents the terrible catastrophe. Later, when pursuing the culprits, Helen once more takes her life in her hands by throwing a lasso from the handcar on which they are pursuing the freight over the brake beam; and then crawling hand over hand to the top of the [box] car. [35]

Episode #72 -The Detective's Peril. Helen is helping the detective (Robyn Adair) untie him from the rail on a bridge girder.

Helen spent some time in between episodes, breaking a bucking bronco for an upcoming scene in *The Hazards of Helen*. According to those who were watching, "she came close to breaking several portions of her anatomy.[36] Helen provided a name for her latest horse. It will be called, *Hazard*. "She declares that this is not only appropriate, but it expresses completely the feeling of anyone attempting to ride the animal. [37]

Episode #73, *The Trapping of Peeler White*, was Kalem's April 1st release. This Hazards episode introduced a new writer for the series. His name is Herman A. Y. Blackman and his scenario style is in keeping with all the previous episodes in this railroad action series. True Boardman, Percy Pembroke, Harry Schumm and Ray Watson supported Helen in this one reeler. [38]

Dick Benton is making a game attempt to start life over again, after escaping from prison where he was confined for a crime he did not commit. "Peeler" White, who was really guilty, and who aided Benton to escape without telling the reason for his interest, stumbles across the young man who is now an express messenger.

"Peeler" threatens to disclose his knowledge unless Benton aids him in a fake hold-up. The young man pretends to be a willing victim, but really warns the railroad detectives and "Peeler" and his companion find themselves in a trap on the train the following day. They turn the tables on the sleuths, however, and throw one of them from the speeding train. The detectives succeed in sending a warning down the line, and when Helen receives it she decides to make a bold attempt to capture the culprits.

Speeding to the bridge, she arrives there before the train and drops to the top of the onrushing cars. Throwing a noose of the rope she carries over the ventilator of the baggage car, she swings through the air and in the door of the car. Covering the crooks with her revolver she signals ahead to the engineer and the train is brought to a stop. The capture of "Peeler" also results in clearing up the mystery of the crime for which Benton was jailed. [39]

In her next weekly episode, Helen does it again with action that wasn't in the original scenario. The brave cameraman cranked away during the action and the players experienced a thrill within a thrill in *The Record Run* #74. [40]

Episode #74 -The Record Run. Helen is pictured half way in between her transfer from a push car (speeder) to the train engine.

The story is built around the rivalry of two railroads, and the record run that is to decide the awarding of large mail contracts. Helen learns of the rival road's plot to delay the mail train and speeds on an electric car which is derailed, almost costing Helen her life. The plotters send a wild engine down the track towards the mail train.

Helen boards a small handcar from which she leaps to the speeding runaway. The mail train is almost upon her, so she reverses the engine and speeds the other way. Momentarily, the distance between the two engines is growing smaller, and collision seems certain when Helen's signal is seen by a switchman and her engine takes a flying switch a second before the mail train roars by. [41]

The making of "The Record Run," produced by James Davis, was brought to an unexpected climax when a speeder driven by Helen Gibson jumped the track crashing into the camera and destroying it, and barely missing the director and cameraman who were standing beside it. Miss Gibson "came up smiling" in the midst of the wreckage and was not hurt. The stunt was to have the speeder coming at full speed, and the machine driven by the crooks was to cross the track just ahead of it, one of the men throwing out an automobile cushion to throw the speeder from the rails and prevent Helen from reaching a point at which to give warning of their escape. The speeder, however, took the matter into its own hands and jumped the rails before the crossing was reached. Miss Gibson jumped clear of it and beyond the camera being reduced to splinters. No one was hurt. [42]

After an investigation it was found that the film was in good condition almost to the moment the camera was struck, due to the cameraman's courage in continuing to grind away at the event. This film footage was used in the episode. [43]

The Kalem Company received a letter from a Photoplay fan with a warning for Helen Gibson. The letter postmarked "Waterloo, Iowa, indicated that Helen should give up her dangerous ways and exercise some caution. It appears that Helen is working in the "thirteenth mile of Hazards."

Dear Miss Gibson. I have just read in a motion picture paper where your series of railroad pictures was one year old in November. Now, I am pretty good at figures and I have just done some and I am writing to you to be careful during the next pictures. If you don't understand I will tell you why you should be careful. Every week for 64 weeks up to April you have been in a 1,000 foot picture, which makes 64,000 feet of film. Now, in April you will start on the sixty-fifth thousand and you will see that figuring 5,000 feet in a mile that will make your thirteenth mile. Now you see why I warn you to be careful and not take any more of them terrible risks like you do, because the number 13 is over you. I like you very much in pictures and your wonderful courage, but would not like to see you hurt, so please be careful.

But Helen merely smiles and refuses to be careful. She laughed as she read the letter. "Of course," she said. "I have my pet superstitions, but thirteen is not one of them, and the letter writer will have to try again to get me worried. In fact, as far as my part is concerned, I hope to make the thirteenth mile of 'Hazards' the most thrilling yet produced." [44]

The "thirteenth mile" didn't seem to affect Helen at all. *The Race for a Siding #75*, released in mid-April gave those hard core Hazards fans more of what they came to see. [45]

Through an accomplice the band of conspirators preying on railroads succeed in having the box-car loaded with auto tires sidetracked at Lone Point instead of being taken on to its rightful destination. They are getting away with the valuable shipment when Helen takes a hand in the affair. While each of the trio carries a load of tires back to the autos which are in a sheltered spot, Helen hurriedly climbs the side of the box-car and releasing the brakes, the car, with its heavy load, starts down grade at great speed.

Later, when the conspirators overpower the detectives sent to capture them and send their engine running wild down the tracks it seems certain that Helen, alone on the box-car, is doomed to death. Fortunately, her signal is seen by the switchman and without a foot to spare, the box-car takes the siding just as the engine tears by. Helen throwing to the winds, leaps to the tender of the engine and in a moment it is brought to a stop. [46]

Episode #75 - The Race for a Siding. Helen (on top of the box car) is about to leap onto the tender of the of the engine.

In her next episode, Fearless Helen adds a motorcycle to her horseback pursuit in *The Governor's Special* #76. Helen sets in a high-powered motorcycle after the automobile containing the crooked contractor and his aides. [47]

> When Nash, the crooked contractor, learns that the detectives on the way to the Capitol with the evidence that will convict him must stop off at Lone Point to make train connections, he determined to make use of the opportunity. He speeds in his automobile to the connecting point, and at the proper moment, his aides set on [Detective] Stanton and succeed in making away with the bag in which the documents are carried.

> Tom Arnold, a tramp who has earned Helen's gratitude by aiding her in preventing an attempted robbery of the station, comes to the detective's aid, but just in time to be arrested himself as one of the thieves. Helen, convinced of his innocence, sets out on a high-powered motorcycle after the automobile containing Nash and his aides. His perilous

ride is the beginning of a pursuit that reaches the climax when Helen leaps from horse-back to the speeding Governor's Special, barely grasping the hand-rail and pulling herself aboard in time to escape injury. But she succeeds in bringing the real culprit to justice and setting Arnold on his feet again. [48]

The Gayla Johnson Collection
Episode #76 -The Governor's Special. Second from right is Hoot Gibson, one of the heavies trying to get Helen off her motorcycle and into the car.

Episode #76 -The Governor's Special. Helen, Lone Point Telegrapher about to make a transfer from her motorized hand car to the train engine.

Episode #76 - The Governor's Special. Helen Gibson (far left) trying to get away from the car full of heavies.
Hoot Gibson (man with no hat, arms extended) trying to pull her off her horse.

The following episode, *The Trail of Danger* #77, released on the last Saturday in April, finds Helen using her horse and a crane to foil the bad-guys. [49]

Following the wreck of the pay-car, it is rifled by a band of conspirators. All but one of the band later succeed in making their escape from the town by automobile, but this one is forced to jump aboard a freight train to which is attached to the wrecked train and huge crane. It is planned for the automobile to follow the train and when far out in the country, he will jump from the car and rejoin his companions.

The conspirator's actions in waving to his companions as the train is just beyond Helen's station aroused her suspicions and she remembers the warning sent out from headquarters. Jumping on her horse, she sets out cross-country on a shortcut to warn the engineer and crew of the train. As she passes the automobile, the bravest of the conspirators jumps from the speeding car to the horse's back and soon forces Helen to stop. In the scuffle she has dropped her revolver but the spurs applied to the horse throw her captor to the ground and, leaning far out of the saddle, regained the revolver.

A short-cut brings her up with the train, but she cannot attract the attention of the engineer, and crew of the wrecked car, grasping the situation, turns the huge crane out over the road and dropping the chain within her reach, swings her through the air to the speeding train. It is but a few moments before the train is brought to a stop and the band captured. [50]

Episode #77 -The Trail of Danger.

CHAPTER 5

The Hazards of Helen May – August 1916

Helen is usually not pestered by fans at the studio, but finds that other people with different motives are getting past the front office.

> Publicity as the most daring actress in pictures has its advantages. Helen Gibson is thinking of engaging a guard of strong-arm men to keep away from her studio the agents for all sorts of patented safety appliances to make her work in "The Hazards of Helen" entirely without danger. Besides the agents for apparatus on the market already, Miss Gibson must also hear from inventors with little more than the idea of a 'drawing' of a new device. Some want advice, others seek to interest the star in making investments, while many are willing to let the star use their apparatus solely for sake of advertisement. [1]

It was only a matter of time before an episode looked at the circus for inspiration. Helen puts a new twist on an old circus stunt in *The Human Telegram* #78. The circus stunt is known as "The Slide for Life," but for this episode it is to be on a much larger scale.[2]

> To prevent a three mile journey around the mountain, the telegraph wires at the construction camp have been strung over the precipice from the station to the mountain top. The operator is discharged when the superintendent suspects him of treachery and Helen is transferred to the station.

> Later, after the former operator has enlisted the aid of crooked brokers to use his knowledge in ruining the value of the road's stock, he receives an opportunity to get revenge on the superintendent. A car loaded with lyddite has been shipped to the camp to aid in the construction work and while the superintendent is inspecting it the operator rolls the door shut and starts the car and engine off around the curve.

Helen, from her post up on the mountain, sees that a collision with the President's Special is certain. She conceives a daring plan and grasping a heavy length of chain climbs the telegraph pole and starts the long slide down the wires. The nerve gripping scenes end when she finally reaches the track and climbing out on a rope is just in time to drop to the top of the runaway car which is quickly brought to a stop.[3]

The Marc Wanamaker Collection

Episode #78 -The Human Telegram.

The Bridge of Danger #79 followed a week later, giving Helen another opportunity to use her nerve and skills to apprehend and capture those bad guys. She seems to be very capable of performing any hazard concocted by the Kalem writers from episode to episode, and shows steady improvement in her acting ability.[4]

The new superintendent is an apostle of Efficiency. His first order on taking the post eliminates the men whom he terms odd, which costs "Pop" Bates his job as Helen's relief operator. His next declaration is that active railroad work is no place for women, and Helen is also dropped from the service. While Helen is breaking the news to Bob Bates, the new superintendent is bustling about the road yard speeding up the work. "Put more snap in your switching," he tells the men.

51

A minute later, while he is making an inspection inside a box car with defective air brakes, a switching engine rams the car. The force of the impact — heightened by the recent orders — throws the superintendent to the floor stunned, and starts the car on the down grade. In a few moments, it is speeding along the road and there is consternation among the men for a washout down the road means that it is headed for certain destruction.

Helen prevails on Bob to set out in pursuit in his engine on the parallel track for a daring plan has suggested itself to her. After a thrilling pursuit they arrive alongside the box car and Helen throws a lasso over the break beam. Climbing out from the cab she then goes hand over hand to the box car. There is a tense struggle with the brakes before the car is brought to a stop within inches of the washout point. Needless to say, the superintendent's idea of efficiency is somewhat altered by his experience.[5]

The next episode, *One Chance in a Hundred* #80, accomplishes its mission in thrilling and complete style.[6] If it were one chance in a thousand, it would be all the same to Helen – she'd take it and make it! [7]

Episode #80 -One Chance in a Hundred.

Billy Warren, timekeeper on the construction job, arouses the enmity of Brent and Easton when he resents their bullying of the other men. Pay day finds the men celebrating in riotous fashion, and Brent in a crazed moment breaks into the station and attacks Helen. Her cries bring Warren, who trounces the bully. Brent and Easton then lay in waiting for Warren and, after a vicious blow has made him unconscious, throw him on a flat car which is started down grade, gaining momentum every second.

Helen learns of the action and, on wiring ahead, finds that a passenger train is speeding towards the flat car so that only desperate measures will save the day. She climbs quickly to the seat of her motorcycle and sets out over the tracks after the flat car. Just as she is overtaking it an express depot looms up ahead and seems certain to halt her progress along the side of the track. But without hesitating a second to count the risk, Helen drives straight ahead, up

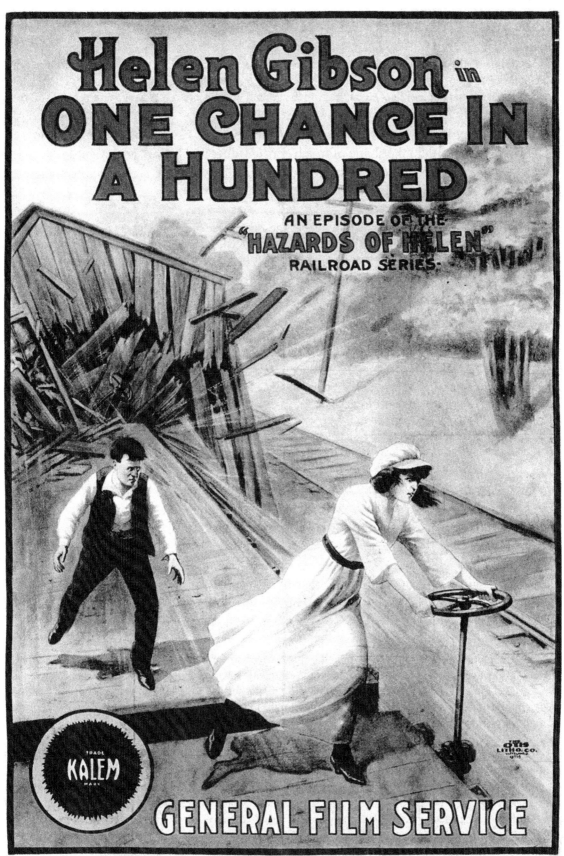

11 by 14 inch Poster Reproduction

the runway of the baggage platform and, as she reaches the top and comes abreast with the flat car, swerves quickly towards the tracks, dropping to the flat car as she passes through the air above it.

While she is struggling with the brakes, a track walker sees her peril in time to send the flat car on a siding just as the passenger [train] speeds by. Before Helen can bring the car to a stop, however, it smashes through the two-story signal tower at the end of the siding. Helen leaps to the ground with the injured Warren just a second before the crash.[8]

The last Saturday of May, *The Capture of Red Stanley* #81, was released. This "Hazards of Helen" number has thrills to start with in the shape of much daring riding and later the story settles down and leads up to a climax of great sensational power. In addition to the thrills that the reel contains, there are unusual night effects with its camera work.[9]

Red Stanley's band has successfully robbed the express car and the members are making good their escape when they come upon Helen and her girl chum riding in the woods. The girls are set upon but they succeed by desperate riding in making their escape temporarily and, when danger seems near again, are saved by the approaching railroad detectives searching for the Stanley band. A running fight results in the capture of one of the band, but Stanley and his chief aide escape.

Under cover of darkness, as Helen is working alone in the desolate station, the two enter and bind and gag her. They are driven off, however, by the approach of the night train. As she is riding the following day, Helen is captured once more by Stanley and hand cuffed, while the horse's reins are tied to a tree. Helen sees the two crooks board a freight train preparing to start from the station. After a tense struggle she succeeds in getting her foot up so as to slip the horse's bridle off and, using her feet and voice to guide him, sets out at great speed towards the train. She drives the horse straight up the baggage platform and aboard a box car just as the train sets in motion.

As the train speeds along, she manages to loosen the gag and her cries bring the train men to the top of the box car. Guided by her directions, they find Stanley and his aide and make them prisoners.[10]

Since the new rules at the Kalem *Hazards of Helen* studio specify that all scenes are supposed to occur at night, they must really be taken after dark. Helen Gibson and her fellow players averaged one and two nights a week of work that lasted until after midnight. "And still they say a picture player's life is a cinch," moans Helen.[11]

Edward W. Matlack, the old reliable writer of "Hazards," returned in the next episode as the author of The *Spiked Switch* #82. Matlack once again supplied a story line for this one-reel drama which evolves in an exciting manner.[12]

Trent returns to the throttle too soon after his recovery from illness. On the following day Ruth, his daughter, and Hume plan to elope. Trent, with a new fireman, is suddenly taken with a weak spell and when the fireman becomes panic-stricken, there is a scuffle which ends with the fireman thrown to the ground while the fast freight speeds on. Trent, a moment later, is overcome, and lies helpless in the engine cab. Flagmen notice that there is something wrong when the express whizzes by without the least attention to signals.

Word is sent ahead to Helen to derail the freight to save the passenger (train), the same train on which Ruth and her lover are eloping. But trouble with the switch had caused the construction crew to spike it earlier in the day and Helen finds it impossible to send the express on a siding. The down grade suggests a plan, and with the aid of an automobile she sends a box car speeding down towards the freight while she rips loose a plank from the top of the box car to prepare for a perilous leap. She braces the plank under the platform on top of the box car and as the flying express speeds by makes the thrilling leap, landing in a tumbled heap at the bottom of a coal car. It is but a few seconds before the train is brought to a stop.[13]

With the title of episode #83, *The Treasure Train*, had an idea there would be something of great value that would involve the Lone Point operator. Helen again at the risk of her neck puts the railroad in her debt by preventing a robbery. This scenario was written by S.A. Van Patten.[14]

"Red" Byrd and his aides learning that a large treasure is to be shipped on a certain freight car under special guard, they overpower the relief operator at Helen's station and tamper with the signals so that the treasure train stops, while the crew runs ahead to investigate leaving Spencer alone to guard the treasure. The crew walks right into "Red's" trap, and the members are made prisoners. Spencer suspects trouble, and hurriedly slams the door of his car, barricading himself inside.

The conspirators, temporarily foiled, plan a dastardly scheme. The last two cars of the freight are uncoupled and started down grade, when by skillful maneuvering they succeed in causing a collision that stuns the guard and all but smashes the treasure car. Helen, arriving for duty, senses something amiss as she nears the station, and learns the truth before she is seen by "Red's" aides left to guard the train crew. Running down the track, she boards the engine and sets out after the treasure car.

By a leap to the car, and her quick wits, she succeeds in frustrating "Red" and in bringing the gang to justice.[15]

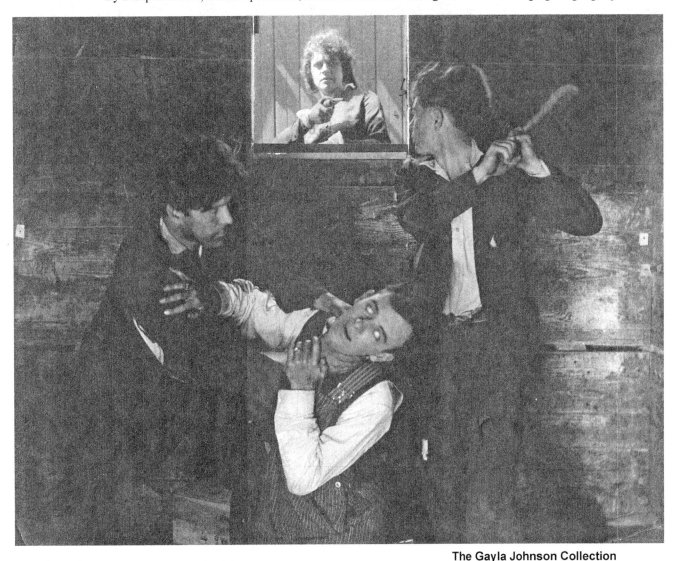

Episode #83 -The Treasure Train. Unidentified actor chocking Percy Pembroke, with Hoot Gibson swinging at Helen Gibson.

Episode #83 - The Treasure Train. Helen watches the door while Percy Penbroke holds a gun on the unidentified actor and Hoot Gibson.

Up to this point in Helen's *Hazards* scenarios, she had not gone to the air for her daring stunts. Ruth Roland used an airplane in several of her serials. In that serial which is considered lost, she transferred from the top of the moving train to a plane passing over the train, using a rope ladder. Pearl White used a hot air balloon in an episode of *The Perils of Pauline*.

The Hazards of Helen episode released in June, 1916, *A Race Through the Air*, was more than Kalem had ever expected.

Helen Gibson last week forced her way into the front pages of the Los Angeles newspapers with a feat which she herself is willing to let stand as her last word in thrills. An aeroplane flight with a twenty foot drop to the top of a speeding freight car constituted the exploit – and a sprained ankle is the only injury that Helen can boast as proof of her daring.

Two weeks ago earlier Helen was prevented from performing a railroad feat by the declaration of railroad officials that would surely mean a wreck and the loss of her life. After that picture with a substitute thrill that brought danger only to her and none to the road equipment, Helen set out in search of an exploit that would be far removed from the domain of bothersome railroad officials.

A scenario calling for an aeroplane flight offered the opportunity. Arrangements were quickly made with Thomas, the famous Coast flyer, for a flight. But when the aviator learned that Helen planned to drop from his machine in mid-air, he balked and refused to consider the undertaking.

Finally it was agreed to make the flight but abandon the plan for Helen to drop from the machine. But the biplane had barely left the ground when Helen succeeded in secretively slipping loose the safety straps that held her in her seat.

"Now," she said to Thomas, 'you had better go through with the drop as I first planned or I'll jump out right here. The camera's grinding so we're going to have a thrill of some kind. It's up to you to say what it will be."

Thomas told of his dilemma afterwards with a sheepish grin. "What could I do? If I had tried to land quickly I'd bumped into a freight train and I let her drop as she wanted to. But, believe me, she may have only suffered a sprained ankle, but I came close to heart failure in the few seconds I had to think."

Episode #84 -A Race Through the Air.

"A Race Through the Air" is the working title of this issue in *The Hazards of Helen*, and it will be a late June release. Having gone as far as the air in search of thrills, Helen is now stumped in finding a more exciting feat. "But I'll think of something while I rest for a few days with this ankle," she laughs.[16]

Helen didn't follow through with a bigger and better stunt in her next episode, but she made many more attempts at it. The eighty-fifth number of the "*Hazards of Helen* Railroad" series exposes a clever attempt to cheat a railroad company. In order to secure the evidence to convict the guilty persons, Helen again risks her life. *The Mysterious Cipher #85,* refers to a telegram in cipher code which gives the operator at Lone Point the first clue that a crime has been committed. Homer Von Flindt is the author of a scenario that has many points in its favor. The agile Miss Gibson shows the same old alacrity in risking her life again.[17]

> Chilton, a shady dealer in antiques, is in financial difficulties. He evolves a daring scheme to recoup by defrauding the railroad. He ships a carload of worthless furniture which he places in the insurance statement at a $30,000 valuation. When Chilton learns the number of the car in which his furniture is being shipped, he wires ahead to Blanding at Lone Point, telling him in cipher message to be certain that the car does not pass that station.

> Blanding maneuvers a fire which completely destroys the supposed valuable shipment, and then goes into hiding to await another cipher telling him the claim against the [rail] road has been paid. Chilton and his partner succeed in getting the money from the [rail] road and are making their getaway. But Helen's suspicions have been aroused by the receipt of the strange cipher at Lone Point and she begins an investigation. How her sharp wits – and, when the moment of peril comes, her bravery in the face of certain death – save the day for the [rail] road.[18]

Helen received a letter from upper management of the New York committee for the "round-up" to be held in August at Sheepshead's Bay, New York. It was an invitation for her to represent the western women riders and to participate in the events. This time her schedule didn't allow her to attend.

> "If there is anyway on earth that we can get far enough ahead on productions for me to steal the time necessary for me to make the transcontinental trip, you can count on me to be in on the big doings at Sheepshead."

> Miss Gibson also states that should she be successful in completing arrangements to take part in the monster round-up, she will not confine her efforts to the Studio Directory contest but will place at stake her title of "Pacific Coast Women's Champion," gained from emerging victoriously from three Los Angeles County rodeos.[19]

The First of July release of *The Engineer's Honor* #86, has scenario author Herman A. Blackman enabling Helen the Lone Point Telegraph Operator, to risk her life to clear the name of a young handsome engineer accused of robbery. Blackman still has her leaping from a moving car in this one-reel Kalem melodrama.[20]

> Circumstances make Helen think that Jack, the engineer and son of the road's auditor, is guilty of the theft of $50 that comes to light through a shortage in her accounts. Gypsy Joe, the real thief, gathers his followers to seek vengeance on the train crew for having thrown him off the train. In the fight which follows, Gypsy Joe's followers are vanquished, but the leader succeeds in overcoming Jack, the engineer, and making away with the engine. Jack, who lies stunned on the floor of the cab, gradually recovers his senses and pounces on Joe. A blow renders Gypsy Joe unconscious, but a second later Jack also drops once more to the floor of the cab, for the struggle has been too much for his ebbing strength.

> Trainmen notice the wild engine and the word is sent ahead to Helen to derail it to save the passengers. At the moment, Helen is confessing to Auditor Blake that she believes his son guilty of the theft. Blake pleads with her not to derail the engine, and they determine on a daring plan. As the engine approaches, they climb into Blake's auto and start down the track. Helen climbs out on the hood and when the train comes within reach quickly leaps to the cowcatcher, while the auto swerves from the track into the path of the onrushing locomotive. In another second, Helen brings the engine to a stop within inches of the oncoming passenger "train". As they prepare to bandage Gypsy Joe's wound his bandana head covering is removed, and with it is disclosed the stolen money.[21]

Episode #86 - The Engineer's Honor.

Sometime in between the last couple of episodes, Helen has been working on a Kalem one-reel western where she doesn't play the Lone Point telegraph operator. One-reel Westerns were in demand.

The steadily increasing demand among exhibitors for productions of the Western type, noted by experienced exchange men for some time past, has caused Kalem to take steps in this direction that should meet with great response. The first of the Westerns announced by Kalem for forthcoming release is a single reel drama, "Notch Number Nine," scheduled on the General Film Program Wednesday, July 5. Helen Gibson is among the stars seen in this story of a "two-gun man" of the old West.[22]

There is gunplay aplenty in this one-reel Western drama. The leading character is an expert at "getting the drop" on his enemies, as the nine notches on the handle of his revolver bears witness. Lovers of a lively Western drama will find the picture quite to their taste.[23]

To Save the Road #87, has Helen outwitting the local sheriff while aiding a Senator who can save the railroad. The rival railroad company has a different idea. It was advertised as, 'nothing like it has ever been seen on a screen in this city. A lone highwayman is the cause of all the excitement.[24]

The vote stands a tie on the railroad bill that would mean ruin to the Western line should it pass the State Legislature. By getting Senator Brown, who is aboard a liner quarantined in the bay to the Capitol, the day will be saved. The road superintendent takes a daring chance and aboard a motor boat succeeds in smuggling the Senator ashore and to a Western special which speeds off towards the Capitol of the neighboring state. The rival corporation wires ahead to the sheriff to stop the train at Lone Point and arrest the Senator for breaking quarantine.

Helen foils the plan and the "Special" shoots ahead, but the sheriff and his deputy climb aboard another engine in pursuit. By taking a shortcut across the hills in an auto, Helen succeeds in getting aboard the Senator's Special with an important message telling of the relay "Special" that is waiting for him just across the State line. As they near the

Episode #87 - To Save the Road.

line of safety, the sheriff overtakes them. With his deputy, the officer climbs down on the cowcatcher to jump aboard the Senator's "Special."

Helen conceives a daring plan and quickly puts it into execution. She climbs to the top of the engine cap and jumps to the guide ropes swung across the track, a second later dropping to the cab of the pursuing engine. In another minute she is at the throttle backing the engine up while the sheriff sees his quarry speeding across the State line to safety.[25]

Just before the filming of episode #88 began, George Routh, an actor for Lubin's western play was hired as an addition to the *Hazards of Helen* acting crew.[26]

The Broken Brake #88, released on July 15, 1916, had its scenario created from railroad workers and a dynamite explosion. A variation of a theme was used earlier in the series. The story leading up to the big situation where Helen Gibson performs the hazard which gives this one-reel railroad drama its punch is clear cut and full of excitement. The cheerful way in which Miss Gibson risks her life for her beloved railroad should make the company present her with a life pass, if nothing else.[27]

In a scuffle between the assistant foreman and a discharged employee at the mountain construction camp the latter's revolver is fired, bringing about a dynamite explosion that severely injures many of the men. The crude medical aid of the camp will not suffice so the foreman and his assistant determine on the dangerous expedient of loading the men on a freight car and coasting down the grade to the Lone Point station. After word is sent ahead to Helen to secure surgeons from headquarters, the start is made. When the car is hurling along at great speed, the foreman and assistant discover that the brakes will not work.

60

The assistant leaps to the ground, and, though badly hurt, succeeds in getting word ahead by tapping a wire. With the special bearing down the medical staff rushing towards the station, Helen's bravery and quick wit are put to a stern test in averting almost certain disaster. An audacious leap from horseback to a freight train and back again, and the manipulation of flying switches that shows the trains missing collision by a matter of inches form the thrilling climax of this "Hazard."[28]

Episode #88 - The Broken Brake. George Routh rides along side the train allowing Helen to transfer to the hand hold on the box car.

Helen's episode of *The Hazards of Helen*, *In Death's Pathway*, #89, has S.A. Van Patten as the author of the scenario. The title of this one-reel railroad drama does not overstate the risk taken by Kalem's fearless actress.[29]

Burkett, superintendent of the Western railway, opposes his daughter's friendship for Dick Benton, one of the company's lawyers, favoring the latter's fellow-worker, Guy Warren. Warren succeeds in putting through a scheme which results in Dick's discharge. The lovers plan to elope and enlist the aid of Helen. But Eleanor's father learns of the move and wires ahead to police officials to board her train and arrest her while he follows in his special. By a daring leap from a handcar to the train, Helen succeeds in warning Eleanor of her peril, but is too late and Helen and Dick are forced to stand idly by while Burkett starts on the return trip in his special, carefully guarding Eleanor.

While Benton and Helen speed in an auto on the road alongside the track, they suddenly see the engineer and fireman of the special flung to the ground by a bursting steam valve. Their warning cries unheard by the passengers on the special, Helen decides on a desperate course and they take a shortcut, bringing them to a bridge over the tracks before the wild train. Benton climbs over the railing and allows his body to sway in mid-air, while Helen drops until she has only a perilous hold on his feet. As the speeding train whizzes by beneath her, she abandons her hold and lands atop the tender. In a few seconds the train is brought to a stop. Helen's pleading combined with the evidence of Dick's courage soon breaks down Burkett's stubborn will and the lovers are happy. [30]

The Gayla Johnson Collection
Episode #89 - In Death's Pathway. Percy Pembroke slowly lowers Helen to the top of a passenger car.

In an interview during the last week in July, Helen Gibson got some interesting press. Some of what she says and some of what she did included her horse, and her automobile crashes at the Kalem Studio.

Helen Gibson confesses that possession of a six-cylinder car is causing her to waver in her loyalty to "Black Beauty", the spirited horse she rides so often in "The Hazards of Helen." [31]

The automobile bill of the Kalem Company isn't all eaten up in gasoline and tires. Just now it has taken on huge proportions because two directors decided in the same week that they had to smash cars to get the proper thrill.

One smash-up occurred in California, at the "Hazards of Helen" studio, the other in Jacksonville. The pictures, "A Plunge From the Sky," and "The Girl and the Tenor," are released the same week. Helen Gibson and Ivy Close are the respective stars.[32]

In the episode, *A Plunge from the Sky* #90, Helen once again takes to the air. It is very evident that Miss Gibson is ready to take any kind of a chance that the director is able to invent. The thrill is all there in this episode when theater audiences saw it on July 29, 1916. [33]

Agents of a foreign power are seeking to get possession of the plans of a new aeroplane motor invented by Dick Benton. Under cover of darkness, they succeed in their scheme and are escaping in their automobile when it plunges over an embankment near Lone Point. The conspirators jump to safety just in the nick of time, and seeing an aeroplane from Dick's plant pursuing them, they cut loose an engine in the yard and race away. When the aeroplane arrives, Helen boards it and the pursuit is taken up.

The aviator arrives over the Melinus drawbridge before the engine, and Helen, having formed a daring plan, dives from the air [craft] to the waters of the river. She raises the drawbridge, thus forcing the conspirators to stop, and at the same time preventing a certain collision with the Limited approaching on the same track. The agents reverse the engine and speed back down the track, but Helen quickly lowers the bridge, and uncoupling the engine of the Limited gives pursuit and overtakes them.[34]

Episode #90 - A Plunge From the Sky. Helen makes her leap.

The Kalem Studio has just finished filming *The Broken Pencil*, the title referring to the only clue to the murder of a Mexican. Helen Gibson aids the sheriff in capturing the murderer by a series of thrilling events. George Routh, appearing in the role of the heavy, is wearing splints on his wrist as the result of two broken bones caused when he swung into a train.[35] Somewhere between the filming and the release, the episode title was changed.

A Mystery of the Rails #91, a murder is committed and the blame thrown on an innocent man. Helen discovers the culprit and brings him to justice with enough plot to supply a three-reel drama.[36]

Jud Hendricks, foreman of the construction camp, is being blackmailed by Gypsy Joe, who knows of a dark page in Hendricks' past. Hendricks and Tom Ransom are rivals for the favor of Helen, with Tom in the lead. The latter, an engineer, is about to take his train out when he finds Gypsy Joe hiding in a box car. He throws him off and there is a brief scuffle. Later Gypsy Joe comes upon Tom from behind with a knife and a fight follows, which leaves Joe senseless on the platform, while Tom strides to the station. Hendricks, who has witnessed the fight, sees his opportunity to settle two grudges, pounces on Gypsy Joe and a minute later informs Tom that "the man he was fighting is dead."

Searching around the body, Helen finds the broken half of a pencil and holds on to it as a possible clue. Tom is arrested, while Hendricks, proclaiming sympathy, stirs up the gypsy workers at the construction camp and a lynching is planned. Hendricks, pretending sympathy, hurries to Helen's station to send a telegram for help, which he knows will be too late. He starts to write the message, taking the broken half of a pencil from his pocket. Helen snatches it from him, and finds that it matches the one in her possession. Seeing that exposure is certain, Hendricks rushes from the station and boarding an electric handcar is seen speeding away.

Helen attempts pursuit on horseback, but is rapidly being left behind, when an approaching train offers a solution. Climbing on a telegraph pole she swings out on a wire and drops to the train. As it comes alongside Hendricks, she throws a lasso that drops over him just as he is about to leap to the ground, and he is pulled from his seat to the speeding train. The train is then quickly brought to a stop and speeds quickly back to the scene of the attempted lynching. Here a spirited battle has been going on, and the arrival of help is barely in time to save Tom. [37]

Episode #92 became a bit more involved than the director planned. After waiting close to a month for the production of a final scene for, *Hurled Through The Drawbridge*, in the hope that a real auto race might be held on the Coast. Director James Davis finally decided to hold a race of his own solely for this picture. A dozen race cars and professional chauffeurs were engaged in San Francisco and Los Angeles. The event was won by Glen Gano, the well known Pacific Coast auto racer and aviator, in a Mercedes car. Director Davis had a battery of ten cameras stationed at various points around the twenty-five-mile course, and secured a number of thrilling scenes for the single reel "Hazards." [38]

Learning that the driver of the Comet car has been disabled on the eve of the big race, Sinton, a gambler, bets heavily on its rival. But his plans go awry when Gordon, the owner of the Comet car, meets Naroche, a celebrated French driver, and engages him to pilot the racer. Sinton, facing heavy losses, desperately instructs his unscrupulous aides to use every means at their command to prevent Naroche and the Comet reaching the scene of the race. The conspirators lay plans to delay the special [train] bearing the Gordon party. Helen, at Lone Point, learns of the plan and speeds in a handcar to the Mellus drawbridge to give warning. Sinton's aides attempt to forestall her by overpowering the bridge tender and raising the draw. Helen, tearing ahead at great speed, plunges through the open draw, barely escaping death as the heavy handcar overturns and strikes the water. Swimming to the opposite shore, Helen races down the track and succeeds in stopping the special in the nick of time. Later, in a race filled with thrills the Comet car sweeps to the finish victorious.[39]

CHAPTER 6

The Hazards of Helen September – December 1916

Some things seem to follow actors and actresses around. The subject of superstition tended to follow Helen around. The studio and Helen both voiced their opinions on this subject.

Perhaps if you had to risk your life every day you would be superstitious too. For our part we know we are entirely too superstitious to even attempt the perilous feats that Helen Gibson performs to keep "Hazards of Helen" to their thrilling standard.

But Helen doesn't worry in the least. In the first place she has been risking her shapely neck and two hundred bones month after month without a serious accident to report – removing from considerations the sprains, bruises, and lacerations that she takes as a matter of course. And in the second place. Helen is on most intimate terms of all the prominent superstitions and never by the slightest move dares to shock their gentle feelings.

"But it's a trying worry," confesses Helen. "If the studio carpenters could only invent ladders under which no one could walk, doorknobs on which bits of apparel could not be hung, and dressing room tables on which people would not set slippers or shoes, my mind would be eased. But what are you going to do when a black cat wanders into the studio and you treat him royally for a few days only to have the ungrateful animal disappear? You know it's good to have a black cat walk in but a terrible bad omen to have him walk out. And it's worse still to have him run across the road before your auto when you are starting out to a location to film a thrill scene."

"There are two superstitions that I haven't got. One I don't possess because I am not a man, and that is the idea among actor folks that it portends misfortune if three men light their cigars from one match. Then the awesome figure "13" has never worried me in the least. A fan wrote me several months ago and warned me that after considerable calculating he found that we were staging the thirteenth mile of 'Hazards' that month. There are a thousand feet in each 'Hazard' and by figuring five thousand feet to the mile he had discovered that I should take no dare-devil scenes that month if I wished to dodge the wrath of the figure 13." [1]

In episode #93, *With The Aid of The Wrecker*, Helen switches her attention from race cars to a pair of jewel thieves. Then with the aid of a wrecker, thwarts them. As usual to accomplish this, Helen displays her nerve with the stunts that exemplify this Kalem railroad series. [2]

Greggs, returning from abroad with a large consignment of precious stones, thwarts the first attempt of Gentleman Joe and his accomplices to rob him at his hotel, but they follow him aboard the train the next day. When he is alone on the observation platform they attack him, and a struggle ensues in which Greggs is finally thrown to the ground from the speeding train. Helen, riding through the hills in an auto, comes upon him before Joe and his pal can alight from the train. Greggs gives her the diamonds and tells her to speed away and rush help back to take care of his injuries. The thwarted conspirators hold up a following auto and speed after Helen. Rounding a dangerous curve, Helen momentarily glances back, and the next moment her auto is dashed to splinters over an embankment, while she jumps in the nick of time. Apparently at bay, a wrecking train approaching on the bridge above offers a means to eluding her pursuers. She climbs a telegraph pole, and the trainmen, seeing her frantic signals, swing out the huge derrick and she whirls through the air to the train. Joe and his accomplice, facing capture, jump into their auto and start to flee, but the chain from the derrick descends and hooks under the hood of the auto, swinging it into the air. The trainmen soon descend and make the pair captives. [3]

Helen returns with her trusty motorcycle in *At Danger's Call*, #94, and takes on the task of saving a life before he is blown to bits by a dynamite car. [4]

Episode #94 - At Danger's Call. Helen (right) has just been fired by Superintendent Waller (George Williams) on the left.

Helen, discharged by the superintendent without justification, comes to the rescue when a flat car, loaded with dynamite, is tearing to certain destruction down the grade, bearing the mischievous son of the superintendent.

She boards her motorcycle and races down the track. The drawbridge is being raised as she reaches it, but without a second's hesitation she speeds across, the motorcycle whirling through the space separating the bridge and tracks. Helen then boards an engine and reaches a railroad trestle by means of a painter's rope, she succeeds in grasping the superintendent's son and swinging him to safety. A second later the flat car, sent on a siding by the railroad men, has struck a box car and exploded with a deafening roar. [5]

Episode #94 - At Danger's Call. True Boardman Jr. (second from left) watches Helen (right) being helped up after her motorcycle crashed.

Episode #95, *The Secret of the Box Car*, begins with a bank robbery far away from an intrepid girl telegraph operator. But, when the robbers reach Lone Point they must deal with Helen and her multiple skills. They were not aware of how she treats crooks. [6]

Escaping after an early morning bank robbery, Gentleman Joe and his pal succeed in boarding a freight train headed toward Lone Point. Fearing rightly that a warning has been sent down the line, they secrete their loot in a box car, and, after noting its number, alight and seek cover until after the pursuit has cooled. Later, when they plan to resume their journey, they are seen by the telegrapher, but a struggle follows in which they overcome him. Boarding an unguarded automobile, they speed down the track towards Lone Point. The telegrapher, recovering, sends a warning ahead to Helen. The car, No. 11165, has been placed on a siding at Lone Point but is now being taken up by the freight engine. Helen, giving chase, succeeds in boarding the caboose and warning the train crew.

Meanwhile, the crooks, abandoning their auto by the roadside, have boarded car No. 11165, and are about to get away with their loot when the train crew, headed by Helen, comes upon them. There is a struggle, but Gentleman Joe escapes and runs across the tops of the cars, carrying the loot. The mail train is roaring along on the adjoining track as Helen comes upon Gentleman Joe from behind and deals him a blow that momentarily stuns him. Helen grabs the bag of loot and runs along the flat car seeking to attract the attention of the mail train crew. Joe gets to his feet and pursues her, but, in the nick of time, the mail crew puts out the "arm" which seizes the mail bags and Helen swings to safety. [7]

Episode #95 - The Secret of the Boxcar.

Helen's early September release, *Ablaze on the Rails* #96 continues to electrify regular serial fans. The stunt Miss Gibson performs is not new to this railroad series, but the thrill is all there. The suspense throughout the thousand feet film is kept at fever heat. [8]

A railroad station safe is plundered by a trio of crooks, but one of the thieves turns informer and attempts to help a company detective recover the money. They are overpowered by the two robbers, bound securely in a freight

68

car and the car set on fire. As it rushes down the grade past the station at Lone Point, Helen sees it and starts in pursuit. Helen, by a courageous leap from a motorcycle, reaches the burning box car in which the detectives are imprisoned and succeeds in applying the brakes in time to bring it to a stop and save them from almost certain death. Her bravery also enables Detective Kent to secure a coveted reward for the capture of the famous crook, which puts the seal of a "happy ending" to this romance. [9]

The Hoodoo of Division B #97 episode was written up with Helen again risking her life which audiences were told must be seen to be appreciated. [10]

> The new superintendent scoffs at the men's fear of Engine 3615, and declares that it must be put into service at once. Engineer Kent, a veteran of the road, refuses to take the throttle and is discharged. Dick Benton, a young engineer is induced to take the engine out and "kill this talk of a hoodoo." But the engine lives up to its name, and after a series of exciting incidents runs wild with Benton disabled in his cab. Helen, who receives word of the impending disaster, saves the day by a daring exploit that brings her within inches of death. [11] She chases the runaway train on another engine and brings it to a stop, after a series of feats. [12]

Defying Death #98 is described in the trade journals as a hair-raising situation. There isn't the slightest doubt about the ability of the reel to deliver a thrill. Helen gets the bad guy by lying face down on an electric handcar. [13]

Episode #98 - Defying Death.

Dick Benton, a young attorney of the railroad, is on his way to the Capitol to deliver evidence involving Riggs in a conspiracy arising out of a fight with the railroad over a franchise. At Lone Point he learns that by leaving the package to be picked up by the express it will reach the Governor sooner than he can bring it on the local. He leaves it in Helen's care. But Riggs, who has been following Benton, succeeds in getting away with the box and boarding an auto standing outside the station. He has scarcely gone a hundred feet when a momentary loss of control causes the car to ram a telegraph pole.

Helen recovers the box, but looks up to find another automobile with Riggs' aides bearing down upon her.

While they are tending the injured Riggs, she [Helen] boards an electric speeder, a development of the handcar, and races down the track. In a moment, the conspirators are after her. Suddenly the express swings around the curve, on the adjoining track. Ahead Helen sees the switch which will send her to almost certain death under the wheels of the express unless her speeder is brought to a stop. She tries frantically to apply the brakes, but they will not work, and in a twinkling she is at the switch and tenders the express. By a matter of inches she escapes the wheels of the train and races along the other track space with the express above her. When she has finally mastered the brakes she calls the trainmen above her, and both express and speeder are brought to a stop together. The trainmen quickly effect the capture of Riggs and his fellows. [14]

Episode #99 - The Death Swing.

70

On the following Saturday, September 30, 1916, *The Death Swing* #99 is released with a slightly higher level of thrills that are associated with this railroad series. More hazardous than many of her preceding feats is the stunt performed by Helen in this number of the *Hazards of Helen.*"

The crew of a freight train is taken from the engine by a disappointed suitor of Helen. [15] Stallings' plot to foil the demonstration of Dick Benton's newly invented safety stop for trains seems certain of success when the locomotive is sent running wild down the tracks. Helen saves the day by climbing out on a wire stretching across the tracks and dropping to the speeding engine. The shock of landing momentarily dazes her but it is only a matter of a few seconds before she has brought the train to a stop. [16]

Most normal people who take time off from work are looking for somewhere to relax, but not fearless Helen Gibson. She signed up for a rodeo on her short vacation.

The Gayla Johnson Collection

Helen really liked those wide brimmed Stetson hats.

Helen Gibson, heroine of Kalem's "Hazards of Helen" railroad series, has taken a week's vacation from the studio to take part in the big Western rodeo and stampede now being held in Bakersfield, California. Miss Gibson will defend her title of Pacific Coast woman's champion in a number of events.

As she will be pitted against the cracks of the Western world, the screen star will be put on her sternest mettle to retain her honors won in the last four years when the rodeos were held at Pendleton, Ore., Boise, Idaho, Vancouver, B.C., and Salt Lake City. [17]

A short article in the newspaper summed up the Bakersfield, California Rodeo.

Helen Gibson, the heroine of railroad pictures, went into the recent Bakersfield, California Rodeo in fear and trembling lest she was to lose the title of Pacific Coast woman's champion which her horseback riding had won for her in the past four big rodeos.

But after a grueling week's contests, the point score finds Helen clinging to her laurels by a single point, victories in the "Standing Roman", relay and bronco-busting events having placed her in the lead. [18]

While away at the Bakersfield, California Rodeo, Kalem released *The Blocked Track* #100 where Helen attempts to stop a hold-up and finds herself up a tree, a real tree. [19]

71

On a visit to the State Prison with Superintendent Melvin of the construction camp near Lone Point, Helen gains the friendship of Butler, a former telegrapher who had been wrongfully convicted on circumstantial evidence. Butler is soon to be released and Helen promises to aid him. She does so by securing a position for him as telegrapher operator at the construction camp. Here Strang, an ex-convict, recognizes Butler, and attempts to force him to aid his plan to rob the pay car. [20] The thrill in this reel comes when Helen prevents a gang from holding up the pay car. During the action of the melodramatic story she is chased by one of the plotters. She climbs hand over hand across a wire to a telegraph pole, down the pole and up into a tree. The branches of the tree overhang the railroad track and Helen, forced out on the end of a limb, leaps to the tender of the locomotive that is hauling the pay car into the trap set by the hold-up men. She foils the plot. [21]

Just like in today's world, reporters are constantly looking for stories especially when it involves a film celebrity. The world of 1916 and Helen Gibson was no different.

Helen Gibson has fully recovered from an injury to her ankle received in the Bakersfield Rodeo and is once more tempting fate at the "Hazards of Helen" studio. [22]

In several newspapers, *To Save the Special* #101, was written up as one of the best and most thrilling of the "Hazards of Helen" series.

In this reel Helen Gibson's undoubted nerve is given a severe test, and she responds with a realism that makes the nerves tingle. She is called upon to stop a runaway team from the back of another horse. Credit is due for the manner in which these scenes were photographed too, for they are quite close-up and the action of the girl and the horse registers with unusual power to thrill.

There is more to the story in this number than there was in many of the recent "Hazards." The real action starts when a driver at a mine gets a load of dynamite from the siding at the Lone Point station. The driver has been given an unruly horse by the stable-keeper. The horses are frightened by a train and run away. Down past the station they speed, and Helen jumps on another horse and is after them. She leaps to the back of one of the runaways and diverts their course from the railroad track just as they are about to crash into the special train. The villains are killed by the explosion when the wagon turns over. [23]

The runaway horse scene in *To Save the Special* appeared to have a great deal of realism on the screen. From behind the scene, there was also a tingle to a cold chill from the director, James Davis.

Helen Gibson, railroad girl for Kalem, while riding running horses for a picture, fell between them and was severely injured. She only saved herself from death by clinging to the mane of one of the speeding animals. She is in a precarious condition. [24]

There was no evidence in the research that the studio delayed the filming of the next episode of this railroad series. No further mention of Helen's severe injury.

Seven year old Billy Boy returns to the Kalem Studio to be the focus of episode #102, *A Daring Chance*. [25] This reel is refreshingly lacking in the deeply villainous themes seen in the series heretofore.

Excitement reaches a high pitch when the little boy, through a series of circumstances, is left alone on a racing gasoline-driven handcar. He is traveling to certain death through collision with a stalled train, when Helen is notified of the little fellow's plight. She boards the engine of the special and starts after the boy. The engine and the handcar race side by side. Just as the handcar is about to collide with the stalled car, Helen reaches down from the cab of the engine and swings the boy to safety. [26]

72

Episode #102 - A Daring Chance.

The Lost Messenger #103, contained more stunts than recent releases of the series. The story holds the interest throughout, and to the melodramatic material is added a compelling element of mystery. [27]

Benton, the express messenger, is known to be in money troubles, so that, when he disappears with a valuable package, circumstantial evidence points to his guilt. Helen, while delivering a telegram on motorcycle, is crossing the drawbridge when she finds the missing package. A wharf gang, which has secreted the package there, pursues to recover it, while one of their number raises the bridge to prevent Helen's escape. But that plucky girl dives to the river, and swims ashore to her motorcycle. The pursuers follow in an automobile.

Coming to a flimsy wooden bridge over the railroad tracks they attempt to cut her off, and Helen swerves aside and crashes through the rail, barely missing the wheels of a speeding train. The trainmen come to her aid and capture the wharf gang. The third degree brings out the fact that Benton had fallen from the express car at the bridge and been rescued by the wharf men who made him a prisoner in their cabin. His delirious ravings about the valuable package caused them to secrete that until a favorable opportunity came to dispose of it. [28]

Episode #103 -The Lost Messenger. Helen being given a hand by George Routh.

It didn't take Helen long to get back from delivering telegrams to catching crooks again. *The Gate of Death* #104 is a typical "Hazards" and is therefore melodramatically interesting. It was released in the first week of November, 1916. [29]

Helen succeeds in frustrating an attempt to rob the construction camp paymaster, and escapes with the money-bag, the crooks in close pursuit. Apparently all is lost when Helen comes to the edge of the precipice, but a huge four hundred foot chute has been built as a delivery shortcut down the mountainside to the railroad tracks offers a hazardous chance. [30]

With *The Gate of Death*, Helen has completed fifty-six one-reel episodes. She didn't have a lot to celebrate personally, but Kalem did. They decided to celebrate the "Hazards" for a far different reason.

November is being celebrated at the Kalem Studio in Hollywood, California, as the second birthday of the "Hazards of Helen." This month the company starts work on the production of the 105th episode of the one-part [reel] railroad series and makes the first step on its 3rd year of life.

Helen Gibson declares that her part in the birthday celebration will consist of crowding as many thrills as possible into the second anniversary month. "I started with the 'The Lone Point Mystery,'" she says. For in that episode there is not one big thrill, but three. The first comes when I am run down by a runaway box car, and grabbing the brake beam, swing under the car as it drags me along."

74

"The second film finds me helpless before an oncoming express train. I fall into a culvert between the railroad ties just in the nick of time, and then have to stay there while the director takes close-ups of the train whizzing along above me. And then for good measure I have to jump from the pilot of a speeding train to an automobile. If that isn't celebrating, I'd like to know what is."

Helen Holmes was the star in the first few episodes of this series. [31]

Kalem started the third year of "Hazards" with the release of *The Lone Point Mystery #105*, on November 11, 1916. In her stunts, she performs as always, "Fearless Helen." [32]

Episode #105 -The Lone Point Mystery. Helen being tired to the railroad track by George Routh.

Arnold schemes to defraud the insurance company by disappearing under circumstances that point to his death. He hides in a shack near Lone Point while awaiting the collection of his $100,000 policy by his brother. By shrewd deductions, Helen succeeds in learning his identity and frustrating his plot. [33]

She [Helen] is bound to the track in the path of an oncoming freight train, but manages to squeeze her body between the ties in such a manner that the locomotive does not touch her. The train cuts the rope and Helen grabs the brake beam of one of the cars, is dragged along for a ways, but manages to get the engineer to stop the train. Then the locomotive, with Helen on the pilot, pursues an automobile. Helen makes a flying leap from the locomotive pilot into the tonneau of the automobile. She captures the man who falsely tried to collect life insurance. [34]

The title of the next "Hazards" episode, *The Runaway Sleeper* #106, is a peek into the type of stunt Helen Gibson will perform faced again with a runaway car. [35]

A hot box and disabled brakes on the Greyson special attached to the Limited cause it to be dropped at a lonely point on the road. While waiting for the arrival of the repair gang and another locomotive to take the special on its delayed journey, the men of the Greyson party determined to get in a little fishing, leaving Greyson's daughter alone in the car. Spug and his hobo pal seize on the opportunity to board the special and get their fill of Greyson's food and wine. They decided to run the special down the tracks out of danger, but once started down grade, they find the disabled brakes will not respond and the special tears along at great speed. Helen learns of the runaway and sets out in an automobile in pursuit of the special. By a daring leap through the air she lands aboard a train speeding on an adjoining track. She jumps to the runaway and then with the aid of a rope brings it to a stop. [36]

Episode #106 -The Runaway Sleeper.

In *The Forgotten Train Order* #107, Helen goes back to her trusty motorcycle to perform another thrilling stunt. [37]

Dick Benton, crack operator of the United Syndicate, is forced by a breakdown to accept a position as operator at Lone Point. In a conflict with roughs from the construction gang, he is worsted and neglects to deliver an order to the local to take a siding and allow the Limited to pass. Helen sets out on her motorcycle to overtake the local. It has been her custom to race the local to the drawbridge frequently, and when the trainmen see her pursuing they think she is racing them and the engineer puts on increased speed. But Helen finally overtakes them and succeeds in boarding the train by a thrilling leap. [38] This prevents the collision between two trains, which, through a forgotten order, would otherwise have collided. [39]

The same day that *The Forgotten Train Order* was released to theaters, Helen was engaged in a completely different feat. She was not aided by a bank of cameras cranking away while she did some of her famous leaps. Helen was involved somewhere between a product endorsement or an exciting challenge. It might also have just been a celebrity stunt.

Helen waves to the reporters and photographers as she starts her trip up the mountain.

Richmond Times Dispatch - August 8, 1917 - Page 3

KING EIGHT CYLINDER

THIS is a photograph of Mr. F. W. Reuwer, 1928 Logan street, this city, who knows King quality and personal satisfaction, from his own experiences with a King. He says:

"All automobile owners have that Pride of Satisfaction after they have made their selection to realize their choice must at no time cause them embarrassment.

"Therefore their car must be powerful, it must be reliable, it must be easy to operate, it must have smart lines with pleasing refinements.

"But to those automobile owners who have mishaps, who sometimes have to walk or use street cars, I say 'Investigate the eight-cylinder King. I have one and am happy with the car and the service that is back of it.'"

Ease of Operation—
Proven by Tests—
Luxury and Comfort—

Helen Gibson arose one morning before breakfast, took her eight-cylinder King to the bottom of Lookout Mountain, in California, and scaled this grade on the high gear.

It was some achievement for Miss Gibson and her King roadster—To date no other woman has attempted to put her car over this mountain on the High Gear.

And now the eight-cylinder King is dubbed "Essentially a Woman's Car."

REX GARAGE & SUPPLY CO.
1917 NORTH THIRD ST. HARRISBURG, PA.
GOOD YEAR SERVICE STATION

Harrisburg Patroit - August 22, 1917 - Page 9

While automobile manufacturers are delving into the problems of proper exploitation methods for the coming year, like a thunderbolt comes the announcement from southern California that Helen Gibson of Los Angeles has conquered treacherous Lookout Mountain in a sensational high-gear in an eight-cylinder King," said M.L. Killy of Noyes-Killy Motor Company. "While the stunt itself is unprecedented and one deserving much applause, the thought that comes from it to the automobile manufacturers may change the present methods of exploiting motor car ability and advantage – turning the spotlight from the male pilot to what women can do in the shape of sensational and hazardous driving."

"Early in the morning, with a handful of friends and Los Angeles newspapermen, Miss Gibson started on her trip. The shifting lever was removed and the gears sealed in high. Miss Gibson took it easy and increased her speed as she went upward. Her arrival at the tavern in the summit of the mountain was a surprise for the inmates, and when she told them she had made the trip in high gear they were surprised, but convinced when they saw the lever was removed and the gear box sealed. Skillful driving, combined with the powerful mechanism in the eight-cylinder King, is the combination that allowed Miss Gibson to make this perilous ascent in high gear." [40]

Whatever a woman does in this era is looked upon with considerable interest. It places a human interest in the feature that, no matter what it is, its accomplishments by a woman is of far greater importance than if made by a Barney Oldfield or any other male human. Therefore, it is possible that Miss Gibson's climb may be the foundation for a series of events in friendly competition in the feminine world. Miss Gibson's climb will go down in the record because she made it first and because it was a problem that reality brought forth driving ingenuity. [41]

"Why I don't see any reason for making such acclaim over my driving the King eight up here," Miss Gibson said as she slid from under the steering wheel after bringing the car to a stop at the summit. As far as its being difficult, I don't see that it was. There never was a second when I thought of the necessity for shifting gears might arise."

"They told me to be careful at the turn leading to the long incline before coming to the switchbacks. Well, I was careful to the curve of going into it at about twenty miles per hour. I swung wide so I could cramp the front wheels and so the back wheels would not lose any traction. The car actually picked up in speed as soon as we made the turn and it kept on gaining." [42]

In *The Trial Run* #108, Helen Gibson again uses a horse and an automobile to save the day using two dare-devil feats. The episode was released during the first week on December, 1916. [43]

Superintendent Purdy informs Lane that unless he brings in a big express contract for the [rail] road he will lose his job. At Helen's suggestion, Lane calls on Manager Morton, of the United Fruit Growers. Later, on an auto trip, Morton's machine rams a telegraph pole and turns turtle on the railroad track pinning Morton beneath. Helen happens by on horse-back, and is vainly attempting to lift the auto when she hears the whistle of an oncoming train. Leaping on her horse, Helen hastens down the track to warn the train. But the trainmen miss her warning and she is forced to board the train by throwing her lasso over the brake rail and swinging herself to the car.

The train is stopped in time and Morton tells Helen, "Have your friend arrange for a trial run and if your [rail] road can beat the time on deliveries that we are now getting, the contract is his." On the day of the trial run, a dynamite explosion near the tracks hurls rocks on the top of a freight engine, stunning the engineer, and sending the train running wild down the track towards the trial run special. Helen receives orders to derail the engine, but to save the engine she decides on a desperate move. By a shortcut, she overtakes the runaway in an auto and leaps from the speeding machine to the freight, which is quickly brought to a stop. [44]

Danger is brought to Helen's attention in *The Lineman's Peril* #109, by a large dog. Helen responds as usual with another leap to save the lineman's life.

Teddy, a Russian wolf-hound, is Helen's companion at the Lone Point station. Dick Benton, the lineman, takes Teddy with him when he goes down the track to fix a damaged wire. The breaking of his defective safety belt plunges him to the ground. He attempts to crawl to his hand-car on the tracks, but collapses on the rails after scrawling a hurried note that he is injured.

Teddy takes the message, written in the lining of Dick's hat, and hastens down the tracks to Helen's station. With uncanny intelligence he succeeds in forcing her to read the note just as the Limited roars past the station towards the injured lineman. Helen sets out in pursuit aboard the engine of the officer's special on a siding near the station. By a daring leap to the top of the Limited's coach, she succeeds in getting the engineer's attention in time to bring the train to a stop within inches of the lineman's prostrate form. [45]

The following Saturday, December 16, 1916, *The Midnight Express* #110 was released. A robbery and Helen's trusty motorcycle play a big part in this one-reel railroad melodrama. Helen made a comment in a newspaper article about the photograph below. "Oh, bless those roomy skirts", breathes Helen, "I couldn't have done this a few years ago." [46]

Episode #110 - The Midnight Expess. With one hand on the boxcar ladder Helen steps off the flatcar.

Through the tapping of the wires a gang headed by Gentleman Joe learns of a shipment of a large amount of currency on the night express. By a daring scheme, they hold up the messenger between stations and succeed in making their escape. They go into hiding near Lone Point waiting for the investigation to blow over. Through a clue furnished by Helen, the railroad detective stumbles upon them but in the fight that follows he is overcome and the two crooks, boarding an engine in the yard, make their escape.

Helen sets out in pursuit on her motorcycle. As she nears the speeding train a flat car looms up ahead to block her path. But a plank running from the flat car to the ground offers a solution. Without a second's hesitation, Helen runs her motorcycle up the plank to the flat car, and as the machine tumbles to the ground on the far side leaps through the air to the handrail of the train. In a second, she has the crooks covered with her revolver and the train is brought to a stop. [47]

The Vanishing Box Car #111, is yet another episode in which the main interest is Helen Gibson making a leap between two large moving objects. The latest entry into the "Hazards of Helen" railroad series. [48]

Episode #111 -The Vanishing Box Car. George Routh chased Helen on his motorcycle and caught up with her car as she is leaping to a flat car.

Dick Benton succeeds in getting a big award for his Vulcan Iron Works by underbidding Hedley, but it is necessary that he makes his first delivery within three weeks to hold the contract. Powden, Hedley's henchman, causes an explosion at the Vulcan Works that destroys vital machinery. Additional machinery is shipped in boxcar 2535 to Lone Point, but before the car reaches Lone Point, Powden uncouples it and switches it to an abandon spur track running into the mountains. After the car is taken, the tracks are torn up leaving no trace of the theft.

At Lone Point, it seems the car has vanished into thin air. Without it, Benton will lose his contract. Helen starts out on a search on her motorcycle and comes upon Powden in the mountains near the car. She escapes in Powden's automobile, while he pursues on her motorcycle. She reaches the railroad tracks just as the fast freight is passing. As Powden overtakes her and leaps from the motorcycle to the car, Helen jumps to a flat car on the freight. The car, without a hand at the wheel, swerves, and is hurled over a cliff. Reaching Lone Point, Helen tells of her find and a party sets out and recovers the [box] car. [49]

In *The Race With Death* #112, add jealousy, a galloping horse, wild freight car, and a drawbridge and you have all the elements for Helen's latest episode. [50]

The unreasoning jealousy of the ranch foreman, in love with Edith, is aroused by the coming of the new night operator at Lone Point. So that, when it appears that the night operator has robbed Purdy, the rancher, the foreman's jealousy blinds him to further investigation, and he sets out with the punchers to deal frontier justice to the night operator. The latter is thrown into a box car at the Lone Point siding, which is then sent down grade to certain destruction. Helen arrives at the station in time to learn the terrible deed and sets out in pursuit on her horse. She finally overtakes the locked [box] car and leaps from her horse to the handrail. But before she can put the brakes on the open drawbridge looms up ahead, and it seems that her sacrifice will be in vain for there is barely time to bring the [box] car to a stop. Tugging at the brakes, Helen halts the car within inches of the edge of the tracks. [51]

CHAPTER 7

The Hazards of Helen Series Ends - 1917

Helen and Hoot were living at 1307 Hawthorne Street, in Los Angeles where they each left the house in the early morning. The couple went in different directions to the studio where they were starring in separate films. [1] After leaving Kalem, Hoot went over to Universal Studio and worked as a double and did stunt work in Harry Carey westerns. "At that time, I moved over to Universal, which had been built, in the mean-time, in the valley." Carl Laemmle had paid $156,000 for over 200 acres in the San Fernando Valley adjoining his back lot. "I went out with Harry Carey, who was the big western star in those days at Universal. I got a job there as a stuntman and also riding in the pictures. Finally, Harry Carey gave me a part in *Knights of the Range* 1916."

Harry Carey

In August 1916, without Helen, Hoot and Art Acord entered the rodeo competition in New York at Sheepshead Bay. After winning second place in the bronc riding event, the two men received only 24 percent of their winnings. The rodeo cashier carrying the receipts of over $100,000 was held up. So, the two boys headed back to Hollywood and the Universal Studio where they had better income. Upon his return Hoot got a part, and with better pay, in John Ford's first feature film, *Straight Shooting*, in 1917, which also starred Harry Carey. [2]

In the first week of the year, 1917 there is talk of a brand new Kalem Studio in Glendale, California, to be built right away. This would allow more films to be shot on a daily basis in a given area. Upon completion of the Comedy Company and "The Hazards of Helen" company now operating in Hollywood will be transferred to Glendale. The Hollywood studio will be closed.

The Mongol Mountain Mystery #113 is the first release of the New Year, 1917. Helen is engaged in a fight with those bad guys who want to destroy the Mongol Mountain Mine. This time Helen's dramatic stunt is swinging and not just leaping. [3]

Bret Morgan and "Squint" Booth are freight agents for rival railroads concerned in getting the contract for hauling the gold ore produced by the Mongol Mountain Mine. The contract finally falls to the [rail] road employing Morgan upon his promise to have cars in operation over an abandoned spur track within three weeks' time.

"Squint" leans that there is a law on the statute books that says that a railroad's right of way reverts to the owner of the adjoining property if no trains run over the rails within five years. He purchases the adjoining farms but falls under the suspicion of Helen, the telegrapher operator at Lone Point. Helen telegraphs her suspicions to the division superintendent who looks up the law and determines to send a special train over the abandoned spur track before four o'clock of the same day that the five-year period will expire.

"Squint" has left one of his lieutenants on guard at the mine to watch developments. Learning that the "special" has started and realizing that he must prevent its completing the trip at any cost, he forces Helen, on duty, to stand by while he telephones his aides to release the brakes on an empty car at the mine.

As "Squint" and his confederates run out of the station, Helen runs down the track towards the onrushing runaway car. In her desperation she can only think of one thing to do and Fate wills that a lineman repairing the telegraph wires shall be the one to aid her. Proceeding a bit further up the track she orders the lineman to climb a pole and to lock his legs around the cross arm in such a manner that his hands and arms are free. Helen then climbs to the top of the pole and as the runaway car, bearing a box of dynamite that "Squint" has placed in it, rounds the curve she reaches up her arms for the lineman to grasp.

With the pole swaying beneath its extra weight, the lineman takes a firm grip on Helen's wrists and swings her out over the track and drops on the runaway car as it passes. In a few minutes she has recovered her breath and is tugging at the brake wheel. She stops the runaway within inches of the oncoming special, thereby earning the gratitude of both Morgan and the division superintendent. [4]

In *The Firemen's Nemesis* #114, Helen's challenge is to save one of the railroads personnel when she takes to her trusty motorcycle to save the day. [5]

Joe, the Wop, employed in the roundhouse near Lone Point is notified he has been promoted and will take his place that night as a fireman on the local freight. On his way home, he stops at the station to tell Helen, the operator, his good fortune.

As Joe starts down the track towards home, Scarlotta, a member of a notorious vendetta that has marked Joe for death, shoots him from ambush. Helen sees Joe fall in the middle of the track and barely succeeds in dragging him to safety out of the path of the Limited.

Joe's wound was not serious and that night he takes his place as fireman on the freight. Determined to "get" Joe, Scarlotta visits the station where Helen is still at her key and after binding her and locking her in a closet, throws the switch so that the freight will collide with the cars on the siding. Helen frees herself by tipping over the clothes closet and saves the freight and its crew by reversing the switch.

Thwarted again, the vendetta agent climbs aboard the engine the following morning, overpowers the engineer and ties Joe to the drivers' seat after dumping the engineer out the side door. As the runaway engine [Scarlotta] has uncoupled it from the train proceeds to certain destruction. Helen gives chase on her motorcycle. After a perilous ride across a high bridge, she leaps for the engine cab and pulls herself by the rope that Scarlotta has used to tie up Joe, the fireman. She is just in the nick of time for the remorseless Italian had tucked a stick of dynamite to Joe's belt and set fire to a short time fuse. As Helen hurls the dynamite from the [engine] window it explodes, tearing a great yawning hole in the right of way. [6]

The title of Helen's next episode is *The Wrecked Station* #115, which gives moviegoers a possible idea to the stunt of stunts Helen will perform. The episode begins with a steam shovel and ends with a freight car full of dynamite. [7]

Helen, the telegraph operator at Lone Point, receives a telegram for Stanley Wayne, superintendent of the Graham Gravel plant, advising him that the plant has changed ownership and that Stanton Grey, and his daughter, Edith, is on their way to Lone Point to inspect the property.

Wayne is startled because he has gambled away the company's money and realizes that his books will not balance. Fortune appears to favor him when Grey is carried into the station unconscious as the result of an automobile accident. He extracts Grey's wallet from his pocket but Cole, the gambler, who has trailed Wayne, gets a photograph of him in the act.

With the photographic evidence, the gambler tries to blackmail Wayne. Helen and Edith, who suspect Cole and have followed him to the gravel plant, see the men fight and seize the evidence with Wayne in close pursuit. Helen climbs to the top of a steam shovel to elude Wayne and falls through it into an open dump car and from that into a car loaded with dynamite. Unconscious of her danger, she releases the brakes on this car from which she leaps to another train just before the wild car crashes into the Lone Point Station, blowing it to smithereens. [8]

The wrecking of the Lone Point Station was so well done that the Kalem Company has just built a new depot for the "Hazards" players and while they were about it they made it quite an elaborate affair. [9]

With *The Railroad Claim Intrigue* #116, Helen is involved in saving a life and catching two crooks who are trying to falsely get money out of the railroad. [10]

Barstow, a crook, conceives the idea of buying old automobiles, staging "accidents" with them, and settling with the railroad.

At the Lone Point crossing, one of his machines is hit by the train and the flagman is discharged because it appears he had been negligent.

Helen, the telegraph operator, gets the day off and starts for the hills on horseback. She meets Duncan, a railroad detective sent to investigate the increasing number of crossing accidents. Through Duncan's field glasses they see the discharged flagman set upon by Barstow and one of his associates, rendered unconscious and driven towards the Lone Point crossing.

Realizing that the fast freight is due and the crooks are planning another fake accident, Helen rides to a point ahead of the crossing. As the freight passes, she leaps from the saddle and clasping her arms about a stick of lumber protruding from a [railroad] car, draws herself up, dashes forward and warns the engineer just in time. [11]

Marjorie Daw   Wallace Reid   Charlie Chaplin   Syd Chaplin   Mabel Normand   William Duncan

It wasn't all work and no play for "fearless" Helen Gibson. You can't continually, week after week leap from horses, automobiles or motorcycles every day and not find something else a little more calming.

Widespread ambition seems to have descended upon the film folk on the West Coast with the following results: Marjorie Daw has taken up drawing, Wallace Reid, oil painting, and Stiles Dickenson, portrait painter of film folk, is acting as friendly critic.

Charlie and Syd Chaplin, William Russell, Anna Luther, J.S. Epping, M.E. Gibson [who is the Kalem Studio manager], Mabel Normand, William Duncan and Helen Gibson are frequently to be seen cavorting about the rink at the Los Angeles Ice Palace. [12]

A short newspaper article concerning the Kalem Jacksonville Studio, Florida went unnoticed by Helen. Even if she had read it, there was no indication that her association with Kalem was short lived. [13]

It is understood that the United States Film Corporation, producers of Black Diamond comedies will take over the Kalem Studio in Jacksonville, Florida, when the Kalem lease expires there April 27. [14]

Helen Gibson continues her stunts from horseback in her next episode, *The Death Siding* #117. There are two spectacular acts in this one-reel episode using a horse and a rope. [15]

Helen, the telegraph operator at the Lone Point Station, shields Miguel, a Greaser, under suspicion of having stolen some horses, until the real thieves are caught. Miguel is, never the less, told to clear out.

Up in the hills the crew of a freight train set out with a lumber car whose load of poles has shifted dangerously. Passing down the mine siding, a premature blast blows the brakeman off the deck and the car runs wild back to the main track. Miguel sees it and, prompted by gratitude to Helen, races his horse to the Lone Point Station ahead of the wild car.

Accompanied by Helen, whose horse is tied back of the station, Miguel races down the track and succeeds in lassoing an upright of the lumber car. He circles away from the car, holding the rope taut while Helen leaps from her saddle and pulls herself hand over hand to a foothold.

After that, nothing is too good for Miguel the Greaser. [16]

It wouldn't be an episode of "Hazards of Helen" if Helen Gibson didn't leap from a horse or automobile to a moving train. This episode, *The Prima Donna's Special* #118, is no different, and also includes a reunion of father and daughter. [17]

Helen, station agent and telegraph operator at Lone Point, is in despair over a broken sounder when [hobo] Morley, who has dropped off a passing freight, offers to fix it for her. Recognizing in him a man whose skills point back to happier days, Helen encourages him to tell her his story, promising to get him the position of relief operator if he cares to accept it.

Morley's story takes him back several years to the time he gave up his position as an operator following the death of his wife. He has never seen his little daughter since turning her over to the care of a rich brother.

Later Morley is installed as Helen's relief. While Helen is on duty she sees Morley through the station window talking to some tramps. He shakes his head in an emphatic negative. That same day Helen gets a wire that [Prima Donna] Mlle. Gazle, traveling on her "special," will pass through Lone Point.

The tramps board the engine of the fast freight and throw the engineer and fireman out in an endeavor to uncouple some cars loaded with silk. Helen receives word that the runaway is headed for Lone Point. With "Dad" Morley's help she appropriates an auto standing at the station and races down the track to meet it. Morley pilots the car as near the train as he can and Helen, straining every nerve, leaps the gap and brings the engine to a standstill just in time to save the "special" with the prima donna aboard. She proves to be Morley's daughter and there is a reunion. [18]

This episode of "The Hazards of Helen," *The Side-Tracked Sleeper* #119 contains the usual, normal, every day death defying stunts of Helen, the telegraph operator at Lone Point, but there is an absence of bad guys. This 1000 foot drama introduces the audience to an effective human touch. [19]

Last of the popular "Hazards of Helen" series, featuring Helen Gibson, which has been running 119 weeks, will be shown at the Lyceum theater tomorrow. [20]

Rupert Winslow, traffic superintendent of the railroad that employs Helen as operator at Lone Point, receives a telegram stating that his wife, who is ill, will be on the midnight express. He calls in Summers, a veteran brakeman on the passenger run and instructs him to watch over Mrs. Winslow and to side-track her sleeper if she requires medical attention.

Near the Lone Point Station, the superintendent's wife takes a turn for the worst and Helen, on night duty at Lone Point, is appealed to. She rouses Dr. Harris, whose headquarters are at the Burro Mine nearby. Meantime the sleeper has been set out on the Lone Point siding. Helen telegraphs Winslow, who charters a "special."

Careless switching at the Burro Mine sets two [railroad] cars running down the siding upon which the sleeper stands. Helen makes use of the doctor's automobile and manages to switch the runaway cars onto the main track. Having saved the sleeper, she sets out to warn the special. Reckless of her own danger, she makes a flying leap from the hood of the auto to the ladder of the box car and, climbs up, sets the brakes. Running forward, she signals the approaching special, which is brought to a grinding stop with only a few feet to spare. [21]

During Helen's seventy episode reign in the title role of Helen, the telegraph operator in Lone Point, was supporting actor, G.A. Williams. He played a part in forty of those episodes.

Exhibitors and fans, perhaps, have wondered at the ease and assurance with which G.A. Williams handled himself in various roles in the "Hazards." For his versatility there is a good reason. He has always been fascinated by railroad life and has had actual experience in almost every branch of train service.

Back in 1887, the show he was with became stranded in Wisconsin. Never afraid of hard work, he secured a position with the North Western railroad, and from a humble "brakie" he rapidly rose to a position of passenger conductor.

His first moving picture work was in the Kalem railroad series, and he has often remarked that it is a delightful compromise between actual railroading and stage life.

The work of these two players, Miss Gibson and Mr. Williams, in stories written by men acquainted with railroading, insures to every episode of the "Hazards of Helen" that realism so greatly sought after and so regularly found in Kalem productions. [22]

George A. Williams

There was no mention as to why the "Hazards of Helen" railroad series was cancelled and replaced with "The Daughter of Daring." Also no indication as to whom at Kalem made that decision, since the series was still very popular with film goers. At first one might think that the destruction of the Lone Point Station in *The Wrecked Station*, #115 might have indicated a change in location. But the new series takes place in Lone Point with Helen Gibson playing the girl telegraph operator.

At the Kalem Glendale Studio, two new series pictures are under way. The first will be heralded as "The American Girl" series, with a splendid cast supporting Marin Sais, a Kalem favorite. Frederick R. Bechdolt, a recent addition to Kalem's staff of contributing authors and already prominent in the world of fiction for his masterful tales of the golden west, is preparing the stories. The episodes will be in two parts, each telling a complete story, but retaining virtually the same players throughout the series.

The other series, to be issued in one thousand foot lengths [one-reel], will feature Helen Gibson, heroine of many dramas of the rails. In "The Daughter of Daring" the Kalem Company believes it has selected a selling title that will stand the test of competition and one that is eminently suited to the high grade character of the stories to be presented. A number of prominent writers will prepare the material on which these short length features will be built up, and Miss Gibson will have the opportunity to make scores of new friends with demonstrations of her fearless characterizations. Like "The American Girl" series, each episode of "The Daughter of Daring" will tell a complete story, making it possible for an exhibitor to book the released episodes in any order that he chooses.

Helen Gibson, whose daring has startled the civilized world, will have in her supporting cast, G.A. Williams, George Routh for the heavy parts, and L.T. Whitlock in the juvenile parts.

Copies of both "The American Girl" and "The Daughter of Daring" will shortly be in the hands of all the General Film exchanges and exhibitors will then have an opportunity to judge for themselves the seat-selling power of Kalem's newest series pictures. [23]

The new series of *The Daughter of Daring* had not yet been released to theaters as the weekly hype continued.

Following close upon the announcement emanating from the Kalem offices that a new two-part series called "The American Girl" and a new single reel series to be known as "A Daughter of Daring" are in the making, comes the news that no limit has been placed upon the number of episodes of either to be produced.

Judging from Kalem's record as a producer of series pictures, there will be at least twenty-five episodes of each new series before the two are brought to a close.

The Kalem organization, it is understood, will furnish several of the general exchanges with additional prints of its new productions so that there will not occur any disappointments when two or more houses set aside the same day of the week as "Kalem Day". [24]

While touring the new Kalem series, work on the Glendale, California studio is very near completion.

According to the latest reports from lower California, Kalem's new enclosed studio at Glendale is rapidly nearing completion. It is 100x150 feet. The present outdoor stages have been built so as to conform to convenient working with the new indoor studio.

Helen Gibson as A Daughter of Daring

Because of these important structures, many minor stages have been built on different parts of the grounds. Landscape artists will be employed for the beautification of the grounds. Speaking editorially of the Kalem enterprises as an asset to the picturesque little city of Glendale, the "Glendale Sun" says: "The establishment of the head offices of the Kalem Company in Glendale [producing division] has a wonderful meaning when the whole situation is analyzed. It means the steady employment of hundreds of people with a weekly payroll of approximately $40,000. All home labor is being employed in the building of this model institution and local talent will be given the preference in the production of the various pictures wherever practical." [25]

Moving Picture World - February 24, 1917 - Page 1157

A Good Title is Half the Battle

You can't expect to make money with poorly titled pictures

A DAUGHTER of DARING

Series of One-Part Railroad Dramas

ought to pack them in on the strength of its name alone.

But it has more to recommend it than a good, catchy title.

It has Helen Gibson for its star—

It is produced in Kalem's thorough style—

And each episode tells a complete story.

Short Length Features

These one-part dramas by contributing authors familiar with the technique of Railroading, are just as truly features as productions six times their length.

And we urge you to say so in your local advertising. We also want you to see the first episode—

"In the Path of Peril"

featuring HELEN GIBSON

Your General Film Exchange will be pleased to make an appointment to suit your convenience.

NOTE: All Kalem productions can now be booked independently of the other releases furnished by the General Film Company.

KALEM COMPANY
235 W. 23d Street, New York

Moving Picture World - March 3, 1917 - Page 1327

The hype concluded with an announcement from Kalem that the new Helen Gibson series, *A Daughter of Daring*, will be released during the first week of March, 1917.

The title selected for the first complete chapter of "A Daughter of Daring" is "In the Path of Peril," from a story by Herman A. Blackman, featuring Miss Helen Gibson. Not only is the main theme quite refreshingly new, but several genuine novelties have been incorporated into this release that will certainly be well received. [26]

The Robert S. Birchard Collection

A photograph of Helen Gibson taken in 1917.

CHAPTER 8

A New Direction - 1917

The *Moving Picture World* trade magazine pointed out to its readers that the new series was the "Hazards of Helen" railroad series with a new name, *In the Path of Peril* #1, and was being directed by Walter Morton. He directed *The Hazards of Helen* railroad series beginning with episode #105 when he took over from James Davis.[1]

Gypsy Joe and his band go into camp near the Lone Point station. Anita, the Queen, and one of the other women, spy on Helen chatting with Engineer Compton, enter the station and offer to tell Helen's fortune. The young engineer, who admires Helen for her pluck in sticking to this outpost of civilization, rewards the gypsies for their very flattering word picture of him in the role of a successful suitor.

Back at camp they tell Joe only a girl stands between them and the money in the station safe. Waiting until the freight has pulled out, Joe leads his men in an attack. Compton's fireman spies the gypsies. As the fireman takes the throttle, Compton jumps off and puts the band to rout. Joe is locked up in the jail. Anita contrives to pass him a saw in a bunch of flowers. That night he files the bars and escapes.

Joe later plans to wreck the freight, climbs aboard and puts Compton out of the way. Near Lone Point he throws the switch when the train is but half over it. Instead of derailing the cars, the rear truck of the flat car takes the siding and is cut loose. Unconscious of the accident, the engineer proceeds with his train broken in half and the flat car dragging on the ground.

Helen is informed of the wreck by telephone and immediately sets out on her motorcycle to overtake it before the Limited shall crash into it. Seeing the dragging flat car she puts on a burst of speed and rides up the slanting surface, abandoning the machine to catch the ladder grips of the freight car ahead. In a few moments she has reached the engine cab, freed Compton and brought the runaway to a stop. The gypsies are apprehended and Helen is thanked by the crew of both trains. [2]

In *The Registered Pouch* #2, in the new series, Helen uses a handcar from which she will leap. The girl telegrapher of Lone Point is teaching a small boy the art of telegraphy and he in turn assists her in this one-reel drama. This boy is a girl when not on screen, who adds that human interest touch. The episode was released a week before the end of March, 1917. [3]

Episode #2 -The Registered Pouch. Helen and the Kalem crew are listening to George Williams discuss the next scene using the velocipede (hand car).

Kinney, the old section boss, is delighted when Helen agrees to take his boy, Jimmie, in hand and teach him telegraphy. The boy provides an apt pupil and soon masters the code, but is heart-broken when the Chief says he is too young to take a regular shift. Jimmie swallows and helps Helen and the lineman construct a "loop" over to her house, and often remains in the station while she slips home for her meals.

Jose, a Mexican track hand, reports for section work much the worse for liquor. Kinney fires him. He hangs around and learns that a registered pouch has been lost off the mail train. While Jose plans a search for it, Jimmie shows up from a fishing trip with the lost sack. Helen locks it in the safe and leaves Jimmie in charge of the station. Jose and his gang bind up Jimmie and leave him in the lineman's room above the station office, where Helen's private wire terminates. By some good contortion work, Jimmie reaches the key and telegraphs the alarm to Helen. A hobo has seen the gang board a passing freight and helps Helen put a gasoline handcar in commission for giving chase.

94

Running down the siding, Helen leaps from the handcar to the freight. Seeing a switch, she tumbles off, but recovers in time to throw it and cause the rear of the freight to side-swipe the handcar in which the Mexicans are attempting a getaway. The bandits are completely done up, the pouch is recovered, and Helen makes sure that Jimmie earns the reward of a job. [4]

The Borrowed Engine #3, has the girl telegrapher at Lone Point getting involved in a freight contract with a rival company who tries to delay a planned test train at the water tower.

Dick Patterson, the "dude" engineer of the Midland, saves the superintendent's daughter, Grace, and one of her chums from drowning when their boat capsized on the lake that parallels the railroad. Helen, the operator at Lone Point, in answering Grace's questions about her rescuer, lauds him to the skies. Dick accordingly receives an invitation to a lawn party to be given by Grace. Having been suspended for two weeks for some slight inattention to duty, he is at liberty to attend.

On the day of the party, the Midland plans to run an important test train to cinch a big freight contract. Graves, business agent of a rival [rail] road, plans to delay the test train and thereby garner the contract. Graves, arriving early at the Cummings affair, calls one of his lieutenants aside and instructs him to see that the water tank near Lone Point is emptied. Grace overhears the plot and immediately phones to Helen just as she is about to be relieved, so that she can come over to the lawn fete.

In the meantime, Dick dressed in his afternoon togs, is pressed into service to run the test train, the regular engineer having been taken sick. Helen, ever loyal to her [rail] road, rushes off to the water tower after receiving Grace's message. There she is set upon by Graves' hirelings and made a prisoner on top of the tank. Dick brings his train under the spout to take on water and assists Helen to the ground. In their hurry to get away, the crooks have left their auto on the nearby road. Using it to good advantage, Helen and Dick overtake a special on the rival line and by a ruse, they persuade the engineer and fireman to climb out of the cab. Without further ado, Dick takes a crossover switch and is soon proceeding on his test run with a "borrowed" engine. [5]

Besides the new title of her series, Helen will also get a new director for episode #4, *The College Boys' Special*.

Scott Sidney, formerly of Morosco and Triangle, has started production on the new Kalem railroad series, "The Daughter of Daring," in which Helen Gibson is the featured player. [6]

Back of Mr. Sidney's selection as the directing genius of Kalem's one-part railroad dramas, there is the earnest desire of his employees to inject an atmosphere of freshness and spontaneity into the new series that will lift them far above the ordinary pictures dependent upon thrills for their drawing power.

Mr. Sidney joins the Kalem Company after compiling an enviable record of successes produced for other firms. His experience goes back more than twenty years when he was an actor, manager and director on the legitimate stage. For three years he was under the New York Motion Picture Company banner and in that time produced eighty one and two-reel subjects. More recently he has been with Pallas-Morosco and prior to that connection he directed some big productions for Triangle. He therefore comes to Kalem well fortified for the demands that will be made upon his ingenuity by the "Daughters of Daring" scripts.

A new camera man has also been engaged to start simultaneously with Director Sidney, and the supporting company for Miss Gibson will be increased as necessary. Exhibitors, it is said, will be able to note the effect of this new blood immediately. Mr. Sidney is an indefatigable and completed his first release in jig time. It is now being trimmed and will be shipped several weeks before its showing date. [7]

A big surprise was waiting for the new director when he arrived at his new place of employment.

All filmland, or that part of it near the Kalem Studios in Glendale, California, is enjoying the neat joke perpetrated on Scott Sidney, who is directing Helen Gibson in her new series, "The Daughter of Daring," by two bold robbers, undoubtedly amateurs of the first water.

When Sidney arrived at the "Lone Point" station used in this series of railroad dramas, one day last week, to begin work on a new episode, he discovered that the baggage room, used for storing props, had been systematically burgled of its movable contents. Even the station safe, which is never locked, gave evidence that it had been tampered with and Helen's motorcycle was also missing. [8]

The plot for the episode, *The College Boys' Special* was built around a college prank.

This one-reel episode of the "The Daughter of Daring" series is the best one yet. Helen Gibson, besides furnishing her usual thrills, shows us that she has histrionic ability as well. The story, too, is better than usual, and contains more interesting material than have any of the preceding releases. Besides seeing Helen Gibson's stunt of leaping to a wild freight car from her horse, we are given several minor thrills by other members of the cast. The story tells of the pranks of a bunch of college boys, and how Helen finally brings them to terms when, through her daring, she manages to sidetrack a freight car which they are in just in time to avert a collision with the Limited. [9]

Episode #4 -The College Boys' Special

96

The Mystery of the Burning Freight #5 takes place in a striking scenic backdrop of natural beauty from a story by Herman A. Blackman. The episode released on April 14, 1917. [10]

As a freight passes Lone Point, a young man falls from the brake rods. Helen, the operator, helps him into the station. The stranger reads the headline of a newspaper lying on the desk. Relieved at not finding the item he had expected he turns to thank Helen for her kindness, saying: "My name is Victor Brown. Can you help me secure a position?" The scene shifts to the ward of a hospital in a city several miles distant from Lone Point. A nurse is restraining a patient who in his delirium keeps repeating the name, Victor Brown! Victor Brown!"

Time passes and Brown, thanks to Helen, is holding a job as fireman on the local freight. One day when Helen and Brown, off duty, are cantering along the road a shot rings out and Brown pitches off his horse to the roadway. Thanks to a gunmetal cigarette case, Brown is uninjured and he tells his story to Helen. The man who shot him must have been Jim Selby, a gambler, smarting for revenge over a knockdown at Brown's hands. In falling, Selby struck his head on the pavement, rendering him unconscious. Thinking he had killed him, Brown fled. Sympathizing with Brown, but believing that he should explain matters to his worried father, Helen telegraphs Amos Brown to come to Lone Point.

The next day Selby and two hired thugs board the local freight. One of the thugs stays in a coal car while Selby and his confederate work their way over the tender into the engine cab, pitch the engineer out bodily and subdue Brown. After cutting the train [loose] just back of the coal car and running ahead a mile or so, they stop the engine and tie Brown to the pilot. Then they open the throttle and leap off. As the engine and its few cars gather momentum, a wisp of smoke curls upward. A cigarette stub has set off the refuse strewn on the floor of the car.

Helen hears about the runaway and leaping on a horse she rides down the track to prevent the almost certain destruction of the special bearing Amos Brown to Lone Point. As the freight whizzes past her, she leans out from her saddle and grasps the ladder of the last box car. Crossing this, the wall of flame confronts her. By lassoing the brake rod of the box car ahead of the fire trap, she has provided a perilous way of crossing, but it calls for superhuman nerve to accomplish this feat. However, she does it and reaches the engine in time to close the throttle, throw on the air [brakes] and bring it to a stop within inches of the oncoming special. There is a happy reunion between father and son in which Helen joins. [11]

Newspapers were quick to pick up a story about a fearless woman doing stunts and risking her life on the movie screen. They called her the girl who would not take a dare.

That Helen Gibson, the famous heroine of the General Film – Kalem series of railroad life, bears a charmed life is the opinion of every employee of the Kalem Company engaged in the making of this popular series which is now running at the principal motion picture theaters in this city.

Miss Gibson is known around the studios as the "girl who will not take a dare" and scarcely a day passes that she does not risk her life in some manner during the making of the picture. There may be a few skeptics left who do not believe that motion picture players take any chances and that most of the feats which astound picture patrons are film tricks, performed in laboratories. If so any of those doubting Thomas' could have been turned into believers had they witnessed the making of "The Mystery of the Burning Freight," a coming episode of "The Daughter of Daring."

In this picture, Miss Gibson was called upon to perform two hazardous feats in one day. The scenario of the picture called for Miss Gibson to ride a horse at breakneck speed after a runaway freight and leap from the saddle to the swaying side of the speeding train. But then her task was only started for a car in the middle of the train is a mass of flame and she must pass to get to the engine cab and stop the runaway. The burning car is a burning gondola so she lassos the brake rod of the car ahead and making her lariat fast, swings hand over hand above the burning car to the boxcar ahead and from there over the top of the train to the engine cab. Miss Gibson suffered severe burns in performing this feat but she simply had them dressed by the studio doctor and went on with her work as she considers a few bruises or burns as merely a necessary part of her work. [12]

The release dates for the next six episodes of "The Daughter of Daring" were advertised in the movie trade magazines. However, in reality they were never released to theaters until later in the year.

The action continued in *The Lone Point Feud* #6, but chasing crooks was replaced by an interesting situation between an elopement and a local feud. Both involved the railroad and Lone Point Station. This episode was not given a release date. [13]

Benton, the new superintendent of the railroad that employs Helen at Lone Point Station, will not designate Lone Point as a regular stop for the Limited. Squire Briggs, in retaliation, gets a village ordinance passed requiring all trains to slow down to four miles per hour within the corporate limits. Patton, an engineer, is fired for disregarding the ordinance and the war is on. Benton's next move is an order closing Lone Point as an agency and curtailing the passenger service to one train, and that in the dead of night.

But Benton and Grace, the Squire's daughter, have planned an elopement. Helen assists the lovers to board the Limited that stops on orders to pick them up. Squire Briggs gets the news and shows up at the station with the sheriff. Engineer Patton is about to take his freight train out of the siding when he finds himself looking into the muzzle of the sheriff's revolver. Under compulsion, he takes the Squire and Sheriff aboard and starts out to overtake the elopers. They pull out just as Helen gets word that a broken rail is sending the Limited back to Lone Point.

Helen goes in pursuit on her motorcycle, leaps from a bridge over the railroad into the tender of the speeding train, and gives a warning just in time to avert a collision. Benton and the Squire, thankful for their lucky escape, bury the hatchet forever. [14]

The Railroad Smugglers #7 contains one of the most dangerous stunts performed on a motorcycle by the girl operator at Lone Point. Helen's stunt is the centerpiece to this one-reel drama. This episode was not given a release date. [15]

News has just reached Lone Point that a force of Mexican bandits raided one of the American border towns the previous night, killing several people. Helen saves the newspaper containing the story to show to her friend, Julius Heckler, a rancher who is coming over that morning to unload a car of agricultural implements.

Heckler is disturbed by the news. He then asks that Helen bring any messages she may receive for him over to the freight shed where he will be working. The message arrives over the wire. As Helen is taking it down, a stranger peers into the window. He understands the Morse code. When Helen starts for the freight shed, he is disappearing down the road on a motorcycle.

On her relief period, Helen starts for the Heckler ranch to visit Mrs. Heckler. Returning to the station for a moment, she takes down an official order to hold the Limited for a special car containing a party of naval officers. At the ranch, the face of the mysterious stranger is again seen peering in at Mrs. Heckler and Helen. They run out. On her way home, Helen spies the stranger walking and leading his motorcycle towards the ranch. She follows.

She is astonished to see Heckler and a Mexican set upon the stranger and bear him into the barn, shouting: "Now we've got you – you American spy." Peering in the window, Helen sees that the place is a veritable arsenal.

Heckler and his son chase Helen, who has seized the stranger's motorcycle and started for the Lone Point Station. Hearing the freight train whistle, Helen at once thinks of the naval officers and rushes to Lone Point. She rides up the freight incline onto the loading platform, through the open doors of the now empty freight car, and leaps her motorcycle to a flat car on a passing freight. Crawling back over the tops of the intervening cars, she gives a warning to the officers. The train is stopped, an automobile is commandeered and the officers arrive at the barn just in time to save Holmes, the secret service agent, from death. Helen stamps out the fuse lighted by Heckler when he saw his plans failing and [Helen] receives the congratulations of all for her bravery. [16]

Scott Sidney, who was engaged temporarily to direct Kalem's railroad series, "The Daughter of Daring," has left the company, and James Davis, who formerly directed "The Hazards of Helen," is now directing the new series. A.C. Gage, who has had many years in the Kalem School, is assistant director. O. Zangrelli, one of the most expert cameramen in the industry, has been brought from Jacksonville, Florida, to photograph the railroad series. [17]

Along with her multitude of fans, the manufacturers of Helen's motorcycle were also paying attention.

Helen Gibson, better known as Hazardous Helen, has been asked by the concern that manufactures the motorcycle she always uses to run down wild locomotives to furnish a number of pictures of herself and the machine. These, the author of the letter states, are to be used in advertisements all over the country. [18]

Episode #8 -The Munitions Plot

The Munitions Plot #8 was not advertised in the *Moving Picture World* Trade Magazine except that its title lived up to the explosive one-reel drama plot. No release date given.

An investigation is held at Hart's Junction to solve the blowing up of ammunition trains. Helen, the operator, is questioned by a detective. Belding, the "brains" of the dynamiting gang, and Steele, his accomplice, approach and note what is taking place. Helen is excused. Crossing the platform to meet the incoming train, Helen sees Belding and Steele. She gets on the train for Fardale. Belding and Steele get in an auto.

Wertz, another member of the gang, "listens in" on the [telegraph] wire near Fardale and gets information regarding the munitions trains. Merkel, a lineman detective, sees Wertz. Merkel attacks him.

In an exciting chase, with the gang fleeing on a freight, Helen climbs a telegraph pole and gets on a carryall arrangement which runs along a cable stretched between two poles on either side of the tracks. She starts the carryall, and when she is over the train, one of the gang shoots and cuts the rope. She drops and lands atop one of the cars. She recovers and succeeds, with the aid of others, in capturing the plotters. [19]

The following episode, *The Detective's Danger* #9 involves the Secret Service and involves Helen on a typical horseback stunt.

There are a lot of fights in this film, including several that take place on top of moving trains. Helen Gibson's stunt this time is a good one. She leaps from the back of a saddle horse to the back of one of a team hitched to a wagon that is traveling alongside of a train. She jumps to the second horse's back and then to the train. In this manner, she is instrumental in bringing about the release of a Secret Service man who has been locked in the [box] car. [20]

Many fans of Helen Gibson along with those who like to write scenarios often send them to the Kalem Company. How many are ever used is not known. But Kalem isn't just looking for ordinary stories.

Phil Lang, in writing concerning a story rejected as not suited for the Helen series, writes an author as to the company's wants. Much might be applied to other companies making a special line of pictures. The correspondent wrote that he sent a story into Kalem "because it was a railroad plot." That was all it was, and Mr. Lang wrote:

The ordinary railroad story does not appeal to us. Each plot must be based upon a daring exploit of the girl telegrapher, and as we have made a couple of hundred of these already, there is little we have not used. We do not expect the outside writer to keep in mind all of those plots, but he should at least be certain that the stunt that forms the basis of the plot is sufficiently thrilling to be out of the ordinary. We have no use for plots without this punch. We do not write a railroad play and then put in a stunt, but rather we find a stunt and that suggests its own plot. We want the plot with the stunt when we buy from the outside, but we are primarily buying stunt ideas. And you must remember that Helen has jumped from bridges to moving trains so often that this is no longer regarded as a stunt, but rather as regular business. This also holds true of a jump to a train to do some eleventh-hour switching. We have gone far beyond the stage where either of these frayed-out thrills will be accepted as the reason for a story. It must be something new and daring – something that only Helen is apt to undertake.

In the same way, it is to be noted that other companies with special production kinks do not want any story along the general lines of their productions, but only real novelties. [21]

In *A Race to the Drawbridge* #10, three bank robbers and a runaway handcar set the stage to test *The Daughter of Daring's* knack to apprehend the bad guys once again. [22]

Helen is seated at the telegraph instrument in Fardale Station when a train pulls in. She delivers orders to the engineer and sees three men climb from beneath two of the cars and hurry away.

Chuck, Pug, and Brandon, three crooks, cross the field to their lair. Brandon, the head crook, has been wounded in the arm. An examination is made by his pals and it is decided to obtain a doctor. Chuck drives to Fardale Station and requests Helen to wire for a doctor, giving her a new ten-dollar bill to pay the charge.

Helen has received a message stating that U.S. Treasury ten-dollar bank notes of a given series have been stolen. In making change, she notes the newness of the bill and upon examination discovers that it is one of the notes stolen. She wires for a doctor and also a detective. They arrive: the detective takes the doctor's place and drives to the hut with Chuck.

Johnson, the detective, is discovered. The crooks tie him to a push car, and send it down a grade on the main line. Helen discovers the plot and races to the drawbridge which is drawn up as the push car and Johnson approach. She uses a lariat, throws it over the end of the drawbridge, lets herself down as the drawbridge goes up and as the car bearing Johnson, who has freed himself from the ropes, comes to the bridge, Helen slips her arm through his arms, which are handcuffed, and saves him from the plunge into the river beneath. [23]

The next episode, *The Deserted Train* #11 was a departure from the thrilling stunts displayed in the first ten one-reel episode of "The Daughter of Daring."

Helen Gibson's stunt was evidently faked in this [11th episode] number, which is very unusual in this series. Helen is supposed to jump from a barrel on a trestle to the end of a speeding train, but she jumps behind the train and the next flash on the screen shows her landing on the platform of the train. However, the number [11] is a worth-while offering. [24]

A small article appeared in the *Moving Picture World* Trade Magazine which may or may not have solved the mystery of Helen's last faked stunt.

Stop! Helen is Here!

The most startling complications and hair-raising situations confront Helen Gibson in every scene in her latest and most marvelous railroad adventures.

You'll feel like waving your hat and cheering when she comes through at the last breathless moment with the miracle of skill and daring that averts impending calamity by the fraction of a second.

A DAUGHTER OF DARING

is a brand new series of railroad adventures in which this popular Queen of the Rails performs astounding feats. Produced by Kalem, whose short pictures are famous the world over.

Don't miss this series. It's the biggest thing yet. Every episode is new —see one each week.

Rockford (IL) Morning Star - March 11, 1917 - Page 18

Helen Gibson, at her Glendale home, is recovering from a recent operation at Thornycroft Hospital and expects soon to resume her hazards in Kalem's railroad series, "The Daughter of Daring." [25]

Upon returning to the Studio lot, Helen was told that her one-reel railroad series, "The Daughter of Daring" was cancelled and her contract ended. [26]

A photograph of Helen taken in February, 1917, for a possible magazine cover.

CHAPTER 9

Riding With Universal - 1917

When Helen returned to the Kalem Studio, she found several major changes had taken place during her absence.

Kalem seemed to be another of the pioneer film companies to feel the keen competition in the film market. Soon after the closing of the Jacksonville Studio, business was almost completely suspended at the Glendale, California studio of the company. Helen Gibson, successor to Helen Holmes in the "Hazards" series, went to Universal, the company headed by Marin Sais, [Helen Gibson] was turned out to pasture and the Ham and Bud partnership alone remained to keep the plant open. [1]

There was no obvious reason why Helen's series was abandoned and the entire acting crew and director released. However, after all the facts were gathered it became quite clear there was not one single reason but a long, slow chain of events.

According to testimony given by picture magnates in the 1917 legislative inquiry as to why there should not be a tax on pictures in New York, more money is lost than made in pictures.

It was learned that "Mysterious Myra," a film made by the International Film company mysteriously made much money. The Kalem Company admitted that a film called "Social Pirates" with True Boardman and Marin Sais, contrary to the general conception of piracy, lost considerable money.

Mitchell Mark, president of Strand Theater Company, boldly averred that fully 85 per cent of the producers are losing money.

Yet between 10,000,000 and 11,000,000 people daily attend picture shows in this country. The average price of admission is between eight and nine cents. Just figure out for yourself the amount of money that passes from the people to the producers. At a fair average, $900,000 changes hands daily. Somebody gets that money. [2]

Helen appeared ready to move on, and wasn't out of work for long. Henry McRae, studio manager at Universal called and offered her a three-year contract at $125 a week. This was $75 more than she was making for the Kalem Studio. McRae wanted her for two and five reel Westerns. [3]

In addition to the *Daughter of Daring* premature series end, the last six episodes had not yet been released to the theaters through the General Film Company. However, Helen and the complete crew had been fully paid for their work on those episodes. [4]

The newspapers made it known that Helen Gibson was no longer a Kalem star.

Helen Gibson, "stunt" star with Kalem so long, is now a Universal player. [5] Helen Gibson, a noted daredevil of the films, has been engaged by Universal to appear in railroad thrillers. [6]

The Western Heritage Museum and Cowboy Hall of Fame

The Wrong Man.

Helen's first picture for the Universal [Bison] studio was announced as "Mettle and Metal."

Her first picture is known by the provisional title of "Mettle and Metal" – the first applies to Helen, of course. The little stunt she performs so nonchalantly in the second reel is merely riding furiously to an overhead derrick, catching the hook which is dangling from it by leaping right out of her stirrups, and swinging on the hook over the track on which a runaway engine, with a wounded man inside it, is coming. She drops from the derrick and enters the cab, steering the engine safely into a siding just in time as the Limited tears by. M.K. Wilson will play hero to her heroine, and the other members of the company include Jack Dill, Marc Fenton and Peggy Custer.

"One thing," says Helen, smiling, "I know that as long I'm doing railroad thrillers for Universal I'll never get bald. I'll be in the hair-raising business!"

Never cleared by the Pennsylvania State Board of Censors of Moving Pictures, this film was not released to the theaters. However, it did re-appear later in 1917 with a new title. Helen's first released film from Universal [Bison] studio was a bit part in *The Wrong Man* with Harry Carey in the lead role. [8]

The Perilous Leap.

Helen found herself in a good situation at the Universal studio. The type of film she was involved with was in demand.

The widespread revival of interest in good Western subjects has brought about a rearrangement of the Universal schedule so that hereafter a Bison feature will be released every other Tuesday, alternating with a Gold Seal drama.

So many requests for full-length Bison pictures have been forwarded from the various Universal exchanges during the past two months that it was deemed advisable to devote more attention to the manufacture of this brand. [9]

On September 10, 1917 Universal [Gold Seal] released *The Perilous Leap* with Helen playing the lead character in this three-reel western with plenty of action. [10]

Joe Mead stood on the porch of "Honest" Dad Shannon's shack, to all intents an agent of a munitions factory in search of quicksilver, but, in reality, the head of a clique of smugglers.

"Dad" Shannon believed in everybody, despite the fact that he knows Le Cruz, not far from the Mexican border, is infested with opium smugglers and Chinese.

He allows the "mercury" to be located in his shed, for Joe says the government is in need of it. Joe warns "Dad" to keep the affair a secret.

Pete Larkins, a renegade brakeman and member of the band, is in love with Effie [Gibson], Shannon's daughter, but she cares nothing for him. But when she meets Ned Donnelly of the Secret Service, the attraction is mutual.

Ned warns the Inspector to watch Mead. That night the Inspector sees Mead and "Dad" lifting boxes from an auto and carrying them into the shed. The Inspector approaches the shed and breaks the locks. He finds the boxes contain opium.

Mead meets Pete, who warns the former that Ned is in town and the two men hasten to look after their stuff. They see someone in the shed, and, when the Inspector comes out Mead fires and misses, then the Inspector shoots and both men fall wounded, while Pete takes the guns and runs away. "Dad" rushes out and Ned and Effie join him. Ned concludes someone has tried to murder the men, for there is no weapon about.

Later Pete tells "Dad" it will go hard if they find the opium in his shed, but he is willing to keep quiet if "Dad" will let him marry Effie. Effie offers to marry Pete to save her father.

Ned receives word that Pete is identified as a member of Mead's gang. He stops to watch him. Ned then urges Shannon to make a clear breast of the whole affair. Shannon tells Ned, Pete agrees to take the opium away and promises to help Ned catch the culprits.

Pete moves the stuff to the railroad yard and prepares to send it out on No. 7 along with some Chinamen. Effie informs Ned and he rushes to the depot where Pete is just resealing the car. Ned holds Pete up with his gun, but a Chinaman suddenly jumps from the car onto Ned, who is overpowered and thrown into the car. Effie has seen this act. She swings onto a car as the train passes, but is seen by Pete who runs to her, trying to prevent her from reaching the top of the car. They struggle. She gets away and climbs to the top of the car, but is caught and Pete tries to throw her in the refrigerator car. As they go under a bridge, Effie trips Pete, then grabs one of the girders and swings from the train, dropping onto the train several cars away from Pete, who seeing her trick, runs after her.

Meanwhile, Ned has had a desperate fight with the Chinaman, who is trying to knife him. Escaping, he climbs to the top of the car and sees the struggle between Pete and Effie. Ned knocks Pete from the train and catches Effie as she swoons. Finally the train is stopped. Pete is forced to confess to everything, exonerating "Dad," and Ned and Effie plan to be married. [11]

Helen's husband, Hoot, had been working on the screen at Universal in Harry Carey Westerns. Off the screen he wanted more action so he joined the Army. He stated years later, "I didn't want to do any walking, so I asked to be put into the tank corps. I thought I had it made riding the big iron monsters, but I was dead wrong, for I never walked so much in my entire life!" [12]

The newspapers told a slightly different story about Hoot Gibson and his enlistment.

"Hoot" Gibson, well-known cowboy actor at Universal City, is among those that have been accepted in the selective draft. Five years ago at the annual Round-up at Pendleton, Oregon, Gibson won the all-around cowboy championship of the world, his feats of horsemanship, rope throwing and steer breaking exciting the wonderment of the hundreds who were present. He was awarded a sterling silver, gold-mounted belt which he prizes as one of his most valued possessions. "Hoot" has been in pictures for about four years and at one time directed his wife, Helen Gibson, daredevil star of railroad pictures, when both were affiliated with the Kalem Company. He is registered as a racing driver, and his chief ambition, now that he is in the Army, is to emulate Eddie Rickenbacher's example and act as chauffeur for a general at the front. [13]

Two weeks after the last film reached the theaters, Universal [Bison] released Helen Gibson's next film, *The Dynamite Special*.

The Gayla Johnson Collection

The Dynamite Special

Jimmy Thurman, the fireman on Bill Manville's engine, is in love with Ruth [Gibson], Bill's daughter. He believes that she doesn't care for him anymore since Ralph Carleton, the son of the district superintendent, has become agent at Wellville. Joe Brooks, the dispatcher, is another who is interested in Bill's daughter, Ruth. So much so he determines to get Ralph out of the running. When Ralph's father comes to see how his son is getting on, Joe tells him that Ruth is keeping the young fellow from his work. His plan succeeds, for Mr. Carleton sends his son to another station. Carleton, meantime, has discharged Joe for drinking, and the man vows vengeance.

A Dynamite Special is to go west the next day and Bill and Jimmy are to pull her over. Ruth pleads with Jimmy to tell her where Ralph is, and he says that Ralph is at Crestmore. That night, Ruth, in overalls and cap, hides in an empty car of the Dynamite Special, and while concealed, overhears Brooks and his companion planning to blow up the superintendent's special, which the Dynamite Special is to meet at Crestmore.

Brooks and Leeds make their way to the dynamite car and steal a box marked "Nitro-Glycerine." Ruth watches them. The men uncouple the engine and drive away, while Ruth rushes to the station to warn her father. Ralph thinks of his father's special. Brooks and Leeds jump from the engine, thus allowing it to speed ahead by itself.

Ruth jumps on a motor-cycle and rides after the runaway. The Special is coming from the other direction. Ralph is unable to help, as the special has already left Hilldale, the nearest station. Gaining on the engine, Ruth jumps from the motor-cycle to the cab, shuts off the throttle, and reverses the engine. She runs ahead with a flag and hails the approaching special. Before she can tell Carleton the trouble, she faints away. Carleton leaves Ralph with Ruth, going to Bill, with whom he shakes hands. Brooks and Leeds are captured. [14]

Saving the Fast Mail.

Saving the Fast Mail. Helen lands on top of the engine cab in order to save the engineer.

In the span of two weeks, another Universal [Bison] film was released. There was brief action in the second reel as the trade papers put it. They went on to report that the production was put on entertainingly and made a good romance of the road. The plot of this film was interesting since it followed the same plot as *Mettle and Metal*, which was released to theaters under the new title, *Saving the Fast Mail*. [15]

Jim Hardy, son of the president of B. and Z. Railroad, went over to the window and looked out upon the busy yards. Then he came over to the desk where his father was sitting, returned the money that his father had given him, and asked for a job instead.

Jim went to work valiantly, no one in the yard, except Jack Day, suspecting his identity. After many months of labor, he graduated from the roundhouse to the position of fireman, and was assigned to the train run by Dan Brown, an excellent engineer. Through Dan he becomes acquainted with Helen [Gibson], the operator at the station, who is immediately interested in him, and he in her. When Dan tries to force his suit and kiss her, Jim interferes and a fight takes place. This is reported, and it causes the dismissal of both Dan and Helen. Dan learns that Jim is Hardy's son, and determines to "fix" him, thinking that it was he that "squealed." When Jim learns of Dan's suspicions, he makes up his mind to acquaint Helen with the facts of the case, and then to give up his job.

Helen practicing her stunt in "Saving the Fast Mail" on the Universal Studio back lot.

Jim steps into the cab of the engine, and a fight is begun between him and Dan. The engineer knocks Jim unconscious and steps off the engine, pulling the throttle open as he does so. Jack sees the engine start off and the cause of it, but is too late to stop it. He rushes to inform Hardy of the affair. The only thing to be done is to derail the engine to avoid a head-on collision with the fast mail train. A message is sent along the line by the dispatcher and Helen thus hears of the trouble.

Riding to an overhead derrick, she catches the hook which is hanging from it and swings over the track on which the engine is coming. She drops onto the engine and enters the cab. The man at the yards throws the switch and Helen drives the engine into a siding as the Limited passes. Jim has now recovered. Hardy arrives. Jim explains the trouble to both his father and Helen, and all ends happily. [16]

Helen emerged two weeks later with another Universal [Gold Seal] offering called *The End of the Run.* This time the story was told in three-reels.

Giles Stafford, a brakeman, sees Portland Pete, a hobo, climb into a baggage car, and begin counting a big roll of bills. When Giles asks him if he is trying to beat his fare, Pete retorts that the money he is counting is counterfeit and that he is circulating it for a gang in the East. Giles says that he will try to get rid of some of it for him, as he believes

110

he has a better chance. Pete cashes a bill at the cigar-stand, and later Giles does the same. The clerks pay no attention to the bills, but later the counterfeit bills are found, and the clerk remembers that he changed two twenties. The sheriff is notified and a Secret Service man, William Craig, comes to carry on a quiet investigation.

Jim Durman distrusts banking institutions. He hides his money in a fruit jar, in spite of his daughter Nona's [Gibson] protests. He has nearly enough to buy the house in which they live. One day, while they are talking about the money, Giles listens at the window. Giles is in love with Nona, but she repulses him. He breaks into the Durman home, takes the money and substitutes the counterfeit bills, but the band of his hat falls on the floor.

Craig finds that the only definite clue leads to Durman or Giles. Giles will bear watching more than Durman, but Craig hasn't sufficient evidence to arrest Giles. One evening, he stops Nona and begins arguing with her, finally grasping her wrist. Craig goes to the girl's rescue and walks home with Nona, who introduces him to her father.

Counterfeit bills are paid to different merchants by Jim, and Craig decides to talk with Durman, though he hasn't confidence in his honesty. Jim shows him the roll of counterfeit bills from the fruit jar, but, though the evidence is enough to warrant his arrest, Craig lets him go out on his run. Craig arrests Pete and finally gets a confession from him, and the knowledge that Giles is going to leave his train this trip and meet Pete in Denver.

Nona has discovered the hat-band on the floor. She jumps on her pony and rides away, meeting Craig and telling him of her discovery. Meanwhile Jim's train is ready to start. Giles swings onto it and climbs to the top. Nona, on her pony, races with the train, while Craig gets a hand-car and starts after the train. Nona lassoes Giles, but he cuts the rope. She at last catches up with the train and, climbing to the top of it, holds Giles up with her revolver. Craig arrives and Giles is arrested. [17]

November 10, 1917, a press release about a new series made by the Kalem Company was issued through the General Film Company. This was "[A] The Daughter of Daring" series made earlier in 1917, before Helen Gibson and the entire crew were let go.

General Film Company announced this week the release in November and December of a new series of one-reel "thrills" featuring Helen Gibson, who has figured in a number of railroad "stunts." Five subjects will make up the series and they will be offered under the general title of "A Daughter of Daring." The dramas were made by Kalem.

The first will be called "A Race to the Drawbridge" and will be issued November 7. Others to follow on the weekly (basis) will be entitled "The Munitions Plot" (November 14), "The Detective's Danger" (November 21), "The Railroad Smugglers" (November 28), and "The Deserted Engine" (December 5).

Miss Gibson first established her reputation for daring in "The Hazards of Helen" series produced by Kalem. She chased trains on motorcycles, dropped from bridges onto speeding trains and performed other daring feats. She has been called "Danger Girl." [18]

The normal release time of Helen's films had been fourteen days ever since joining Universal. Her next film, *Fighting Mad*, took thirteen days longer. Since there were no announced serious studio problems, Carl Laemmle's new studio policy would hold the answer.

Carl Laemmle, president of the Universal Film Manufacturing Company, has issued the following statement concerning the temporary suspension of some producing companies at Universal City.

"Until we know exactly how seriously the war tax is going to affect us," says Mr. Laemmle, "and until we are positively convinced that the exhibitors will co-operate in collecting the money from the public, we intend to take advantage of the fact that we have accumulated the largest reserve stock of negatives in our career by laying off several feature companies for about four weeks."

"The fact that the cloudy and rainy season are about at hand helps us to arrive at this decision, for we have not quite enough electric light stages in Universal City for all our companies. By suspending operations until we have used up a certain amount of our big reserve supply of negatives, we avoid the heavy loss of having several companies lying idle on cloudy and rainy days. This, by the way, happened only last week entailing a loss of approximately $15,000."

Mr. Laemmle continues: "No doubt this temporary suspension will give rise to various rumors, and it is to prevent any possible misapprehension of the true situation that the Universal Company has issued this official announcement." [19]

The film *Fighting Mad* was released on the first Monday in December, 1917. This was a slightly different role for Helen. J.G. Alexander and Fred Myton wrote the story under the original title of *Man of God*. [20]

This five-reel production is particularly good in its faithful reproduction of the atmosphere and character types of the days of '49. Certain of the characters are very well drawn, notably the preacher hero, who comes with his wife to fight the devil in a mining camp, the gentleman gambler, his friend at the dance hall, and other minor portrayals.

The tale begins with the appearance of the preacher and his bride [Gibson] at the camp of Arapahoe Flats. "Doc" Lambert, as the divine is called, takes a small cabin. The gambler, "Clean-up" Carter, is shot in a row over the card table and taken to the minister's cabin. Here he recovers his strength and entices Lambert's wife to leave her home.

The wife is about to become a mother and such is her general depression that she agrees to leave the mining camp. Later she returns, after being deserted by the gambler, and falls on the roadside. She is taken into a cabin by Faro Fanny, the gambler's dance hall friend, and dies after the birth of her child. "Doc" Lambert comes to the cabin after his wife's death and is so angered by the turn of events that he almost loses his reason. He leaves the child on a doorstep and begins wandering about the country, hating and despising everything but the cur dog that goes with him.

Years later Lambert, now a confirmed drunkard, returns to his camp. A young girl named Lily befriends the dog when it is injured and wins Lambert's confidence. "Clean-up" Carter and his friend reappear and the former takes a fancy to Lily. The girl is saved from him, and Lambert, after recognizing Carter, shoots and kills him. Lambert experiences a return to his former self-respect and also discovers Lily is his daughter. [21]

Just before the end of 1917, Helen became aware of a serious problem at the Kalem Studio. The General Film Company had released five of her earlier *Daughter of Daring* one-reel dramas in the name of the Kalem Company. [22]

For an indefinite period, Kalem has decided to cease producing pictures, it is announced. While no reason is given for the action, it is understood that the question of war tax payments entered in. Kalem was one of the oldest companies, an original licensee of the Motion Picture Patents Company in the General Film Company. [23]

Helen continued into the New Year making films while her husband, Hoot, was serving in World War I. [24]

A Universal Studio publicity photograph of Helen Gibson.

Universal Studio publicity portrait of Helen Gibson.

Witzel

To Dear Friend
"Mrs Price"
With My Very B
Wish

The Margaret Herrick Library Collection
Universal publicity photograph displaying a feminine side of "Fearless" Helen Gibson

CHAPTER 10

Helen's Ride at Universal Continues - 1918

In between films, several actresses at the Universal Studio got together for the war effort.

Several of the girls at Universal City, including Priscilla Dean, Neva Gerber, Molly Malone, Helen Gibson and Jessie Mitchell, have banded together for the purpose of "adopting" the recruits to Uncle Sam's Army, who were drawn or volunteered from that film community. Schemes of some sort are constantly being promoted by the actresses who appear in Universal pictures to furnish tobacco, necessities and delicacies to their friends in khaki. [1]

Helen took some time off from the studio to again pursue her second love, the rodeo. With the aid of the United States Marines, Douglas Fairbanks put the rodeo idea together. This event took Helen back to her days with the Miller Brothers 101 Ranch. [2]

Twenty thousand people saw the sports and pastimes of the range enacted at the big Red Cross Rodeo in Los Angeles.

Douglas Fairbanks Sr.

On the field, cow punchers galore in the most outspoken shirts broke broncos, bulldogged steers and shot and yelled to their heart's content. When they tired, a band of fiercely painted Indians enacted a war dance or a crew of clowns amused the crowd with burlesque gun-fighting and bronco breaking.

Trick shooting and roping, fancy riding, Pony Express races and a thrilling stagecoach hold-up were other events that will make the occasion [thrill] one of the long stand in the memories of those attending.

The Rodeo was the idea of Douglas Fairbanks, the famous movie star, and it was due to his untiring efforts that the affair proved so successful.

116

Mr. Fairbanks placed much credit upon his assistants, chief among whom are the United States Marines. As usual, the boys who are "First to Fight" were also first to aid this worthy cause, and did their bit toward insuring the success of the Rodeo.

Enlistments are still accepted for this attractive branch of the service. Recruiting offices are located in Los Angeles, San Diego, Bakersfield and Phoenix. It is well, however, to first write for a booklet concerning the Marine Corps before appearing for examination. These booklets are mailed free of charge. [3]

The Coconino Sun (AZ) January 25, 1918 - Page 5

Upon her return to the studio, Helen began working on a current Universal serial with another female daredevil.

Marie Walcamp and Hazardous Helen Gibson who appear in the tenth episode of "The Lion's Claw" serial called "Through the Flames" and shows her utter disregard of danger in sliding down a rope thru a mass of flames. The charge of the English infantrymen against the moon men is very spectacular. Helen is noted as a dead shot and a rough rider, so while it amazes Easterners to see her stunts on horseback, the Westerners have heard of her before. [4]

Helen rejoins her regular crew to film another action western, "Play Straight or Fight," from a story by Leon De La Mothe. The film was released in the middle of June.

117

The villain of the story frames up a stagecoach robbery on the girl's brother, but the girl gets advanced knowledge of the crime, and prevents same. This is conventional in plot, but is made exciting and generally successful by the graphic nature of the attempted holdup. Fast horseback riding and picturesque scenes are features of the production. [5]

A week later, Universal released "Quick Triggers." [6] This two-reel western had Helen in a secondary role behind Neal Hart and Eileen Sedgwick and was advertised as a film full of "Pep." [7]

Helen was once again back into cranking out a two-reel western each week for Universal. Her next film, "The Midnight Flyer," was released with Helen in the starring role.

Marie Walcamp in *The Lion's Claws*, a Universal serial.

Danny Morgan had escaped from jail, but found a haven with his sister, who was a telegraph operator in the West. When his pal, Duke, got out of jail, he took a liking to Helen, although he was pledged by every tie to Evelyn, who had been true to him during his entire prison sentence. His knowledge of Danny's career gave him the opportunity he sought to win Helen. He forced Danny to hold up a bank and then told the sheriff that it was to take place. On the same day, he forced Helen to run away with him. He had failed to reckon, however, with Evelyn and resolved to kill Helen rather than to surrender Duke to her. Her first shot went wild, and Helen told her how matters stood.

When Duke entered the station to claim Helen, he was met by Evelyn, whose aim had steadied in the knowledge of his treachery. [8]

Universal released "The Branded Man," a two-reel western drama with Helen in the lead. It was action packed, but didn't require our heroine to leap from a horse or car to or from a train. This was Hoot Gibson's last film before reporting for duty with the Tank Corps.

Val Heywood and his confederate agent, Triovio Valdez, are caught at cheating, and Heywood, branded publicly as a criminal, vows in a rage to kill John Ewing, the leader of his ranch gang cowboys.

Heywood and Valdez again join forces and are ordered out of the town by the sheriff [Hoot Gibson]. They send word to Ewing that he is wanted urgently on the edge of town. Then ambushing Ewing, they keep him bound and gagged while they hold up the stage. Ewing is still bound and left in a weakened condition with a mask and the stage loot to incriminate him. Heywood and Valdez escape to a destination high in the hills.

When Ewing's daughter [Helen Gibson], becomes worried about the disappearance of her dad. Then with her sweetheart, Jim Calvert, foreman of Ewing's ranch, they go in search of him. The sheriff is informed of the hold-up of the stagecoach and also starts out with a posse. Sometime later, Ewing is found underneath the underbrush and the posse believes him to be guilty. Helen and Jim notice tracks leading into the hills. They investigate and find – the two men have been hiding away.

Helen decides on a way to catch Heywood, but he dashes to the ranch and goes inside. The posse approaches the ranch and begins firing at Heywood. He quickly snatches up the granddaughter, Sierra, and all shooting stops. The men don't dare to shoot in fear of hitting the child. Jim is slightly wounded. Heywood finally puts the child out of danger and releases her, and as he starts to run Helen lassoes him, yanking Heywood directly from his horse that captures him. Valdez is killed by Jim. [9]

July 20th, it's another Helen Gibson film, "A Shooting Party", [10] which was followed up a week later with another two-reel railroad story, "The Payroll Express." Helen was happy and busy as ever.

A western featuring Helen Gibson as a girl detective sets out to clear up some mysterious train robberies. The plot hinges on mistaken identity, a certain engineer having a double who is in league with the train robbers. This has a number of good thrills, some of which are more entertaining than convincing. [11]

Helen's next film was a big surprise to her fans. It wasn't a western, nor a railroad film. It was a comedy with Helen playing a bit part. It was in theaters in mid-August.

Alice Howell in "Bawled Out," a two-reel comedy, is the latest offering featuring this star which comes from the Century Comedy Company. According to Universal officials, "Bawled Out" is the best Alice Howell comedy released to date. Featuring so popular an aggregation of players as Hughie Mack, Vin Moore and Helen Gibson in support of Miss Howell. Universal regards it as being out of the ordinary.

Hughie Mack enacts the role of the poor unfortunate jailbird, while Miss Howell is his sweetheart who comes to visit him at his "home with the iron windows." This comedy was directed by James Davis, who has a number of successful laugh-producers to his credit. [12]

Neal Hart

With the comedy behind her, it was back to playing another bit part in a three-reel western again starring Neal Hart in the lead role. The film, *Beating the Limited,* was released on August 24, 1918, three days before Helen's twenty-seventh birthday. [13]

Neal Hart plays a wealthy young man, in love with a daughter [Gibson] of a rich man. The crooked secretary gets a hold on the father, but the hero outwits him. There is plenty of action in this, some of the scenes occurring in the East and some on a ranch. The auto chase after the train is well handled. Not an unusual subject, but enjoyable throughout. [14]

Helen returned to the starring role with her regular crew in her next film, "Danger Ahead." It was a two-reel railroad Western Bison film.

Lucille [Gibson] is the daughter of the man who owns a train line in Valley Junction. Tom and Ralph both work for Lucille's father. Both are very fond of Lucille. She is fond of Ralph and thinks Tom is a bully. Tom is jealous of Ralph but tries to hold back his feelings. When Ralph and Tom are on a run together, Tom causes some confusion among the crew on a train run with Ralph in charge. It almost caused an accident.

Ralph is called on the carpet, but insists that he followed signals from the brakeman. The brakeman swears he had not given signals and the conductor and his crew stands by him. Ralph is given a reprimand. Lucille is sure Ralph is not to blame.

The engineer on the Limited is forced to lay off because of eye trouble and Ralph is given the run. This makes Tom furious. A friendly operator tells Lucille that her sweetheart is on the Limited and will come through Valley Junction that day.

When Tom's train starts that evening he is told to look out for the Limited in charge of Ralph. Tom discovers that an oil car is leaking directly over the rail. He sees his chance to hurt Ralph when he hits the slippery rails. Tom is almost caught in his own trap however, for they stop on a hill where they have to double to a next siding. The engine sets out on the first part of the train, the remaining cars standing on the track which is being smeared with oil. Tom and his brakeman apply the brakes, which refuse to hold, and they jump to the cars, which start down the hill.

Lucille, riding in her car, sees the runaway cars coming at a rapid rate. She can't reach the switch to derail them, so determines quickly to try to stop them. In an automobile she goes after them and makes a desperate leap from the motor car. She applies the brakes.

The Limited speeds along. Lucille has let the runaway cars into a siding and has cleared the main line. Lucille is rewarded by having Ralph given a passenger run and Tom is discharged for carelessness. [15]

The hero Ralph (M.K. Wilson) is about to kiss Lucille (Helen Gibson) in the final scene of Danger Ahead.

Fourteen days later, Helen returned to the screen with her regular film crew in the Universal release of "Under False Pretenses." The newspaper ad depicted Helen in action with romance as a big part of the plot. [16]

Helen Gibson and M.K. Wilson are in a railroad drama. This picture contains a very thrilling scene in which Miss Gibson rides up behind a railroad train and leaps from her horse's back onto the train. The story tells of the love of the railroad president's son, working as a lineman, for the telegraph operator. He meets with an accident and the girl [Gibson] compels his father to pay for the operation. [17]

A movie trade magazine advertised "The Fast Mail," as five reels of thrills boiled down to two hurricane reels. Universal released Helen's latest railroad drama in early October. [18]

A stirring two-reel railroad story, based on a tale by Frank H. Spearman. Helen Gibson performs a daring feat in the closing reel, jumping from a telephone pole to the top of a moving train. The story has considerable plot, telling of the struggle between competing railroad lines to get a Government mail contract. Others in the cast are Val Paul, Buck Conners and G. Raymond Nye. A strong subject. [19]

Coming attraction theater glass slide

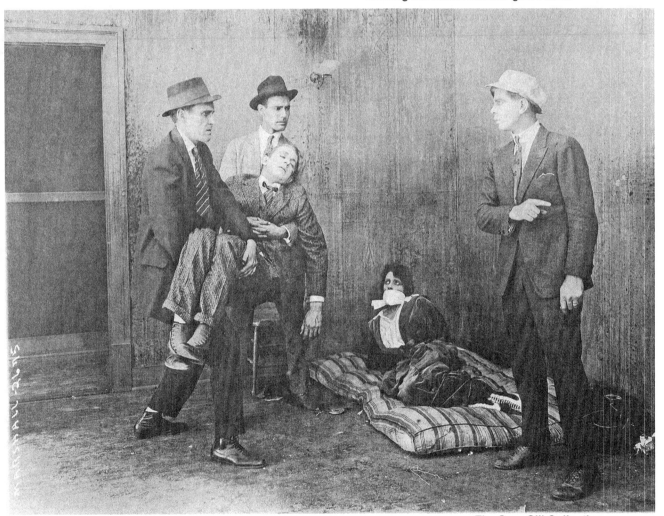

The Sam Gill Collection

G. Raymond Nye and Val Paul are holding Buck Connors as Hoot Gibson (right) is giving orders.

During a four week period, new and re-issued film distribution had been suspended due to the Spanish influenza epidemic in 1918.

The embargo is listed from October 15 to November 9. Branch offices of all film companies will continue to serve exhibitors with pictures regularly released prior to October 14. Serials and news reels, the only exception to the rule, will be issued as usual.

Forty per cent of the film houses in the country have been closed through the epidemic. This caused the producers to take drastic action. However, sufficient films are on hand to tide over the emergency. In fact, there are more than enough to assure excellent programs not only during the barren period, but until normal conditions are resumed and new releases issued. [20]

Helen's next role in *The Dead Shot* was slightly different from her usual railroad drama. She played the part of a stranger with a quick finger on her trigger. This Universal released as a two-reel offering. [21]

Reproduction poster

A dance-hall girl known as "The Tigress" [Gibson] rode into the town of Los Alamitos, forced the biggest man in town to give her his horse when her own stumbled, took possession of the dance-hall and saloon and began to run things.

She ruled with a loaded quirt that cut ugly gashes in leering faces and at times gave emphasis to her remarks by flashing an evil-looking gun.

Jim Thornton, owner of the biggest mine in the country, lives in decency and is planning to marry the village schoolteacher. She does not know that Thornton betrayed "The Tigress" years ago when she was a sweet girl in her teens.

Trouble seems to swoop down on Thornton's mine. The men strike and there are many mysterious explosions. No one but Thornton knows the cause. Behind the work he sees the cool head and quick hand of "The Tigress."

"The Tigress" learns that Jim and the schoolteacher are going to go East to be married, taking with them little Dick, the baby born of Thornton's treachery to "The Tigress."

Thornton is harassed on two sides; by the striking minors and by the demands of his company stockholders that he straighten out the tangle. At the critical moment "The Tigress" comes to him and says that she will prevent the blowing up of the mine.

Thornton, anticipating her demand, says: "I am going to marry a lady."

Then Thornton pointed out to her that his ruin would mean poverty for their son. "The Tigress" races to the mine and saves it from destruction by shooting the glowing fuse from a striker's hand. Then she returned to Thornton. He sat limply in his chair.

"I've been a dog," he said.

The schoolteacher led little Dick to "The Tigress" and told him that she was his mother.

A re-made Thornton and "The Tigress" are reunited. [22]

The Dead Shot.

Helen's next film "The Silent Sentinel" which concerns the rivalry of two men over a girl, was without a railroad in the background. One reviewer stated that the action was of a conventional melodramatic order as the subject was of about average strength. [23]

Barbara Benton [Gibson] lives with her father in a Western cabin. He had been wounded in a quarrel and she was nursing him under the doctor's directions. One day Steve Rollins came by the house, and when Barbara confronts him with a gun he laughs, displaying no fear, and then he introduces himself. He is the heir to the farm they are living on. They then enter into a pleasant conversation.

Ed Morgan, the foreman of the ranch, who has been a persistent pest for Barbara's hand, comes in the room greeting Barbara and speaks to Rollins whom he hasn't seen in quite a few years, saying: "Travelin' don't seemed to improved yuh none, yuh just as ornery as when yuh were a "kid." At that, Steve presses the blade of his knife against

123

Ed, then turns to a bit of sarcasm, saying: "If it ain't ole Ed Morgan up to his same old tricks, always trying to be someone." From then on jealously became a part of Ed and grew deeper and deeper, filling him with revenge and envy, who was rapidly gaining a soft spot in the heart of Barbara and her father.

One day a terrific fight took place at the saloon between Steve, Ed and several others there. Finally Steve got away, and when he met Barbara he told her that all would be well. They both raced off to find Ed. Meanwhile Ed entered the Benton shack, quickly being ordered away by her father when he killed him, and just as he began attacking Barbara, Steve came hurrying back and upon seeing this, a heated fight took place between the two angry men which resulted in Ed's death. The town sheriff and his men had been hunting Steve, and when they finally reached the cabin, they saw Barbara in the arms of Steve, mourning the loss of her father. Everything was explained to the sheriff and the whole matter was cleared, leaving Steve and Barbara to live happily after. [24]

In "Captured Alive," Helen continued not to use the railroad as a plot element. In this two-reel drama, she was in the middle of cattle country. Edward Peil, Sr., played her sweetheart in this Universal release.

HELEN GIBSON IN "THE ROBBER"

The Robber

The ever increasing activities of cattle rustlers in the El Cajon County is the direct cause for an election for sheriff. Dolly Martin [Gibson], daughter of one of the biggest cattle men in the county, campaigns for the election of her sweetheart, Jim Watson, while her father, Charles Martin, remains a staunch supporter of the present sheriff, Bud

Harris. Harris is defeated, Martin, disappointed, makes Harris foreman of his ranch. Harris as the new foreman fires all the old employees, installing men of his own choosing. Dolly becomes suspicious of the new men, discovers that Harris, the ex-sheriff, is the leader of the band of cattle rustlers. Her father is arrested by Jim charged with rustling and attempted murder. Through Dolly's efforts he is freed, and the entire gang captured, thus effecting the necessary reconciliation between her father and sweetheart. [25]

On December 21, 1918, Universal released Helen's next film. "The Robber," a Western without her typical railroad theme. The newspapers advertised this two-reel drama as "an engrossing story of the stage coach days of the West." [26]

This Christmas, Helen received an unexpected gift.

Helen Gibson, the star of "Captured Alive," and a number of other two-reel Universal western dramas, will have a Christmas gift worth while in the return of her husband, "Hoot" Gibson, from an Army encampment at Camp Dix, New Jersey. He left a position in stock at Universal City to enlist in the Tank Corps, and is soon to be discharged, when he will again take up acting in western productions at the Universal Studios. [27]

Hoot obtained the rank of sergeant and was honorably discharged in 1919. He returned to Hollywood, resuming work at Universal with the help of Harry Carey and Jack Ford. [28]

Two days before the end of 1918, "Wolves of the Range," was released. It was similar to her last picture since it didn't use the railroad as part of the plot. This appeared to be a trend in Helen's films.

A two-reel number with Helen Gibson and Lee Hill in the cast. This is a story of the western range and abounds in fast riding and picturesque scenic effect. The plot, which deals with a band of outlaws, is rather conventional and contains considerable melodrama that is not entirely convincing. Its chief strength is in its picturesque atmosphere. [29]

CHAPTER 11

Helen Departs Universal At Year's End

Helen continued to work into the New Year. Nearly a week into the calendar year Universal released *The Secret Peril*. [1] This film was followed twenty-three days later by the release of *The Girl Sheriff*. [2] Universal released Helen's next endeavor, *The Canyon Mystery* on February 2, 1919.

> This two-reel special is a genuine Western picture, two-reels packed full of action and remarkable stunts, one of the most amazing thrills is the leap across the canyon, a picture you do not want to miss seeing. [3]

Helen and her crew were cranking out films on a regular schedule.

However, nearly a month would pass before Helen's next picture would be released. That date was the first day of March. The reason for the wide gap was never explained to newspapers or trade magazines. One can only speculate given current world events.

> The second wave of the Spanish influenza epidemic struck the Pacific Coast with full force, but the amusement business is not being as hard hit as when the disease first made its appearance last October. At one time practically every theater in the San Francisco territory was closed, with similar conditions prevailing in other districts, but it is now estimated that all but about 40 per cent of the moving picture houses on the Pacific Coast are closed.

> The San Francisco film exchanges also serve 11 towns in Nevada which have a population of 25,000 and 15 theaters, as well as two towns in Oregon which have four theaters and a population of 6,500. About one half of these houses are closed, but film rentals have not been affected in like population since most of these theaters are in small communities. [4]

On the day, March 1st, Universal announced Helen's next picture, a Western, *Riding Wild*. [5]

A two-reel story of the West featuring Helen Gibson, Leo Maloney and others. The girl [Gibson] is the daughter of a bandit leader and the hero, a Secret Service man. There is not much suspense in the action, but the number contains some fine riding and a great deal of picturesque scenery. The continuity is too uneven to get the strongest dramatic effects. [6]

A short article in the March 22, 1919 *Moving Picture World* magazine offered a clue as to the absence of Helen during the month of February, and a look at what the studio had in store for husband, Hoot.

Helen Gibson, who has been resting for several months, is back at Universal City and will appear in a new series of two-reel melodramas. Hoot Gibson, recently returned from military duty, will support his wife in these pictures. [7]

Universal released Helen's next film, *The Black Horse Bandit* in mid-March. In the supporting cast was her husband, Hoot, which would be the first of six pictures they would perform together on the screen. Also in the cast was Pete Morrison, who took take over the lead role in the next handful of Helen Gibson films.

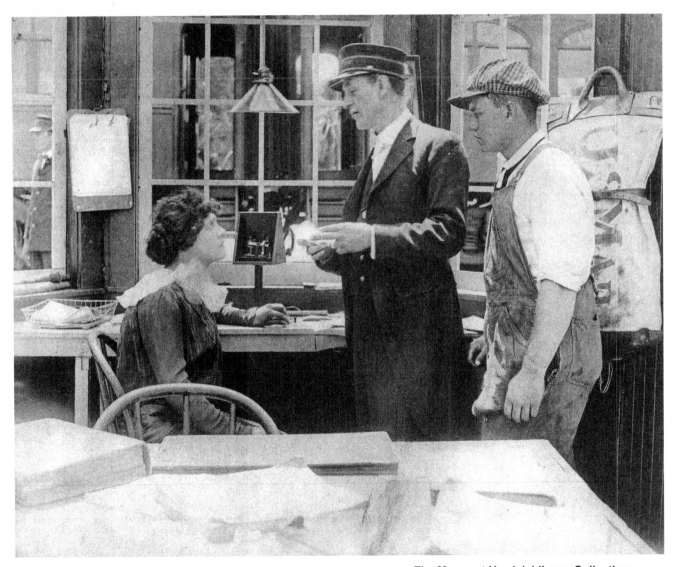

The Margaret Herrick Library Collection

The Black Horse Bandit.

In the little Western town of Jawbone, Bill Graham, the sheriff, is plagued by a mysterious outlaw, who is seen roaming the country. The citizens of Jawbone elect Joe Graham, his son, [Hoot Gibson] as sheriff. Joe, having been raised in the East, is somewhat of a tenderfoot and does not know how to handle the rough Western element.

Two strangers ride into Jawbone, one of them, Hugh Manville, rides a colorful coal-black horse, while the other, Jack Morgan, rides a pinto. Hugh meets Dolly Graham [Helen Gibson], the former sheriff's daughter, and falls in love with her. A bunch of cowpunchers hearing of the new sheriff, come to town with the intention of "shooting up the saloon."

Joe, called upon to quiet them and stop the disturbance, shows his yellow streak and is afraid to stop them. Dolly, his sister, takes his badge from him, and, rushes to the saloon, [and] quells the disturbance.

The country lives in fear of the "Black Horse Bandit," who has repeatedly robbed the stage and made his getaway, and the people are at a loss to understand his mysterious operations.

The stage arrives at Jawbone just having been robbed by the bandit riding the black horse. During the hold-up, Bill Graham is killed. Attention is drawn to the fact that the only black horse in the country is the one which Manville rides. Hugh, led to believe someone else is riding his horse, lays a trap for them. Joe sees Hugh ride out of town on his black horse. Dolly soon learns that Hugh is suspected and follows.

Again a stage is held up, but this time by Morgan, on his pinto. Hugh rides in and stops the hold-up, but Morgan flees, and he and his companions capture Dolly coming from town. Realizing that his plans have been disrupted, Morgan takes Dolly with him to a deserted cabin. Hugh locates her, and along with Joe, who has grown up a good deal, captures Morgan after a gun battle. Dolly and Hugh were re-united. [8]

Helen and Hoot Gibson in The Black Horse Bandit.

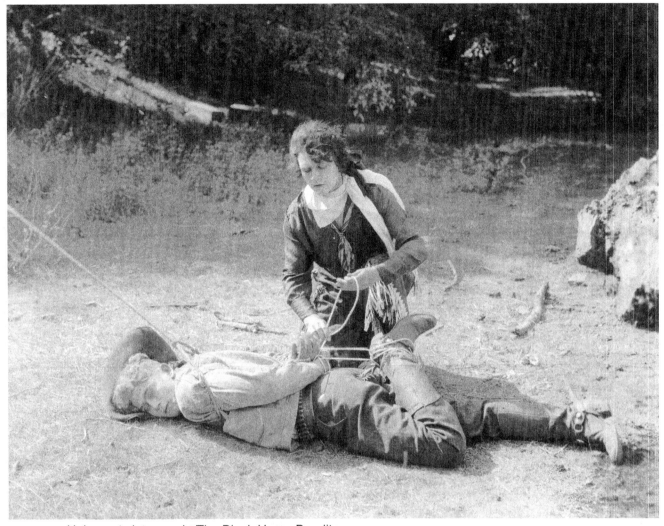

Helen gets her man in The Black Horse Bandit.

To most movie goers it was evident that Universal was grooming Hoot for a starring role in the very near future.

"Hoot" Gibson, husband of Helen Gibson, Universal Western character actress, recently returned from the firing line in France, is seen in support of Pete Morrison in "Fighting Brothers," a two-reel Western drama scheduled for release March 24. Jack Ford directed the production. [9]

Helen was asked in a 1953 interview if she helped Hoot restart his film career after returning from the war.

"Hoot continued to get work as an extra and stuntman until 1919, when he starred in a two-reeler at Universal. From then on, he was on his way up. I didn't know it at the time, but my career was on the way down. [10] His attitude towards me was quite different, and the success of these Universal Westerns further inflated his ego, and ended our marriage. [11]

It was always a good sign when a film company put out the call for short stories for films at the same time they were looking for writing talent. This appeared to be good for Helen since the studio wanted Western stories. Maybe!

Eugene Mullin, the new scenario chief at Universal City, throws open the doors far and wide to scenario writers. He wants new stories from new authors.

While Universal is negotiating with well-known short story writers and novelists for their product, the scenario department is still seeking to develop new talent to prepare dramatic vehicles direct for the screen.

Six-reel melodramas of intensity and novelty are desired for Priscilla Dean. Six-reel Western stories are needed for Harry Carey, while Monroe Salisbury is in the market for six-reel Westerns or for any character stories that will fit his well-known style of acting. Two-reel Western dramas are desired for Pete Morrison and Helen Gibson. [12]

Pete Morrison and Hoot Gibson got top billing on the next five films which included Helen. In mid-April, *The Rustlers* was released, followed by *Even Money* (aka *Rustlers*) ten days later. Approximately ten days into May, Universal announced the release of *Gun Law* (aka *Posse's Prey*). Fourteen days later, *The Gun Packer* (aka *Out Wyoming Way*) made its way to the screen. June 7, 1919 was the final release of the Morrison, Gibson and Gibson films, *Ace High*.

The Gun Packer, the story of a reformed outlaw recruited some of his former gunslinging buddies to look after a small shepherd community from overassertive cattle barons. The film was also reissued in August 1924. [13]

An early June newspaper article described Helen's next Universal film. Neither Pete Morrison or her husband, Hoot, would be in the film with her.

"Destiny's Snare" is the title of the melodramatic story bought by Universal from Alvin J. Neitz and Neal Hart, to be used as a two-reel Western vehicle for Eddie Polo's talents. Jacques Jaccard is directing it at Universal City with Helen Gibson as Eddie Polo's leading woman. [14]

This film, *Destiny's Snare,* was the working title for Universal's *Down But Not Out*. It became chapter 8 of the Eddie Polo, *Cyclone Smith* series, released on June 30, 1919. [15]

In between films for Universal, Helen found time to do some product endorsing for the Racine Auto Tire Company. She appeared with the new Horseshoe Tire. Her ads appeared in numerous magazines over an eight month time span. The ad makers combined Helen and horses to sell their rough and tuff tires. Someone at the ad agency must have

Eddie Polo

remembered Helen's historic drive up Lookout Mountain. [16] [17]

How quickly
you can gauge a
man's motoring
experience by
the tires
he buys

Remember
The Horse-Shoe
Tread

RACINE
HORSE-SHOE TIRES

RACINE AUTO TIRE COMPANY, RACINE, WISCONSIN

The Literary Digest - July 12, 1919, Page 59

The Gayla Johnson Collection

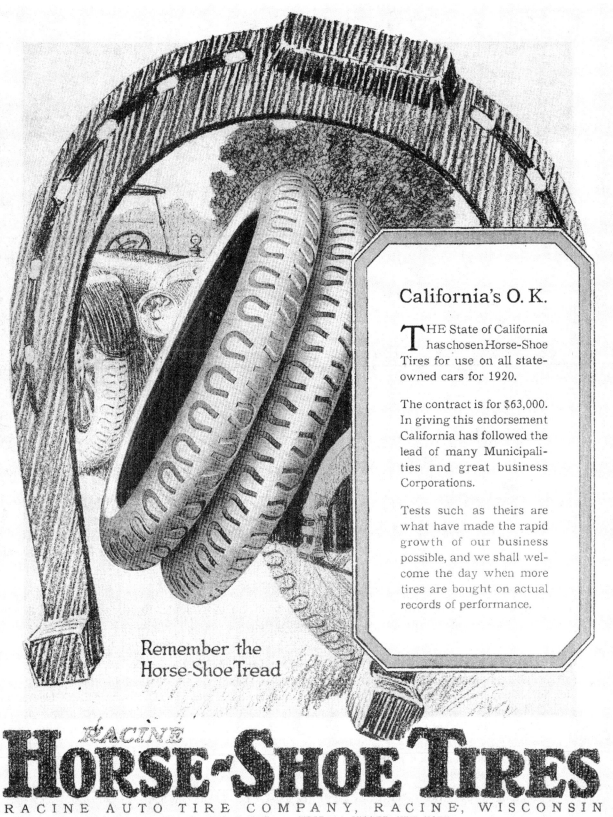

California's O. K.

THE State of California has chosen Horse-Shoe Tires for use on all state-owned cars for 1920.

The contract is for $63,000. In giving this endorsement California has followed the lead of many Municipalities and great business Corporations.

Tests such as theirs are what have made the rapid growth of our business possible, and we shall welcome the day when more tires are bought on actual records of performance.

Remember the
Horse-Shoe Tread

RACINE
HORSE-SHOE TIRES

RACINE AUTO TIRE COMPANY, RACINE, WISCONSIN
EXPORT DEPARTMENT, 144 WEST 65th STREET, NEW YORK

The Saturday Evening Post - February 7, 1920, Page 74

Universal finished the filming of *Loot*, a six-reel production in September. Helen played the part of a maid, a far cry from her horseback riding and thrilling stunts.

"Loot," the well known Saturday Evening Post story from the pen of Arthur Somers Roche, has been completed as a six-reel feature at Universal City by Director William G. Dowlan. In the supporting cast are Gertrude Astor, Wadsworth Harris, Alfred Allen, Arthur Mackley, Helen Gibson, Frank MacQuarrie, and Frank Thompson.

Director Dowlan has provided "Loot" with a great many beautiful interior settings, but it is in the exteriors that the picture is particularly fine. A mob of 10,000 extras was used in the big jewelry store robbery, filmed on one of Los Angeles' principal downtown streets. [18]

The Universal production of Saturday Evening Post's *Loot* was released on October 6, 1919.

In this six-reel Universal subject, entitled "Loot," the producers offered another version of the famous crook story written by Arthur Somers Roche. The leading feature, in which a wholesale jewelry robbery was carried out in broad daylight, was incorporated originally in a film serial, "The Grey Ghost," but has here been made the basis of a separate tale.

There were plenty of action and thrills and the production may be termed a highly successful melodramatic subject, even though at times there were lapses in matters of detail and a certain lack of plausibility. It might be well argued that a robbery on such a gigantic scale could not be pulled off, and yet it was the boldest of conceptions and its swift execution that convinced the observer in spite of himself. After all, it was but an elaboration of such a robbery as occurred in the city of New York but a week ago, when auto bandits made a daring raid on a bank. [19]

The Robert S. Birchard Collection

Pete Morrison

This film was the last for Helen Gibson at Universal City. They didn't renew her contract. It wasn't written in any of the trade magazines as to why Universal let a popular star like Helen go. There is possibly a clue from one of the supporting cowboy actors, Ted French, under contract with Universal, and from its founder.

"Hoot [Gibson], Pete Morrison and I all had the same dressing room at Universal, and that was directly across from Helen Gibson, Hoot's ex-wife, and brother, I'm telling you, every time Hoot came out that door he had to duck, 'cause she was sittin' there just waitin' for him. She'd throw anything she had handy. Pete and I both got took. That old squatty Hooter, he'd just sit back and laugh at us, then he'd come out when she had nothing left to throw. [20]

The Robert S. Birchard Collection
Ted French

It was well known that Carl Laemmle, Universal City founder was grooming Hoot Gibson to be the next great Universal star. Uncle Carl, as he was called, didn't renew cowboy star, Harry Carey's contract when it came due. He gave Gibson the lucrative contract and promoted him to a "star" rating. [21]

Moving Picture World - June 19, 1920
Uncle Carl

CHAPTER 12

Helen Signs with Capital Film Company - 1919

A month before the release of *Loot*, Helen signed a contract with the Capital Film Company in 1919. [1] Helen stated in an article in January, 1968 that when she signed on with Capital they were losing money. [2]

In the face of all the furor and discussion regarding fewer and better pictures, the management of renowned authors and similar prophecies and promises in which producers generally are indulging, the most striking feature of the motion picture business is the increasing demand for short subjects of quality and interest superior to those of precedent years. This is the observation made by S.L. Barnhard, President of the Capital Film Company. [3]

Following negotiations conducted by S.L. Barnhard, President of the Capital Film Company and Harry M. Owens, coast-manager, contracts have been signed with Helen Gibson for the production of twenty-four two-reel dramas featuring that star in a series of episodes of railroad life.

The arrangement is the outcome of the policy of expansion of Capital Film Productions decided upon as a result of the popularity which has made Capital's two other offerings, short subjects, in which Al Jennings and Neal Hart are the respective players, in wide demand.

Miss Gibson, as "The Railroad Girl," is known wherever motion pictures are shown. She will be provided with direction and support of excellent character, according to Mr. Barnhard, who at present is at the studio arranging the final details of the transaction. The stories will each contain that element of exciting action and spectacular effects which have made Miss Gibson's work in romances of the rails so widely known. [4]

It appears that the Capital Film Company had the same problem as that of Universal City. That problem was not enough good scripts to go around.

The call is out for railroad stories. If you have a railroad story up your sleeve or in your mind suitable for production as a motion picture, here is your chance.

There is only one condition: You must know what you are talking about. You must know railroading and you must know the language and customs of railroaders. If you are not a railroad man yourself – or, if not a man, the wife, mother, mother, sister, sweetheart or daughter of a railroad man – your chances are nearly 100 per cent that you will not have a story to tell.

The frantic S.O.S. for railroad stories comes from the studio of the Capital Film Company in Hollywood, where Helen Gibson holds forth. [5]

It was very apparent that Capital wanted to make sure that its three stars be given the opportunity to produce excellent two-reel films.

Recent development growing out of the demand for short productions have made Capital Film Company's film studio one of the most rapidly growing production plants on the West Coast where Al Jennings, Neal Hart and Helen Gibson each are heading short feature production units, and where still a fourth company soon will be at work making comedies.

In addition to the present studio equipment, a large enclosed stage now is being erected in preparation for the rainy season so that production activities will not be hampered, and lighting and other electrical devices are being installed. [6]

The Margaret Herrick Library Collection

The Opium Runners.

The first Helen Gibson Capital film *The Opium Runners* opened in theaters on November 13, 1919, [7] followed two days later with *The Trail of the Rails*. [8] Next up *Daring Danger* on December 12, 1919. [9]

Miss Gibson is known as the "girl daredevil" of the screen and has won her title by numberless intrepid stunts before the camera. [10]

Helen's last film of 1919 appeared in theaters the day before Christmas. The title, *Flirting with Terror*. [11]

The Gayla Johnson Collection

The Opium Runners.

The Opium Runners.

Into the New Year, Capital only released one film in January with Helen Gibson in the title role. The film, *The Clutch of the Law*. [12]

> Because of the scarcity of scripts and the progress made on production, it was decided to close the studio for at least two weeks, during which a vigorous campaign for western stories and railroad stories will be maintained. [13]

Capital found some worthwhile Western scripts during this period and produced three Helen Gibson two-reel railroad films, *The Broken Trestle,* on February 6th, [14] followed by *The Golden Star Bandits,* February 15th [15] and five days later, *The Border Watch Dogs.* [16]

Reproduction Poster

The Broken Trestle.

The Golden Star Bandits.

The Border Watch Dogs Glass Slide

The Border Watch Dogs.

The Gayla Johnson Collection

Helen is ready to duck below the track as the engine passes throught the smoke.

During the month of March, only two films from Helen's production crew were released. One of the films was *The Ghost of the Canyon.* [17]

J.F. Mortimer, Superintendent of the L.A. and S.L. Railroad is in a battle with the C. and L. Railroad for a contract. His daughter Helen [Gibson] and Tim Forrest, assistant superintendent arrive at the office. Mortimer gives the job of landing the contract to Tim. If he succeeds, he has permission to marry his daughter.

Outside the C. and L. Railroad building, Peter Wells, Superintendent of the C. and L. Railroad is talking to two other men. All three men leave in an automobile. Helen and Tim leave the building with Helen behind the wheel. The two cars nearly crash at an intersection. Harsh words are exchanged before both cars drive on. Helen and Tim reach the train yard and talk to the crew about getting the test shipment through. Wells and his two henchmen spy on Helen, Tim, and the train engineer. When the train leaves, the three spies get back in their car and speed away.

Helen Mortimer and Tim Forrest arrive back at the office when shortly a message arrives. It states that the train has passed Frassed Valley Junction station on time.

Wells and his two thugs arrive at a railroad bridge where they have equipment set up. A short time later the Mortimer train approaches the bridge. Billows of black smoke come up through the tracks with a white ghost-like figure hovering in the smoke. The train stops, then shortly backs up returning to the yard. Wells leaves the area in his car.

145

The Ghost of the Canyon. The ghost makers are caught red handed.

Upon his return, the train engineer sees Mortimer, Helen and Tim Forrest to explain the situation. A message arrives indicating that the C. and L. Railroad test shipment blew out a cylinder head. Mortimer knew they still had time to get the contract, but the engineer wouldn't take the train this run. Forrest volunteered.

Mortimer, Helen, Forrest and the engineer drive to the train yard as Wells watches them go, and then he follows. Just before Forrest starts the run, Helen sees Wells spying on them. The train leaves. Wells drives away with Helen close behind. Mortimer and the engineer follow Helen. Wells arrives at the bridge and informs his men the train is on its way. Helen arrives a few minutes later and is captured by Wells and his thugs. They tie her to the tracks on the bridge.

The train approaches as the smoke and ghost reappear. On the other side of the smoke, Helen struggles with the ropes on her wrists. As before, the train stops. This time it continues on. Helen gets herself hanging between the railroad ties and the train cuts the ropes as it passes. She falls to the ground below. Mortimer and the engineer arrive and with Forrest, who stopped the train, capture all three C.L. men. Helen joins Forrest in the cab of the engine to finish the test run. [18]

The Overland Express was released exactly eleven days later. [19]

The Ghost of the Canyon.

April saw only one new film with Helen Gibson. Audiences were able to view *The Payroll Pirates* in late April. [20]

Helen Gibson spoke briefly about the Capital Film Company in an article printed in 1968. "I left Capital in May, 1920 when they went out of business." [21] There was no mention of this in the trade magazines during the month of May or June, but Capital hadn't placed an ad in those same magazines since early February. At that time, it was a full page ad for Al Jennings, Neal Hart, and Helen Gibson. Someone at the company didn't spend much money on publicity. [22]

Reproduction Poster

On May 3, 1920, Capital Film Company released *Winning the Franchise*. [23]

Malcolm Hayes, President of the S.L. and L.B.R.R. wants to win the new mail contract. His secretary secretly works for the L.T. and T.R.R. and overhears Hayes discussing it. Valentine Dunton, Assistant Manager of the L.T. and T.R.R. pays him a visit with a proposal to buy him out. Hayes refuses. Dunton secretly hands the secretary a note telling him to meet in Central Park. Hayes' secretary leaves shortly after Dunton. They meet in the park.

Hayes daughter, Helen [Gibson] arrives to see her father. He tells her she will take the bid envelope to Washington. When the secretary returns, he is instructed to give Helen the special bid envelope. Bob Ferris, traveling engineer for the S.L and L.B.R.R. enters the office. While he and Helen are talking, the secretary removes the special bid envelope from the satchel and puts it in his coat pocket.

Helen and Bob leave for the train station. The secretary also leaves and meets with Dunton where he passes the special bid envelope to him. Dunton and his two henchmen arrive at the train station to see Helen boarding the train. They board in a different car. Shortly after the train pulls out of the station, Helen opens the satchel to find the special bid envelope missing. She asks the conductor to send her father a message. Back at the office, Hayes gives Bob a copy of the bid sheet to deliver to Helen on the next train.

Winning the Franchise.

Helen arrives in Washington and takes a taxi. Dunton and his men follow. Bob arrives a few minutes later and follows Dunton in his taxi. When Helen arrives at her destination, Dunton throws a blanket over her head and throws her in his car. Bob sees the abduction and follows. Dunton and his men take Helen to a remote cabin in the country with Bob following. When Bob's taxi gets a flat, he follows on foot.

When Helen is in the cabin, Dunton leaves the two men to guard her. Bob finds the cabin, hears Helen scream, and breaks down the door. The men fight Bob and end up on the floor, at which time the two make a dash for Bob's taxi. They drive to the railroad office in Washington where they find Dunton. Since there are two bidders, a test run must be made.

A few minutes before the test run, Dunton gives the assistant train engineer who will be working with Bob, a gun. While Helen is boarding, Dunton puts something in the water bag in the engine cab. Along with Helen, Dunton and the two men also board. Not long after they start the run, Bob drinks from the water bag and passes out a few minutes later falling to the floor.

The assistant engineer stops the train. Helen runs to the engine and finds Bob unconscious. She asks the assistant to help her and he refuses. That is when Helen sees the gun in his back pocket. She grabs the gun, holds it on him, and takes the throttle.

Dunton thinks the assistant engineer has double-crossed them. He and his two thugs climb to the roof of the train and head for the engine. Helen at the throttle sees them and shoots a warning shot over their heads. In order to shoot, she takes her eyes off her captive. He struggles with her for the gun. Bob wakes up and fights the assistant while Helen gets on the roof and puts her gun on the three thugs. Bob stops the train and the four men are locked up by the conductor on board. [24]

Winning the Franchise was followed by *Wires Down*. [25] Audiences were unaware that the film *Terror of the Rails*, would be her last film at Capital. [26]

Just before *Terror of the Rails* was released to theaters, the news of her divorce from Hoot made the newspapers.

"It has brought me much money and a good deal of fame, but it has ruined the happiness of my marriage and my prospects of a peaceful home life."

That is the way Helen Gibson, heroine of scores of two-reelers, summarized "the picture game" last night when a reporter told her that her attorneys, Jones, Wilson and Stephenson, had filed for her a suit for divorce from Edmund R. ("Hoot") Gibson.

"As long as we stuck to rodeos and round-ups, as long as we were just plain show folks, we were happy," she said. "Then we got into the picture game and we struck the domestic snags."

"It was jealousy that turned the trick for us. 'Hoot' was jealous of the salary I was making and the publicity I was getting and we quarreled all the time. Then he got to worrying about the men playing with me – and, well, we broke up for good a year ago in March."

Mrs. Gibson heads her own company, making "railroad thrillers" on the Universal lot. Her husband is directing and leading in two-reel Western pictures. [27]

Helen left Capital quietly with no press releases. Several films were still in the can to be released. All three were seen in theaters before the end of 1920.

Reproduction Poster

Those three films were *Danger Signal*, [28] *The Broken Brake* [29] and *Running Wild*. [30] Either the Capital film Company had a low budget on advertising or they didn't advertise in trade magazines. However, in November, 1920, an article was written commenting on some of Helen's outstanding films. They were *The Frustrated Hold-Up*, *The Ghost of Canyon Diablo*, *The Robber of the Golden Star* and *The Run of the Yellow Mail*. That last film listed was adapted from a story by Frank H. Spearman. [31] These last five films account for twenty-two films Helen made for Capital. It is not known at this time if she completed twenty-four, two-reel films from her original contract. Her contract might have been cancelled with two films left.

A short while upon leaving Capital, Helen picked up a brief job endorsing Horseshoe Tires. The Racine Auto Tire Company was organized as a partnership February 1, 1910, and incorporated November 28, 1914. They soon became known as the Racine Horseshoe Tire Company because of the horseshoe shaped tread on the tires. The Racine Company located in Wisconsin produced automobile tires, as well as bicycle and motorcycle tires. They're tire advertisements were very predominate from 1917 – 1922. Helen knew how to change a tire which she demonstrated in one of her last films, *The Ghost of the Canyon*.

After her photo shoot, at age of twenty-eight, Helen was out of work for the first time in her short professional career. In addition she was in the middle of a very nasty divorce.

CHAPTER 13

Hard Times Are Ahead - 1920

Helen took some time off during which she organized her own company, Helen Gibson Productions. She would make her own films and release them through Associated Photoplay Corporation. [1]

> Helen Gibson Productions, recently organized to exploit Helen Gibson in a series of five and six reel features, to be released through the Associated Photoplay Corporation during the coming year, has leased space at the Astra Studios in Glendale and is making final arrangements to start production on their first picture on October 18, 1920.
>
> "No Man's Woman," a story written by L.V. Jefferson and adapted for screen presentation by Ford Beebe, has been chosen as Miss Gibson's first vehicle.
>
> Wayne Mack has been named director, with Leo Maloney as production manager and co-director. [2]

For several years, Helen was saving men, women and children on the movie screen. But during the filming of *No Man's Woman* she did a real rescue act.

> *It isn't always the hero that rescues the heroine.* In fact, rescuing her heroes from all manner of violent disaster is life to Helen Gibson, the young star, whose feats of daring and skill have gained her world fame.
>
> And in real life, for a change of diet, Miss Gibson even lends a hand to the villain.
>
> While the star and her company were on location recently in the mountains of the Mojave for the shooting of the final scenes of her current picture, "No Man's Woman," a three-ton boulder dislodged and catapulted down the mountainside with the unsuspecting Leo Maloney, who plays the heavy and co-directs with Wayne Mack, as its objective. Miss Gibson deftly, if somewhat roughly, swung that skillful right arm of hers and when Leo looked around to see who was trying to pick a fight with him, the boulder crashed by.

The picture just completed, a Western drama in which Miss Gibson as a dance-hall girl fights her way through many obstacles and adventures to the love of a stern-principled prospector, is announced as her best. [3]

No Man's Woman.

No Man's Woman.

No Man's Woman.

No Man's Woman.

No Man's Woman.

No Man's Woman.

159

When the film was nearly completed, Helen was running very low on money. She signed a $1,500 note in order to finish the film's intertitles. However, there was a delay in delivery of the film from Glendale, California to New York. Helen lost everything. [4]

> "My money gave out before my first picture – *No Man's Woman* – was finished. I signed a 90-day note and ultimately lost everything, and had to go through bankruptcy, which didn't help my movie career." [5]

> The year 1920, as many independents were finding out, was a bit late to start one's own firm. The majors were eating everyone alive. [6]

During December, the newspapers made mention of a new movie thriller.

> Present announcements by the publicity department of the Associated Photo Plays include the completion of a six-reel thriller entitled "No Man's Woman," starring that talented young actress, Helen Gibson, in which she reaps new laurels for daring and dramatic achievements. [7]

Associated Photoplays released *No Man's Woman* to rave reviews. It was a big hit.

The Robert S. Birchard Collection
Ed Coxen

> Ed Coxen, as a wronged husband, vows vengeance on the man who stole his wife and child in this drama. Coxen returns home from the gold fields to find that a gambler has fled with his family. His search takes him to a dance hall where he meets an entertainer [Gibson]. Later, the gambler abandons Coxen's wife and child. The woman, taken in by the entertainer, dies of shame. The dance-hall belle cares for the child. The gambler returns and begins to woo the entertainer, but Coxen arrives, learns that he is the man responsible for his dilemma and begins to clobber him. A stranger in the dance hall with a past grudge against the gambler shoots him. Coxen, who earlier had condemned the entertainer for her life-style, forgives her when he realizes she has been taking care of his child. [8]

No Man's Woman was re-released on March 22, 1922 with a new title, *Nine Points of the Law*,* aka *A Girl's Decision*.

With *No Man's Woman* becoming a big success, Spencer Productions hired Helen to star in a film called, *The Wolverine*. [9]

> "The Wolverine," starring the ever daring Helen Gibson, boasts of three of the most daredevil horseback riders in the United States today. Nothing too great can be said of the work of Miss Gibson in her past performances, but to add Leo Maloney and Jack Connolly to her side in one production is a feat hard to be duplicated. In the making of "The Wolverine," which is from the pen of B. M. Bower, Spencer Productions, Inc., saw to it that the best cast and the finest locale possible were brought together. So as to allow both Maloney and Connolly to assist in this wonderful play,

* Appendix B - Re-release Advertisement, page 245

it was necessary to wait three weeks. Helen Gibson whose daring feats of horsemanship have attracted the attention of the motion picture world, is at her best in "The Wolverine," which gives birth to a new and far more interesting type of Western photodramas. It is built in the land of the snow and boasts of wondrous natural settings as a background. [10]

When "The Wolverine" was released to theaters it was advertised as "a story of love, glittering through the great land of the snow, showing the hardships of a girl who cherished her honor above her life." [11]

An ex-convict who has unjustly served a prison term for someone else's crime has problems trying to build a new life for himself in this action drama set chiefly on a ranch. Jack Connolly portrays Ward Warren, the unfortunate ex-convict who gets a job at the Wolverine ranch run by Billy Louise, played by Helen Gibson. She had taken over the ranch after her parents died. When some of the stock are stolen, Ward goes after the rustlers and warns them to clear out. Instead, the rustlers falsely accuse Ward of the rustling. He is away on a hunting trip where he breaks his leg after being thrown from a horse. Billy Louise finds him and stays with him until he is well enough to prove his innocence. [12]

In addition to the story and acting, "The Wolverine" was praised for its use of horses and the consequences of a grueling schedule of filming.

The Wolverine.

The Wolverine.

The finest horseflesh in the end of the great Northwest is seen in "The Wolverine," the six-reel action photo-drama which is the attraction at the Atlas today and tomorrow. Spencer Productions, Inc., in planning for this starring vehicle for Miss Helen Gibson, scoured the land for the finest of Arabian steeds. That they accomplished their purpose is best evidenced by the action of the story.

In spite of the fire of the steeds and the cunning and daring of the riders, it was necessary to give the horses much rest between the scenes. Ten horses were lost by accidents and disease in the making of this great photo thriller. [13]

Victor B. Fischer, general manager of Associated Photoplays, Inc., left recently for Los Angeles to confer with the officials of Spencer Productions, Inc., regarding the second of the series of Helen Gibson features for independent distribution.

The first of the series, "The Wolverine," based on B.M. Bower's novel, "The Ranch at the Wolverine," is now en route from the West Coast. It was directed by William Bertram.

"The Gibson series will be made with no fixed sum given the director," says Mr. Fischer. "We demand the best, but at all times shall try to keep down production costs, so that the exhibitor may secure features of merit at the lowest prices." [14]

The Wolverine.

The Wolverine.

The Wolverine.

march— 1921

SPENCER
PRODUCTIONS, Inc.
Present
HELEN
GIBSON
Supported by
JACK CONNOLLY
AND AN ALL STAR CAST
in
"THE
Wolverine"
Directed by
WILLIAM BERTRAM

Distributed by ASSOCIATED PHOTO-PLAYS INC.

Helen Gibson Scrapbook- page 32

166

Helen's fans loved The Wolverine.

Again Spencer Productions were so pleased with the positive results of "The Wolverine" that they put Helen on the payroll at $450 a week, and cast her for a second film that was to start on April 2, 1921. [15]

Sale of the motion picture rights to his novelette, "The Girl in Gopher City," to Spencer Productions, Inc., was announced yesterday by George Rix, Riverside writer and member of The Enterprise editorial staff.

In this latest story by the local man, Helen Gibson well known Photoplay actress, will be featured. It is to be produced as a five-reel feature, starring Miss Gibson, who has won laurels for her fearless portrayal of Western type girls.

"The Girl in Gopher City" is a stirring drama, most of the scenes of which are laid in a "ghost city," or long-deserted mining town in the midst of the southwestern desert. Several surprising twists have been given to this yarn by the local writer; and mystery, struggle and thrilling situations have been woven into an absorbing tale. [16]

This film sounded like it was made for Helen Gibson to play. But it was not to be. Her string of bad luck was still lingering in the dark shadows.

"But, I didn't appear. My appendix had burst on April 1st and I was in the hospital battling peritonitis. When the studio called the hospital to learn when I'd be back, the doctors were angered and told them I was lucky to be alive. So they offered Helen Holmes my role." [17]

"The Girl in Gopher City" title was changed to "Ghost City" and Helen Holmes Productions made it! Holmes produced it herself and took the lead role with Leo Maloney. "Ghost City" was released November 23, 1921. Her distributor was Associated Photoplays, and it was one of only two movies made by Helen Holmes Productions, and neither was very successful.

Helen Holmes and Jack McGowan left Kalem and started Signal Film Corporation in about 1915. That's when Helen Gibson took over the lead role in "The Hazards of Helen". Signal ran out of money in late 1917. Then in early 1918, Signal's distributor, Mutual Film Corporation, collapsed. Mutual took many small film companies with it. The president, John R. Freuler, resigned on May 1, 1918. Later that year, what was left of Mutual was taken over by Affiliated Distributors' Corporation. The collapse of the Signal Film Company probably hastened Holmes and McGowan's breakup, which was announced in the Los Angeles Times of June 2, 1918. [18]

Lobby card of Helen Holmes playing the lead role in Ghost City.

Helen was able to return to work on the first of June. However, the studio refused to allow her to resume her job. Helen felt that Spencer Productions had broken her contract so she took them to court. The trial began in mid-August.

Helen Gibson, motion picture actress, instituted suit yesterday against Spencer Production Company asking $10,000 for an alleged breach of contract. The contract called for thirty weeks' work during which time the actress was to appear in six 5 or 6-reel feature productions.

She was to have received $350 a week for the first three pictures and $400 a week for the last three, according to her complaint. The contract contained a clause, to assure her of re-employment in case of sickness.

Two months after the making of the contract she was taken ill. Her illness prevented her from rendering services until June 1, when she reported for work, she says. The complaint alleged the company refused to allow her to resume services, thereby breaking the contract. The suit was filed by the law firm of Loeb, Walker and Loeb. [19]

In late August, a local newspaper published an article about Helen's production company. The article hinted that a possible film was to be made in a neighboring canyon.

A.M. Cooper, well known deputy sheriff and owner of Topanga Ranch and Cooper's Camp at the entrance to Topanga Canyon, was a visitor at the BIG THREE office today and incidentally spread some fine news.

The Helen Gibson Productions have arranged to make their permanent home and studio headquarters on the Topanga Ranch, and a score of more of cowboys in full regalia are now registering bravado and such-like before the movie cameras out there in the "staging" of the first production.

Cooper is elated to have a real cow-girl doing real riding at his place. "Miss Gibson is an honest-to-goodness cowgirl," he declares. "She can ride high and fancy; bucking broncos are her favorite pastime and she can bulldog a steer as good as any man that ever flung a rope." Cooper compared present day doings at the ranch with those of two years ago when a famous English actress had to be lifted onto her pony for equestrian scenes. "That was the bunk," he said, "but Helen Gibson is real reel stuff." [20]

In a January, 1968 film magazine article co-written by Helen, she described the story above in a little different manner.

"In September '21, an independent company hired me for a 5-reeler, and folded without paying any of us a cent. I had had to ride in the course of that ill-fated venture and doing so put me back in the hospital on December 14, 1921. I had to sell my furniture, jewelry, and car. Hoot was then at the top of his career, but he avoided me." [21]

From the beginning of 1922 through March, Helen managed to get by with help from her friends. On March 11, 1922, Helen's lawsuit would reach a conclusion.

Two suits directed against the Spencer Productions, Inc., and involving services to have been rendered by two women, were settled out of court, it was indicated today when they were called for trial by Judge Hewitt.

In one action, Helen Gibson, screen star, demanded $9500 for alleged breach of contract, and in the other, Helen Van Upp sought to recover $1850 for writing the continuity for a photoplay entitled "Bluebeard Jr." and for cutting and preparing for distribution, the films, "The Wolverine" and "Ghost City."

The defendant denied there was anything due in the Van Upp suit and in Miss Gibson's case it was declared it had been mutually agreed that her contract of employment would be contingent on a contract the defendant entered into with a distributing company to market the pictures. It was stated the distributing company cancelled its contract.

It further was contended in the answer that Miss Gibson had been ill and was in no condition to work. [22]

Helen Johnson

Another famous Gibson made a newspaper headline, this time it was Helen's ex-husband Hoot.

Riverside, California, April 20 – Edmund "Hoot" Gibson, motion picture actor of Los Angeles, and Helen Johnson, vaudeville actress, were married today. [23]

Many years later in 1962, Helen recalls Hoot's second marriage. At this time in her life, she was Helen Gibson Johnson.

The only real 'Hazard' in my life these days is the confusion that still persists over my marriage to the late 'Hoot' Gibson, the celebrated cowboy star. He then married *another* Helen [Johnson]. I'm still forwarding her mail. [24]

Out of work in Hollywood with no acting or stunting job prospect in sight, but not for long. Helen was contracted to make public appearances in theaters and rodeos for her films, *No Man's Woman* and *The Wolverine*. [25]

The most daring girl in Western pictures is the distinction held by Helen Gibson, who is making a tour of the central West, now appearing at the Strand Theater.

When asked to give some of her experiences while making pictures, she related, among others, on standing on a horse's back running at a fast rate. "I had to ride under a tree, grab hold of a branch and let the horse run from under me. The branch broke and it seemed as if I was falling from an aeroplane. When I woke up, I found myself in a hospital." [26]

At times it is difficult to keep things hidden from the press. While on route from Minnesota to Wisconsin, several newspapers printed her current financial situation.

In a voluntary petition in bankruptcy, Helen Gibson says she has liabilities of $24,063, owed chiefly to picture supply houses; assets, zero. [27]

On one of the tour stops, Helen elaborated a bit more to an audience in Wisconsin by talking more about Hollywood than herself.

Just as though she had stepped from the screen, only a hundred times prettier, Miss Helen Gibson walks into the spotlight at the Unique in the midst of her latest feature picture "The Wolverine." From the peak of her sombrero to the tips of her riding boots, she is vivaciously Western and delightful.

She begs her audience to believe that Hollywood is not as black as it is painted; that the very hazards and strenuousness of the film folk's calling require decent and healthy living just as the life of circus players must. She tells of some of the big risks she herself has run in her wonderful railroad pictures, and suggests her audience try standing upright on the back of two galloping horses as she does in *The Wolverine*. It's a great life if you don't weaken, as the saying goes, but one cannot hear the winsome speaker without a thrill of conviction for what she claims in behalf of her coworkers.

For herself, Miss Gibson begs "And when you see me in pictures, please remember it's Helen Gibson doing the stunts with no doubles and no dummies." [28]

During the month of May, Helen had made her way into North Dakota and more audiences were eager to see her in person.

Movie Star Here – Miss Helen Gibson, moving picture actress, began a three day personal engagement Monday at the Strand Theater in connection with her picture, "The Wolverine." She gives a brief address on Hollywood at each performance. [29]

Helen took a side trip in August 1922. "I visited old friends at Miller Brothers' 101 Ranch in Ponca, Oklahoma." She made it just in time for a round-up. It didn't appear to be a coincidence.

Bliss, Oklahoma, August 21 – Henry Grammar, Western Osage county ranchman and squawman, former cattle roping champion of the world, has accepted the challenge issued by several other cowboys of arena fame to rope two steers daily, during the third annual 101 ranch round-up and Indian camp, for a riding purse of $2,500 and the championship of Oklahoma. The dates for the round-up are Saturday, Sunday and Monday [Labor Day] September 2, 3, and 4. Grammar has his own string of trained roping horses and will transport the entire string to the 101 ranch buffalo pasture for this event. Miss Lucile Mullgall is also bringing her horses for this round-up, but Miss Helen Gibson, the movie star, will use 101 ranch horses in her events. [30]

Ponca City, Oklahoma, September 2 – Helen Gibson, star of many thrilling motion pictures, will appear in the three-day rodeo roundup and Indian celebration starting at 101 Ranch here today.

When asked of the danger of performing "stunts" in the "Hazards of Helen" and other movie breath-takers, Miss Gibson said:

"Oh, I was lucky, I never have been hurt much, just several ribs broken and my fingers and ankles broken now and then."

Miss Gibson said 101 Ranch here has been the training place of many movie stars in Western pictures. It was with the 101 Circus that she got her first "cowgirl" experience, Miss Gibson said. [31]

Shortly after her return from Oklahoma, Helen was contacted by a low-budget studio, Robertson-Cole. [32] They wanted her to star in a film, *Thorobred,* to be distributed by Clark-Cornelius Corporation the Certified Film Exchange. The film was reviewed in the November 4, 1922 issue of *Moving Picture World.* No release date was found in the remaining months of 1922.

Helen Gibson carries off equestrian honors. Her ease and skill as a rider is setoff in some vivid scenes in which a beautiful horse plays an important part. "The Thoroughbred" offers enough entertainment to keep the average Western fan interested.

Pop Martin, the town sheriff, is too sick to hunt down the bandit who has robbed the bank. The enraged citizens are about to take away his star when Martin's daughter offers to take her father's place and insists on a trial. One of the younger men in the group offers to go with her. She refuses, but he follows anyway. She learns where the robbers have their headquarters, and in order to detect their plans she dresses as one of the dance girls at the saloon and gets the desired information. She goes after the bandit the next day and holds him up in his cave. The man who has befriended her from the start proves of valuable assistance. Her father's reputation is saved and the sheriff star remains in the family. [33]

There were no film roles in 1923 but Helen continued to work at odd jobs in the Hollywood area. Her luck for full-time employment was about a year away. [34]

CHAPTER 14

The Lure of the Circus then Vaudeville - 1924

Helen's best opportunity for full-time work came in late April, 1924. She signed a two and a half year contract with Ringling Brothers Barnum and Bailey Circus as a trick rider. The Ringling Brothers organization had a Wild West Show associated with the main circus attractions. [1] However, Helen's trick riding performances were not documented by newspaper reporters, but may only be hidden in personal memories of circus performers.

The after show or concert was a separate admission presentation after the primary circus performance. Customers remained in their seats and paid an extra fee to remain and observe the action. Wild West traveling show activity generally originated in 1883. Circuses added Wild West components to their performances in the late 1880s, owing to the success and popularity of the Cody and other traveling presentations. Annie Oakley, A. H. Bogardus, Pawnee Bill and others appeared in these 1880s-1890s additions to circuses. They were separate and apart from entire Wild West operations, such as Buffalo Bill's, Miller Bros., etc. The circus-staged Wild West concerts rose and fell in popularity, with the rise of film cowboys renewing interest in the style in the early 20th century.

Troupes framed around western activity were simply termed "Wild West." Cody was a leading proponent of not using the word "show" because his presentations were intended to be re-enactments of incidents and scenes from history.

Little survives of 1920s RBBB employment and business records. Some basic information about the Wild West after show, or concert, with RBBB in the 1920s will be found in the show's programs. The concert roster was sometimes printed as part of the reviews published after the season opener in Madison Square Garden.

Many of the cowboy movie matinee idols had experience with Wild West and circus activity. They included Hopalong Cassidy, Hoot Gibson, Buck Jones, Ken Maynard and more. When you examine the published rosters, people will definitely recognize more celebrities if a person is familiar with the larger Wild West and rodeo field. A few, like Jones, Maynard and Tim McCoy ended up fielding a show in their own name. Thus, Helen Gibson's traveling show employment wasn't as much an exception and unique, but a common right of passage for western stars [2]

Buck Jones   Ken Maynard   Tim McCoy

Helen was still a very recognizable star among the press and very approachable. A reporter in Chicago stopped her for a quick statement about her hat and hair.

Chicago, May 1, 1924 – The shingle bob hasn't affected the hat sizes among cowgirls as yet. They're wearing two-gallon sizes over their latest coiffeurs, according to Helen Rose Gibson, former wife of Hoot Gibson.

"Sure, my hair's bobbed," said Miss Gibson on her arrival here today.

"That's no reason why I should try to squeeze into a hat of the pint size when a cowgirl's supposed to wear a two-gallon hat."

Miss Gibson is on her way east with a Wild West Show. [3]

The 1924 Ringling Brothers circus season was over on the third day of November in Greensboro, North Carolina. Instead of heading for the circus winter quarters, she traveled to Omaha, Nebraska. Fans still wanted to see her.

Helen Gibson, motion picture actress, who was known as "queen of the rails," ten years ago, when she made thrillers for the old Kalem Company, will appear in person next week, starting Saturday at the Moon Theater.

In conjunction with Miss Gibson's appearance will be shown "Perilous Leap," a film she made for Universal in a series of western pictures. Miss Gibson displays her clever horsemanship in this picture. In all her motion picture career, she has never used a double. In her talk, Miss Gibson will tell of the thrills and dangers of picture making. [4]

The 1925 Ringling Brothers schedule began in late-March, in New York City, at Madison Square Garden. It ended in October in Salisbury, North Carolina with no incidents reported. [5] The 1926 season started in Madison Square Garden, with the next stop Philadelphia. They arrived on May 3rd, the same date that Helen had an accident.

174

Helen Gibson, of the Ringling-Barnum Circus* has been in the St. Luke's Hospital, Philadelphia, with a broken ankle, received thru falling from her horse while doing a one-foot slick saddle stand. The ankle was to have been put in a cast last week and Helen was expecting to rejoin the show at Newark Arena, May 18.

Among other accidents to the Wild West contingent folks with the show, Ted Elder, trick rider, received two broken ribs while in New York, Thelma Hunt had her horse fall on her during trick riding at Madison Square Garden – no bones broken – and Ed Bowman was jumped on by a bronco. [6]

Helen received a pleasant surprise while the circus was playing in Blair, Nebraska in late-August. She had two visitors from the past attend the show and help her celebrate her thirty-fifth birthday.

Mr. and Mrs. H.J. Gibson spent Friday in Omaha with their [ex] daughter-in-law at the Ringling shows, Mrs. Helen Gibson being one of the many equestrian riders in the show.

To say that they had a most enjoyable time is putting it very mildly. They were introduced to all the circus folks, who all seemed to be friends of Helen Gibson and her (ex) husband of the movie world. Mr. H. Gibson and the Blair folks were made to feel that they were a part of the aggregation.

The show company is made up of fifteen hundred people and the cast is as good as money can buy and they are cared for as one big family.

The Gibsons went to the dining tent for supper with Mrs. Helen Gibson, who was surprised at finding a mammoth birthday cake at her plate. It being her birthday, the management had taken this method of noting the event. Every courtesy was shown the Blair people and we do not doubt but if H. J. was forty years younger he would become a circus man himself. [7]

Typical Circus/Wild West Show Poster (Reproduction)

* Appendix B - 1924-1926 Barnum & Bailey Schedule, page 246-249

Helen's contract with Ringling Brothers ended in mid-September. She immediately joined a Hopi Indian act. The group was associated with the Keith vaudeville circuit out of Boston. [8]

With the troup of Hopi Indians surrounding her, Helen receives the key to the city from Mayor Gregory J. Scanlon on November 3, 1926 in Holyoke, Massachusetts. In the background, Charles E. Shute, Manager of the Victory Theater looks on.

The appearance of the Hopi Indian snake dancers in Cohen's Theater yesterday, provided a sensational novelty for big houses in attendance. Nothing of its kind has ever been seen in these parts before – the weird and ancient ceremonies of the aborigines of this continent. From the standpoint of the audience, it is a colorful and novel entertainment. The snake dance is the most sacred of the Hopi [peaceful] rites. It is the prayer for rain in the arid and desert regions of Arizona. It is not, the ethnologists say, snake worship. Then came the Buffalo Dance – the prayer for snow. And, the third one of the evening's program – the Wa Dance, a warning to enemies. To the layman in such matters, the study of Indian life, it is the most Indian of them all. The beat of the tom-tom, the shrieking war cries, the tossing of feathered heads – redskins and war. Each and every move is interrupted by Mrs. Helen Gibson, the "Hazards of Helen" of movie serial fame. Her thorough knowledge of the Hopi Indians and her interesting form of explanation indeed make the appearance of the Indians an educational entertainment. [9]

The American Red Man will be seen in all his glory at the Broadway Theater next week, when seven Hopi Indians, descendants of the cliff dwellers, will take part in the performances. [10]

176

The Gayla Johnson Collection

Helen Gibson and the Hopi Indian Troup.*

Six representatives of the Hopi Indians, who recently journeyed to Washington and induced Congress to repeal an order, which it had issued restraining their tribes from performing their age-old dances and rituals, will arrive in Boston today. They will remain here for the balance of the week and will appear with Mrs. Helen [Hoot] Gibson, well-known movie actress, at the Keith-Albee St. James Theatre. The Indians, who danced before Congress and persuaded them to allow the religious rites to continue among their tribe in Arizona, are Chief Soloftoche, Kolcortowah, Sctalla, Ponyah, Quamaquap, and Tewah. They are visiting the principal cities in an effort to acquaint the American people with the dances. [11]

* Appendix B - Two Hopi Indian Newspaper Articles, page 250

Helen appeared to have made plans for employment beyond the Hopi Indian vaudeville group presentations. It was described in a newspaper article earlier in August, 1926.

Helen Gibson informs that after leaving the Ringling-Barnum Circuits in 1926 to accept a year's contract with M.W. Billingsley's Hopi Indian vaudeville act. She has made her home at Burbank, California, to which city she intends to return from the east in December to again enter pictures. While on her way to Washington D.C., recently from New England, where she has been making personal appearances at movie houses, Helen took in the [August 2nd] rodeo at Philadelphia. Pronounced it a good show and met friends, including Florence Randolph, Rene Shelton, Bob Calem and Maud and Ted Elder. [12]

CHAPTER 15

Hollywood, Serials, Stunt Work, and Romance - 1927

Helen arrived back in Hollywood in 1927 and began doing stunt doubling for: Louise Fazenda, Marie Dressler, Edna Mae Oliver, May Robson, Esther Dale, Marjorie Main, and Ethel Barrymore, to name a few.

With this new job, Helen was free to participate in local and distant rodeos as she had in the past. The first big contest was *The Seattle Stampede* for eight days starting on July 2, 1927, with two shows daily. At this event Helen had a chance to be reunited with an old rodeo friend, Yakima Canutt. [1]

Yakima Canutt

> Thrilling, awe-inspiring revival of the great West! See cowboys from every section of America battle with outlaw horses and steers from the championship of the world. [2]

> "I also did character parts and extra work, and in fact, took anything I could get. My hopes of a comeback in railroad melodrama or westerns were not fulfilled." [3]

It could have been a coincidence or maybe luck when Helen got her next job. Only a few weeks after *The Seattle Stampede*,* Helen was hired by Nat Levine's Mascot Pictures as a bit player in the studio's second serial production, *Heroes of the Wild*. The star of this serial was Jack Hoxie whose four-year contract with Universal Blue Streak was up. Levine had an idea for his western serial plots right from the beginning. He would team up a hero, with a horse and a dog, and it worked. His idea also caught on with other studios making western serials.

* Appendix B - Ad for The Seattle Stampede, page 251

179

The dedication of Rolando Plaza, Rolando streetlights and opening of Rolando Boulevard will be tomorrow night. With a program of fireworks, music, dancing, speeches, refreshments and a spectacular illuminated aerial circus for all.

Since the above was printed, arrangements have been made with the Mascot Pictures Corporation to present thirty of its movie stars at Rolando tomorrow night at 8 o'clock. Be sure and attend; meet and dance with these well-known stars, which include Jack Hoxie, Joe Bonomo (the world's strong man), Josephine Hill, Helen Gibson, Linda Loredo, Emily Gerdes, Roy Craft, Art La Forest, Elva Simmonds, Jay J. Bryan. [4]

Joe Bonomo

Chapter one of the Mascot serial, *Heroes of the Wild* was released in theaters on November 1, 1927.

White Fury portrayed a horse called The Ghost of the Gauchos, a wild stallion carrying on his leg the key to a vast fortune, the rightful owner of which was the leading lady, Josephine Hill. Hill's uncle and guardian, played by Joe Bonomo, is in league with a bunch of crooks and they plot to snatch the wealth. Fortunately for all concerned, except the bad guys, Jack Hoxie playing Jack Hale, joined by Tornado and White Fury, are on hand to protect Hill's interest. Of course, at the fade, Hoxie wins both the girl and the fortune. [5]

Helen had gone back to her extra work long before *Heroes of the Wild* was released. She didn't get another bit part offer until the fall of 1928, when Helen got two offers. The first came from Trem Carr Productions Ltd., who was producing films in Placerita Canyon.

The picture offer was a ten-chapter serial, *The Chinatown Mystery*, starring Joe Bonomo and Ruth Hiatt, directed by J.P. McGowan. It was the same director who was responsible for the Railroad series at Kalem, *The Hazards of Helen*.

Cast as Tarzan in a Universal serial in 1928, Joe broke his leg and was replaced by Frank Merrill. Joe was approached by Trem Carr to star in an independent serial for Syndicate Pictures, *The Chinatown Mystery*. Bonomo agreed to do it for 25 percent of the net receipts, a sum he never received. Carr hired Francis Ford to write the story and J.P. McGowan as director.

The story concerned a piece of jade with the formula for the manufacture of artificial diamonds inscribed upon it – a formula sought by the Mysterious Thirteen, led by Ford, who wrote himself in as the chief villain. [6]

The first chapter of *The Chinatown Mystery* was released on September 1, 1928. Helen was just finishing up her second bit part offering from the Mascot Picture Corporation. She was cast in another ten-chapter serial, *The Vanishing West*. By the time this serial went into production, Mascot had a reputation for producing chapter plays equal to or better than Universal Studio. Levine packed each of his chapters with as much action as possible. [7]

As was the case with the small producers, Levine usually cast his chapter plays with former stars who no longer command steady work of any consequence at the major studios. The best example of this type of casting was found in "The Vanishing West (1928)", with Jack Daugherty, Jack Perrin, Leo Maloney, Eileen Sedgwick and Helen Gibson (all one-time box-office greats) all appearing in the same serial. Mascot made good use of the talents of Yakima Canutt, an outstanding creator of dangerous action sequences. His appearance on screen always meant countless thrills for the audiences. [8]

Chapter one of the Mascot Picture Corporation serial, *The Vanishing West,* was released to the theaters on October 15, 1928.

Half way through the month of January 1929, a story had made it into nearly every newspaper across the U.S., Hoot Gibson was being sued for divorce by his second wife.

> A suit for divorce charging desertion has been filed in Superior Court by Mrs. Helen Gibson, wife of the film cowboy, Hoot Gibson.
>
> Mrs. Gibson asserted that her husband left their home more than a year ago. Sam Wolf, Gibson's attorney, indicated that the movie star would not contest the suit, and added "Gibson's strenuous film work caused his absence on location frequently. These absences were the cause of dissension which brought misunderstandings and estrangement."
>
> The Gibsons were married in 1921 and had a daughter, Lois, 5 years old, whose custody was requested by the mother. Mrs. Gibson was an actress before her marriage, but left the screen following the wedding. Mr. Wolf said a property settlement had been made "amply providing for the wife and daughter." [9]

Helen had no comment about her ex-husband and his marital problem.

Helen Johnson Gibson as she appeared in court,

In 1929 Helen found most of her jobs in stunting and not with bit parts. It would be a year she would remember. On October 1, 1929, Helen received word that a good rodeo friend of sixteen years had been involved in an accident.

> Bonnie McCarroll, Idaho's queen of horsewomen, is coming home from Pendleton, her riding days over forever. She will be buried in Morris Hill Cemetery, overlooking the valley where she lived since early childhood. Death occurred in a Pendleton hospital after a rodeo accident.
>
> As a blue-eyed baby, born in a log cabin in High Valley, near Smiths Ferry, Bonnie Treadwell rode the range in her mother's arms. She got her own saddle horse before she went to school. From that time until 1924 when she won the Lord Selfridge Cup as the world's best woman bronc rider at Wembley Stadium, London, she had appeared at fairs and rodeos from sea to sea.

It was after taking first honors at the state fair in Boise in 1913 that she married Frank McCarroll, who rode and swung a lasso at the same fair, together with Art Acord, Hoot and Helen Gibson and other notables of the track and arena. [10]

Bonnie was an extremely popular member of the rodeo family, and adding to the tragedy was the fact that Pendleton was to be her last rodeo. After seventeen years on the road, Bonnie and her husband had already announced they would retire, and she had hoped her winnings would help pay for decorations in their Boise new home.

Immediately after Bonnie's death, the Pendleton Round-up committee dropped cowgirl bronc riding from their programs. Thereafter, the debate continued throughout the profession. Some individuals and organizations supported outright bans of cowgirl bronc riding, while others advocated a change in the rules. One group that could have provided invaluable assistance in the matter was the fledgling Rodeo Association of America, also formed in 1929. The reason for the RAA's opposition to women's contests may never be known, as all of their records are lost. [11]

Beyond Bonnie's death the other big event of 1929 was the stock market crash on October 1st. Helen's stunting work wasn't affected much. The big studios slowed down somewhat, but the small independents shut down or halted operations for an undetermined amount of time.

Bonnie McCarroll

The decade of the 1930s would bring more happiness and some sorrow to Helen. She continued stunting (uncredited) in 1930 as the studios increased production, and beyond 1931, found herself busy playing bit parts for several different Hollywood studios.

It sometimes felt to Helen that a Gibson was in the newspaper more than necessary. On June 28, 1930, Hoot Gibson was back in the headlines after taking a new bride, in Hollywood fashion.

Hoot Gibson who rode from the rodeo chute into cowboy film stardom, and his bride, Sally Eilers, screen actress, are en route today to Canada, where they will spend their honeymoon in the Rocky Mountains.

The couple were married last night at the Hacienda of Gibson's ranch near Saugus. Like a set prepared for one of his pictures, the ranch house was furnished for Gibson's third wedding in the conventional "Old West" fashion. Through the windows of the living room, where the Rev. Hamilton Lash of the Hollywood Congregational Church, read the ceremony, could be seen from the corral where Gibson keeps his string of horses.

Gibson is 36 years old. The bride is 21. It is her first marriage. [12]

Another tragedy for Helen as the New Year of 1931 began with the untimely death of an old rodeo friend, Art Acord.

Acord was a champion bronco buster before entering the movies. In the latter part of 1929, he came into conflict with police and finally was arrested on charges of robbery and liquor possession. The robbery charges were dropped and he later left for Mexico where he said that he would "start all over again".

He went into the mining business in Chihuahua City, but his affairs were understood to have gone from bad to worse. [13]

The *New York Times* reported that his body contained enough cyanide to kill several men. However, Helen Gibson has reason to believe to this day [1964] that Acord met with foul play. She says:

"There are no records any place; as to Art's death, all I can say is I saw the letter M.K. Wilson [her leading man at Universal in the twenties] received through the American Legion. He has passed on and so has Art's wife and everything has been destroyed. Art loved life too much to do that. He was a tough fellow who would fight at the drop of a hat and he always won. He just ran into some bad ones in Mexico." [14]

Hoot Gibson and Art Acord were best friends for nearly twenty years. When asked about his suicide, Hoot replied, "It wasn't suicide – he was found dead in a bed with knife wounds about his stomach!" [15]

Helen received an offer for a bit part in a twelve chapter serial from Mascot Pictures, *The Lightning Warrior*. She appeared in chapter one and two with a speaking role, and did some stunt work also. The serial was released to theaters on December 1, 1931.

A Rin-Tin-Tin serial presented in 12 episodes. The mysterious Wolf Man terrorizing settlers in a western town. With the help of Rinty, young Jimmy Carter unmasks the Wolf Man and foils his evil plot. [16]

Yakima Canutt's stunting in The Lightning Warrior was in top form. Typical of his stunts was his close for the first episode. The camera was mounted on the front of a runaway wagon with Canutt and Helen Gibson aboard, doubling George Brent and Georgia Hale. They were being pursued by hostile Indians. The camera tracks to where the wagon hits a stump, mounted on the driver's seat at the moment of impact. The horses pull forward, taking their harnesses with them, the wagon rolling back slowly and gaining momentum as it hurtles down the hillside. [17]

A lengthy article appeared in the Boston Herald on December 28, 1931. The headline read, *Many Film Stars of Yesterday Glad for Occasional Small Roles*. The article listed nearly three dozen silent film stars, and Helen Gibson was one of the names.

Reproduction Poster

Some live in Hollywood, not far from studios which brought them fame. Others have gone into business, turned to vaudeville, to roles on the legitimate stage or are content to get occasional small parts in films. [18]

Helen's next uncredited bit role was in a Willis Kent production, *The Cheyenne Cyclone* with Lane Chandler in the lead role. The film was also known as *Rustler's Ranch*. It was released in January, 1932. [19]

On the same day, Big 4 Film Productions releaseed *Human Targets*. The film was directed by J.P. McGowan with Helen playing Mrs. Dale.

> The Dales need money for their sick mother and Bart Travis, having found gold, says he will provide it. Duke Remsden learns of the strike and waylays Buzz Dale as he tries to record Bart's deed. Then dressed as Bart, Duke kills and robs a man. With the sheriff after Bart, Buzz escapes capture, finds the clothes worn to impersonate Bart, and heads for the sheriff. [20]

One month later, February 10, 1932, Monogram Pictures released *Single-Handed Sanders* with Helen in an uncredited role. During the month of March, Helen was hired as a bit player by Alan Crosland Productions. This film, *The Silver Lining,* had a very large cast. It was also known as *Big House for Girls*, and was a different type role for Helen. No horses or western backdrop. [21]

> Atmospheric necessities, to give the right and proper setting to every scene, made it necessary for the producers of "The Silver Lining" to employ more than six hundred extras in the making of this picture. They represented nationalities of practically every country on the globe. This Alan Crosland production, made for Patrician Pictures, will be the feature at the Liberty Theater, beginning tomorrow.

> In every sequence, Director Crosland was compelled to use a different group of extra talent, and in so doing has brought before the camera practically every type of human being, as well as every civilized country.

> Aside from the numerous nationalities represented in the picture there is also presented the various stages of human life, from six to thirty years. From the sordid atmosphere of the East Side, the story moves to the penthouse district of Park Avenue.

> It is an engrossing production from every angle. The cast includes Maureen O'Sullivan, Betty Compson, John Warburton, Montagu Love, Mary Doran, John Holland, Cornelius Keefe, Martha Mattox, Jayne Kerr, Grace Valentine, J. Frank Glendon, Helen Gibson and many other well-known players. [22]

Crosland began his movie career at the Edison Studios in 1912. He began directing by 1917, and eight years later was working for Famous Players-Lasky (later Paramount Pictures). Warner Brothers hired him to direct Al Jolson in 1927's *The Jazz Singer*, the film that made him famous. Four years after directing Jolson, Alan Crosland died at the age of 41 in an automobile accident. [23]

Helen had some down time in May and June 1932. The only Gibson to make the newspapers was Hoot Gibson, again.

> Hollywood, May 9 – Success of Sally Eilers, young screen star in "Bad Girl," today was blamed by her husband, Hoot Gibson, cowboy film actor, for their separation.

> "I could no longer please her after she made 'Bad Girl' and attained independent success," Gibson said.

184

Gibson and Miss Eilers separated after a final quarrel Saturday night, he said. Miss Ellers went home from a club dance with Mr. and Mrs. Edward Cline whose automobile was wrecked injuring Miss Eilers and Mrs. Cline.

Miss Eilers declared Gibson was jealous of her, but that she would make no statement to injure him.

Gibson today will be awarded custody of his daughter, Lois, by his previous marriage to Mrs. Helen Gibson, his second wife. He and Miss Ellers were married June 29, 1930.

Sally Eilers Gibson

Gibson said he would contest Miss Eilers' proposed divorce suit. [24] In July, Helen headed for San Diego, California and a two-day rodeo event.

San Diego's first annual July 30-31 Congress of Rodeo Stars opened at Navy Field yesterday with more than 100 foremost international roping and riding aces, of both sexes, battling for championship honors.

This afternoon's session will decide who's who among the contestants. Billie Montana of rodeo and film fame nosed out Bernice Ealy and Helen Rose Gibson, first wife of Hoot Gibson, for first place honors; Ed Bowman, Bill Cox, Sandy Garret, Ace Gardner, Boyd Fury, Slim MacKey, Rube Finney, leaders in the cowboy's division for riding honors.

"Perhaps the keenest rivalry has developed in the cowboy's bronco and Brahma bull riding events; so far," says Undersheriff Oliver Sexson. "Any one of the 67 contestants is champion. Aehora Luline, barefoot rider from Honolulu, has an edge on the cowboy riders from the States.

"San Diego County shows signs of scoring the high-pointers among the roping and wild-cow milking contestants," says Sexson, delegate to the Congress from Warner's Hot Springs, Mesa Grande and Julian being real threats in this afternoon's finals. [25]

It wasn't until November when Helen found another rodeo. She was riding in the rodeo* at the Pasqual Ranch in Escondido, California. [26]

Helen Gibson with horse will ride in Frontier Wild West show to be staged November 18-20 for benefit of the Parent-Teachers milk fund. Dramatic episodes in life of the Old West will be reproduced under the direction of old cattlemen. [27]

Before leaving for the Escondido Rodeo, Helen put in several hours at the Majestic Pictures' studio. She was given a part in a new Jack Hoxie western, *Law and Lawless* where she played Mrs. Kelley. Helen had another opportunity to act alongside Yakima Canutt.

The story, which boasts of an unusual amount of comedy and romance, in addition to its close-packed super thrills, depicts Jack's adventures when Don Jose, owner of the El Rio Rancho, hires him and his pal, Pancho, to check the deviltry of a mysterious band of marauding night-riders known as the Wolves. The presence of Don Jose's black-eyed daughter, Rosita, makes the job even more appealing, but it takes Jack several reels and innumerable dips into a tome entitled "How to Make Love in Spanish", to overcome the rivalry of the guitar strumming Pancho.

Julian Rivero, who portrays Pancho, supplies much of the comedy, while the Spanish Follies beauty, Hilda Moreno, whom the late Florez Ziegfeld considered one of the loveliest and most talented girls he ever glorified, plays the dark-eyed Rosita.

* Appendix B - Newspaper Article of 2-Rodeos, page 252

The great supporting cast also boasts such distinguished names as Wally Wales, famous and popular western star; Yakima Canutt, champion rider of the world and most daring stunt man in Hollywood; Jack Mower, J. Frank Glendon, Helen Gibson, famous old-time serial star, and many others. Jack's Wonder Horse, Dynamite, and his clever little dog, Bunk, are also much in evidence. [28]

Just before the year 1932 ended, Helen was one of the featured horse woman at another rodeo in Southern California.

Helen Gibson, famous rodeo star, is to be one of the feature attractions at Cy Toosie's Farm on December 17 and 18. The former Encino Country Club is being transformed into the famous farm. [29]

After the first few months of 1933, Helen was back at stunting. Over the past few months she hadn't gotten any press, but Hoot had made the newspapers again.

Los Angeles, May 10 – Hoot Gibson, cowboy screen star, today was under court order to pay Mrs. J.L. Johnson, his former mother-in-law, $2500 in settlement of a promissory note signed by himself and Helen Gibson, the actors' divorced wife, in 1928. [30]

It was in the month of May that Universal Studio offered Helen another bit part. It was in an upcoming Ken Maynard picture called *King of the Arena* where Helen played a circus cowgirl.

Mysterious deaths have been occurring in the same towns as Miller's Circus and the Governor has sent Ken Kenton to investigate. Ken joins the show but when he realizes that Bargoff is involved, Bargoff has fled and taken Mary Hiller as a hostage. The trail leads to Baron Petroff who concocted the deadly chemical and Ken quickly finds himself the Baron's prisoner. [31]

Helen Gibson did a fine bit in Ken Maynard's picture "King of the Arena." Her scenes with Frank Rice were exceptionally good. [32]

Only a few short weeks after the release of Maynard's picture, his name and Hoot Gibson's name appeared in the same newspaper article. Both men were good friends and both liked to fly airplanes.

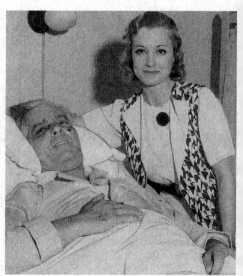

Los Angeles, California. July 3 (AP) – Hoot Gibson, who rode to fame in pictures on a horse, took to an airplane Monday in a special match race at the National Air Races and wound up in the hospital with a concussion or a possible skull fracture received in a crash witnessed by 25,000 spectators.

The gray-haired Hollywood actor, long a sportsman pilot, slipped to the ground after rounding the second pylon in a fifteen-mile race against Ken Maynard, another actor who stars on horseback and spends much of his leisure flying airplanes.

The two were flying for a trophy donated by Will Rogers, film humorist.

Gibson was catapulted from his ship as the motor struck the ground.

Hoot and June Gale

The plane was destroyed. Gibson said he "just couldn't figure out how it happened," but pilots who saw the plane crash believed he had given it too much rudder on a turn while leading Maynard, and slipped into the ground from an altitude of about 200 feet.

Maynard circled quickly and landed near the plane. He dragged his friendly rival from the wreckage and the race ended there. [33]

"Gibson is resting comfortably," said Dr. Martin, "and seems out of danger, but he will have to stay in bed for more than a month. Aside from the fractures, he is black and blue almost from head to foot." [34]

Hoot appeared to make news even from his hospital bed. He just kept making news.

Los Angeles, July 9 – (AP) – Divorce of Sally Eilers, motion picture actress, and her cowboy husband, Hoot Gibson, is planned, Gibson announced last night from his hospital bed where he is recovering from serious injuries suffered in the crash of his airplane at the National Air Races.

His statement was made in the presence of June Gale, 21-year-old San Francisco actress, who agreed with Gibson that they were "madly in love." Miss Gale has been a daily visitor at Gibson's hospital room since the 3rd when his plane cracked up during a race with Ken Maynard, another film cowboy.

Asked if they were going to marry, Gibson said: – "I don't think this is the time to talk about engagements or marriage. I am still married and it wouldn't be fair to anyone concerned to make any statement now."

Miss Eilers, third wife of the actor, left for Europe several months ago. It was rumored then that they were estranged. Gibson said there was an agreement that her trip would be sort of a "trial separation." He said Miss Eilers wrote him from Europe that she felt they would be happier apart. Miss Gale has appeared in New York musical comedies and revues. [35]

Helen's numerous stunting jobs kept her busy for the remainder of 1933 and into the spring of 1934. That is when the Ken Maynard Production Company at Universal Studio hired her to play the settler's wife, a bit part in *Wheels of Destiny*.

Bill, who is about to lead a wagon train to California, has a map to a valuable gold field and Rocky is after the map. When Rocky and his men attack, Ken Manning breaks it up and later identifies Rocky and his men as the attackers. Expelled from the wagon train, they stampede a buffalo herd putting the Indians on the warpath. After the Indians attack the wagon train, Rocky thinks he can get the map. [36]

Wheels of Destiny was the second film in a row for Helen to work with the Ken Maynard cast and crew. They were on location in Lone Pine, California. It would be interesting to hear Helen's description of a day's activity on the set. Maynard was a one-of-a-kind western star loved by his millions of fans and extremely disliked by his fellow actors. At the drop of a hat, he would cuss out casts or crew, or both. When the front office learned about his inflated ego and his rage on the set, he was let go, only to be hired by another studio or rehired by a previous studio. [37]

In August, 1934, Helen got a call again for a bit part. It was Universal Studio with a different star, Charlie "Buck" Jones. She plays a townswoman (uncredited) in *Rocky Rhodes*.

Rocky Rhodes returns to find his father dead and his best friend Joe accused of the murder. The culprit is Murtch who now lets Joe break jail and then has him shot escaping. When Rocky starts to interfere with Murtch's plans, he has Rocky framed for murder. Rocky now has to prove Murtch is guilty while escaping the law. [38]

Reproduction Lobby Card

Helen's stunting, a bit part job routine, was once again interrupted in September, 1934. This time it was serious. Her mother had passed away in Cleveland, Ohio.

> Helen Gibson, former star and first wife of Hoot Gibson, is in Cleveland attending the funeral of her mother, who passed away Sunday. Filmography joins Miss Gibson's many friends in extending its condolences. After internment, Miss Gibson will return to Hollywood and resume her screen work. [39]

As soon as Helen returned from Cleveland she started work on the first of four films for Superior Talking Pictures. The first was *The Way of the West* with Hal Taliaferro (Wally Wales) in the lead role. Helen's small part is that of a townswoman.

> Government agent Gordon, working undercover, is investigating a cattleman-sheepman war. The culprit is Horton and when Horton kills Parker he frames Gordon. His identity revealed, the Sheriff lets Gordon escape to go after the real killer. [40]

In between this film and her next two for Superior, Helen played an uncredited part in *365 Nights in Hollywood*, a Fox Film Corporation film starring Alice Faye. Helen was among forty-four other uncredited actors. It was her last film of 1934.

> Down-on-his-luck film director Jimmie Dale takes a job at a fly-by-night acting school. He is drawn into the plans of the school's owner to bilk a wealthy young man out of the funds he has supplied to shoot a movie starring pretty student Alice Perkins. But Jimmie hopes to bilk the bilkers by actually completing the movie as ostensibly planned. [41]

The first couple months of 1935, Helen went back to her stunt double work. At this same time, a three column article appeared in the print media making it known many former stars are flocking back to film as extras.

> But extras have codes of their own. It is no longer news that they would close their ranks to outsiders, even to late-comers. Sometimes they may appear unjust; but we must not concern ourselves here with ethics. Last week Jean Acker, first wife of Rudolph Valentino, one-time stage, film and vaudeville actress, complained on a Paramount set that it has been easier to hold a $3,500-a-week job than to earn $7.50 a day as an extra. [42]

In March, Helen was called back to Superior Talking Pictures. Her role as Mrs. Carter in *Cyclone of the Saddle* was a much larger role than she had been offered in a long while. She was also reunited with Yakima Canutt who in this film plays one of the bad guys.

> The Army sends Andy Thomas posing as a renegade to find out who has been harassing the wagon trains. He joins the wagon train and soon learns Cherokee and Snake are the ones he is after. But Cherokee and Snake then kill two Indians and blame the settlers from the wagon train and Andy finds the Indians about to attack. [43]

Reproduction Lobby Card

Helen made a quick stop at Universal Studio backlot one evening as one of many villager extras for *Bride of Frankenstein*. It was released April 22, 1935. It was then onto the third film for Superior Talking Pictures, *Fighting Caballero*. She plays Drusella Jenkins in an uncredited role.

> When her mine foreman is killed, the owner arrives to investigate. Also on hand are two agents working undercover as Mexicans. Jackson has taken control over the mine and is using it for his counterfeiting operation. The two agents go to work and soon uncover Jackson's operation. [44]

Helen's last film with Superior Talking Pictures wouldn't start for several months, but the motion picture and her role had been announced in the media.

> Former Western Star – Helen Gibson has just been cast in the role of "Calamity Jane" in the new Weiss Brothers' flicker, "Custer's Last Stand," which faces the camera soon. [45]

While waiting for her shooting schedule, Helen accepted a small role in a Stage and Screen Production. It was called *The Drunkard*, produced by Bert Sternbach, with the operation supervised by Louis Weiss from Superior Talking Pictures.

> In order to make money and put their lazy relatives to work, hard luck theatrical producers decided to stage the 1843 play *The Drunkard*. [46]

Six days before her forty-fourth birthday on August 27, 1935, Helen Gibson would be a bride again.

CHAPTER 16

A Bride, Stunt Work and More Bit Parts - 1935

There was nothing written or in print on how long Helen Gibson dated Clifton Johnson. Nor was there anything on how they met. They were married on August 5, 1935 at Helen's home in Burbank.*

In her home at 212 South Glenwood Place and in the presence of a score of intimate friends, Helen Rose Gibson became the bride of Clifton Johnson of Los Angeles in an evening wedding recently. Rev. J.R. Bostwick of Glendale officiated.

The bride was attired in a formal gown of pale blush crepe with a blue taffeta sash. Her bouquet was of matching pink rosebuds and maidenhair fern tied shower wise with pink ribbon. The only attendants were Mr. and Mrs. Gus Pulliam of Glendale.

After the ceremony, a full-course dinner was served, the table appointments being carried out in shades of yellow, green, and henna. Baskets of gladioli and asters in yellow and bronze, and tall yellow tapers decorated the rooms. A decorated wedding cake was cut by Mrs. Johnson at the end of the evening.

A group of musicians from KMTR serenaded the couple outside the home before the ceremony, and played the wedding march.

Mr. and Mrs. Johnson will take a belated honeymoon in early September, as the bride is working on a forthcoming Universal Picture, "Custer's Last Stand", and the groom's occupation as a boatswain for a petroleum company will keep him placed on the high seas for the next few weeks. Mrs. Johnson has lived here seven years, and is well-known to "Western" film fans.

Among those present at the wedding were Mr. and Mrs. H.J. Gibson, Mr. and Mrs. Jack McIrvin, Mr. and Mrs. H. Strickland, Mrs. Nora E. Goodrich, Marian Hoxie, Dolly Spackman, Arthur E. Turcott, Richard McIrvin, Duncan Pullian, and Bob Rose.[1]

* Appendix A - Marriage Certificate, page 237

Reproduction Poster

Some belated details of the marriage of Helen R. Gibson, formally with the Wild West contingent of Ringling-Barnum Circus and other shows and periodically in pictures, to Clifton L. Johnson, boatswain on a Petroleum Oil Company tanker, Emedio, traveling along the Pacific Coast, were received last week. [2]

Helen and Clifton did get away for a belated honeymoon and the press noticed when they got back.

Mr. and Mrs. Clifton Johnson (Helen Gibson) of 212 South Glenwood Place, who were married here August 5, have returned home from a trip to San Diego and San Francisco which was a belated honeymoon journey. [3]

Early in 1936, Clifton Johnson changed jobs. He became a studio electrician at Universal Studio. It was a better situation where he could be home with Helen every evening and not stuck on a tanker for more than a week at a time. [4]

Chapter one, *Perils of the Plains*, of *Custer's Last Stand* was released in January, 1936. Helen had a speaking role in five of the fifteen chapters.

When some men are attacked by Indians, a survivor obtains an Indian medicine arrow. An Indian tells Blade he has found gold but will not tell him where until he has that arrow. So Blade starts killing the survivors of the attack but fails to get the arrow. One of the men he kills is John Cardigan and Kit Cardigan, a scout for Custer, now starts looking for the killer of his father. [5]

With Clifton at his full-time studio job, Helen accepted a bit part in a John Wayne Republic Pictures film *The Lawless Nineties* which was released February 15, 1936. [6] A few days later she changed hats and resumed her sporadic stunt doubling in Hollywood. Later in February she accepted a bit role for Columbia Pictures Corporation. Helen played a nurse (uncredited) in *Lady of Secrets* which was a non-Western. It was about a lady who goes into seclusion because of an affair she had earlier in her life. [7]

On May 26, 1936, a group of stars from the old studios in Hollywood got together for a joint breakfast. The two groups involved were the Women's Breakfast Club and Riverside Drive Breakfast Club. The sole purpose was to honor Will Rogers and all the old-timers of the silver screen who had passed on.

While Dr. Cleveland Kleihauer tolled off the names of the deceased in a Memorial Week eulogy, "Captain," a horse which appeared in films with Will Rogers, Gloria Swanson, Vilma Banky, Rudolph Valentino and others, was led riderless across the stage in tribute to the beloved cowboy humorist.

Cheerful faces turned serious when Rogers and other pioneers no longer alive were mentioned.

Among those attending Dot Farley, Helen Gibson, Huntley Gordon, James W. Horne, Helen Holmes, Cleo Ridgely, Alice Lake, Florence Lawrence, Ralph Lewis, Mary MacLaren, Robert Middleton, Virginia Pearson, Larry Trumbull, Ruth Stonehouse, Bryant Washburn and Vera Gordon.

Also Charles Chase, Kenneth Harlan, "Baby Peggy" Montgomery, Lois Wilson, Fritz Leiber, Heinie Conklin, Clarence Badger, Kathryn Adams, Edwin August, William August, Victor Potel and Maurice Costello.

As a result of the gathering, Blackton, Washburn, Potel, Cleo Ridgely and Helen Holmes joined in announcing the formation of a new club to preserve yesterday's spirit. It will be known as the "Silent Screen Stars' Organization", and members will include most of the 100 veterans present at the breakfast. [8]

Dot Farley

Huntley Gordon

Helen Holmes

Cleo Ridgely

Alice Lake

Florence Lawrence

Ralph Lewis

Mary MacLaren

Robert Middleton

Virginia Pearson

Ruth Stonehouse

194

Bryant Washburn

Vera Gordon

Charles Chase

Kenneth Harlan

Diana Serra Cary Collection
"Baby Peggy" Montgomery

Lois Wilson

Fritz Leiber Heinie Conklin Clarance Badger Kathryn Adams

Edwin August   Victor Potel   Maurice Costello   Helen Gibson   **BFI**

A couple of months after Helen's Columbia Picture job, she moved to a Western film, *Last of the Warrens*, at Supreme Pictures. She worked with Bob Steele, an up and coming star with the studio. Steele was directed by his father, film director, Robert N. Bradbury and screenwriter who directed 125 movies during his career. [9]

Ted Warren returns from WWI to find that everyone thinks he is dead. The culprit is Kent who intercepted Warren's, rustled the Warren cattle, took over the Warren ranch, and is now after Ted's girlfriend. When Kent's henchmen fail to kill Ted, Kent shoots Ted's father and leaves him for dead. But only wounded, the plan is to have Warren appear as a ghost to get a confession from Kent. [10]

Continuing to get Western bit roles, Helen was hired by Republic Pictures to play a settler's wife in *Winds of the Wasteland*. The lead actor was a rising star in Hollywood after making *His Private Secretary* for Screencraft Productions. The actor in question is John Wayne. [11]

The arrival of the telegraph put Pony Express riders like John Blair and his pal Smoky out of work. A race will decide whether they or stage line owner Drake get the government contract. [12]

It was back to more stunt double work until Universal Studio offered Helen a bit role in *Jungle Jim*, a 12 chapter serial with Grant Withers in the lead role. She would play the part of Mrs. Raymond.

Two safaris enter the African jungle intent on finding a white girl who is the heiress to a fortune. One safari, led by Jungle Jim, wants to make sure she gets the news that she is now a rich woman. The leaders of the other safari want to kill the girl so they can try to get hold of her inheritance. [13]

The stunt women's organization Helen joined earlier received some well deserved newspaper publicity.

Hollywood, October 10 – If you ever have a dangerous job that must be performed by a woman, call Gladstone 6519, Hollywood, and ask for Frances Miles. She'll arrange it for you, or do it herself.

If you want a girl to jump out of a burning building, fall from a galloping horse, change planes in mid-air or anything like that, Miss Miles knows plenty of people who'll risk their necks, and gladly. She's the president, organizer and chief participant of the Riding and Stunt Girls of the Screen, a club recently formed mostly for the financial

* Appendix A - Social Security Application, page 238

protection of women who double for the stars.

The organization expects soon to include every stunt girl in the movie colony. Right now it has 51 members — women who can ride, drive stage coaches, do high dives, perform fancy falls and acrobatics, and train lions. The lion tamer is Mme. Olga Celeste, former circus star.

There are several ex-leading ladies of the flickers who in their best days had doubles doing hazardous stunts for them. Best known is Helen Holmes, serial star of "The Hazards of Helen" and of Keystone and Kalem comedies. Then there are Helen Gibson, Hoot's first wife; Marin Sais, formerly Mrs. Jack Hoxie, and Frances Miles herself used to be a leading lady in Westerns at Universal.

Miss Miles has been smart in her organizing, and under her leadership the stunt girls have established a minimum of $35 for any sort of feat. That's a rock-bottom price; above it, the girls do their own bargaining. They have no set figure for falling down stairs, staging a fight, leaping off a building or boarding a train from a running horse.

"Those are things we can't put a price tag on," Miss Miles explains. "Every stunt's a little different, and every girl has a different idea of what her neck is worth. [14]

Grant Withers as Jungle Jim from episode 2

197

Shortly after that "stunt girl" article appeared in the newspapers, Helen's next uncredited film, Paramount Pictures, *High, Wide, and Handsome*. It had a very large cast and was filmed in Big Bear Valley and San Bernardino National Forest, California.

The setting is a small town in 1870s Pennsylvania. Sally Waterson and her father have stopped in town with their traveling medicine show, but when their wagon catches fire, they find themselves stranded. They are taken in by Mrs. Cortlandt and her grandson, Peter, who is trying to set up a pipeline that will supply oil throughout the state. Sally and Peter fall in love and marry. Neither their marriage nor Peter's pipe dreams flow too smoothly. [15]

The Marc Wanamaker Collection
Rouben Mamoulian, director of High, Wide and Handsome chats with Helen.

198

Helen's next on-screen appearance is in a film from Monogram Ranch in Newhall, California. Director Robert N. Bradbury was filming Jack Randall in a Western. Helen plays Dana Temple in *Danger Valley.*.

When Temple's miners strike gold, they send Jake to file the claim. Dana is in the Recorder's Office and overhears. He and his men kill Jake and forge new deeds. Now owning everything, Dana tries to kick the Temple group off their land. But Jack and sidekick Lucky are on hand and plan to help them fight back. [16]

Helen had entered a three month dry spell until Republic Pictures called for a bit part in Gene Autry's *The Old Barn Dance.* She played a woman at a dance. [17]

In Helen's next film, she gets to show both her acting and stunt abilities. The film wasn't a Western, far from it. The film *Condemned Women*, takes place in a women's prison.

Burbank, January 31 – Helen Gibson, film serial thriller star of silent days, has completed a part in "Condemned Women," new RKO – Radio picture directed by Lou Landers.

Miss Gibson, who makes her home in Burbank, at 212 S. Glenwood Place, plays the part of a police matron in the picture.

A scene from Condemned Women.

A scene from Condemned Women.

The female lead in "Condemned Women" was very familiar to Helen. On the set, both Helen and Sally Eilers took advantage to talk with each other.

Sally Eilers and Helen Gibson, working together in RKO's "Condemned Women," have been talking over old times – and Hoot Gibson. Miss Gibson was his first wife and Miss Eilers was his third wife. [18]

Shoplifter Linda Wilson (Sally Eilers) doesn't care much for life inside or outside of jail until she starts a relationship with prison psychiatrist Phillip Duncan. When the warden asks her to break off the affair, rather than jeopardize Duncan's career as husband of a felon, she reacts by joining a jailbreak that turns into a riot. [19]

Helen Gibson tumbled down the stairs the other day at a Hollywood studio. She collected an abrasion, a bruise and her pay. The next day she did her act again.

Stair tumbling isn't in the repertoire of Hollywood's stars. It's the business of a stunt actress like Helen Gibson.

A scene from Condemned Women.

Those who can remember 23 years ago, and the events in the realm of the theater at the time, will remember Miss Gibson. She was a "Daughter of Daring", one of the serial queens of the day. She did stunts then too.

In "Condemned Women", which comes to the Paramount at 6 P.M. Wednesday, Miss Gibson is cast as a prison matron for the melodrama which features Sally Eilers, Louis Hayward and Alice Shirley. Lee Patrick shoots her, and she tumbles dead from the stairs which she was barring against a jailbreak.

Helen's act, she admitted, was the toughest since the days when she did anything in stunts – for doubles and stunt actresses were not known in her picture heyday.

In 1910, Helen joined Miller Brothers 101-Ranch Show. The late Thomas Ince bought the show after the 1911 season to make Westerns for 101-Bison Pictures.

Each day, Helen and her circus companions rode from Santa Monica to Topanga Canyon five miles away to ride for Ince's cameras. The pay was $8 a week. Rather than be a hardy but womanly pioneer with the covered wagons, she put on the costume of an Indian and rode bareback because it was "more fun".

Later, Helen joined the Kalem Company as a contemporary of the late Ruth Roland. Soon she was made the heroine of a blood and thunder serial, "The Hazards of Helen". Her pay was $35 per week. She jumped from a horse to a railroad train, from a train to a horse, from a motorcycle to a train or automobile, with every variation.

STUNT GAL
Former Circus Rider
Takes a Fall

New York Sunday News - April 3, 1938

1 - Clutching her stomach, Helen Gibson, Playing the role of a prison matron, as convicts flee in horror.

2 - Vainly she grabs at the railing as she falls forward.

4 - She continues down coming to rest at the bottom of the stairs.

3 - Head over heels Helen tumbles down the stairs.

(Newspaper article from Helen Gibson Scrapbook - Page 42)

One day, the studio manager watched her drive a team of horses under a viaduct and grasp a dangling rope, hoisting herself to the street above, he raised her pay $15.

Later Kalem cast her in "The Daughter of Daring", and she continued her hazardous feats, adding the stunt of having her hands tied to a railroad tie to be released when the train cut the ropes.

"When I returned to Hollywood, I found most of my friends and former stars working as extras and bit players," Miss Gibson said. "I just stuck my pride in my pocket and did the same thing." [20]

In "Condemned Women", you'll see a prison matron getting shot and tumbling down a flight of stairs. That's Helen Gibson – a stunt woman at 44. She received $50 for the first fall and $25 for the second take. Not bad pay, but Miss Gibson says she is getting a bit brittle, also a little tired of trying to break her neck.

Oh, yes – the director of the picture, who hired her to fall down stairs, is Lew Landers. When Miss Gibson was a star at Kalem, making thrillers such as "A Daughter of Daring", he was an office boy there. [21]

Helen's hometown newspaper wrote an article about her and her work in film. The reporter noticed Helen had a slightly wistful attitude toward the stars of today.

"When I was a star in Westerns during the old silent days," she declared, "I did all of my own stunts. I didn't have maids, hair dressers and portable dressing rooms following me around. The modern stars aren't allowed to do the stunts. The film companies have too big an investment in them."

"Nowadays they can take any beautiful but dumb girl and make a star out of her. Almost anybody can act under supervision."

Never seriously injured in any of her stunt work, Miss Gibson has jumped from train to train, from a horse to a train and visa versa, and fallen off cliffs times too numerous to mention. She will allow herself to be "murdered" and then fall down a flight of 16 steps for as little as $50.

In about a week, Miss Gibson expects to return to Hollywood hoping to find work as a willing "murder victim," a bit player, or stunter. [22]

It was back to Universal Studio to work as an uncredited bit player in chapter nine of the fifteen chapter serial, *Flaming Frontiers*. Johnny Mack Brown took the lead role in this film production taken from a story by Peter B. Kyne.

Tom Grant has found a rich gold vein and Bart Eaton is after it. Tom's sister, Mary, heads for the gold fields and Eaton and his men follow. Eaton teams up with Ace Daggett who plans to double cross him and get the gold for himself. They frame Tom for murder and then try to get him to sign over his claim. The famous scout, Tex Houston, is on hand, escaping the attempt on his life, saving Mary from various perils, and trying to bring in the real killer and clear Tom. [23]

Clifton and Helen celebrated their third wedding anniversary a little differently than most couples.

A totally unexpected anniversary present was received by Mr. and Mrs. C.L. Johnson of 12 South Glenwood Place Friday night when they attended a North Hollywood theater and won a new gas range.

By way of celebrating the wedding that took place three years ago, the couple and their two attendants, Mr. and Mrs. Gus Pulliam of Glendale, had a reminiscent dinner together at the Tick Tock, later going to the theater where they took home the appliance. [24]

Reproduction Poster

On Thursday, August 18, 1938, *The Riding and Stunt Girls of the Screen* held an official meeting.

Helen Holmes, star of silent screen days, today was president of the Riding and Stunt Girls of the screen, an organization of 40 women who perform stunt work, riding and doubling for present-day motion picture stars.

Marin Sais, silent pictures star listed today as a bit-player, was elected vice-president. Ann Ross, acknowledged one of the best stunt women in the industry, was chosen secretary. Helen Gibson, former star with Kalem and Universal Film companies, called and conducted the special meeting at 6030 Hollywood Blvd, after former officers had resigned, and will continue in her office of treasurer.

"Membership in the organization formed 11 months ago, is open to any women, that may qualify," Miss Gibson stated. [25]

Margaret Herrick Library Collection
Marin Sais

The Riding and Stunt Women of the Screen held another meeting the next day for a very important reason.

Riding and Stunt Girls of the Screen today were "on their own" following the disbanding last night of their organization at the close of its first year, according to Miss Marin Sais, silent-days screen star who served the group as vice-president.

"One year ago we organized with the object of acquainting studios with the wok and capabilities of our members," Miss Sais stated. "Today we have listed the name, address, phone number and qualifications of each girl with every casting director and every agency, and our purpose is accomplished."

The final meeting took place at the home of Helen Gibson, treasurer in Burbank. Helen Holmes, acting president, Ann Ross, acting secretary, and Miss Sais and other members were present. A club roster included the names of the screen's outstanding "artists," aerialists and stuntwomen, many of whom were part of early day pictures. [26]

Stunting kept Helen busy until a bit part in front of the camera was offered. She would take either of the offerings to keep busy. Her next uncredited role was a film that most film historians consider one of the best Westerns ever made, *Stagecoach*. Helen plays a girl in the saloon.

A simple stagecoach trip is complicated by the fact that Geronimo is on the warpath in the area. The passengers on the coach include a drunken doctor, two women, a bank manager who has taken off with his client's money, and the famous Ringo Kid, among others. [27]

It is also unconfirmed that J.P. McGowan played a bit part in *Stagecoach*. He was seen on the set, but by time the film reached the theater screens, he was out of film as an actor. [28]

John Wayne

Helen as the girl in the saloon in Stagecoach.

It was like clockwork. Helen finished one job and another was close behind. Republic Pictures had a part for Helen in *Southward Ho* with Roy Rogers. She would play Mrs. Crawford.

> In post Civil War Texas a former Union officer is the government's chief law enforcement official and tax collector. Roy discovers that the man is also the head of an outlaw gang. [29]

Universal Studio's *The Oregon Trail* with Johnny Mack Brown in the lead role was Helen's next uncredited bit role. In chapter six of this fifteen chapter serial, Helen is seen as a wagon trail pioneer.

Roy Rogers

> Wagon trains are not making it to Oregon and Jeff Scott has been sent to investigate. Morgan, the representative of an eastern syndicate, controls the fur trade and does not want the area settled. So he sends his men led by Bull Bragg to stop the latest wagon train. Scott is quickly on to Bragg and repeatedly captures him only to have him escape before he can reveal who is responsible for the attacks. [30]

206

Within a month Helen bounced back to Republic Pictures for a bit part in *New Frontier*, part of *The Three Mesquiteer's* series. She plays Jed's wife. [31]

RKO Radio Pictures was the next studio to offer Helen a bit part. She played Mrs. Bentley in an upcoming Western, *The Marshal of Mesa City*. [32]

Helen's next two jobs were back at Republic Pictures. Her first was an uncredited role as a woman at a party in the film *Saga of Death Valley*. [33] The second activity was in another of *The Three Mesquiteers* film series. In the film *Cowboys From Texas*, Helen played the uncredited part of a settler. [34]

Reproduction Lobby Card

It was a few months after the New Year, 1940 that another bit part was offered to Helen from the Monogram Studio. The film, *Covered Wagon Trails*, features Jack Randall in the lead role. Helen had worked with Jack Randall in *Danger Valley* two years earlier. She also worked with his brother, Robert Livingston in *The Three Mesquiteers* films. In this film, Helen is a woman in the wagon train.

A wagon train of settlers is approaching Prairieville and rancher Allen is out to stop them by having some of his men join the train and poison the horses. When Jack Cameron arrives in Prairieville with replacement horses, he learns his brother who was with the train has been murdered. A piece of his brother's clothing identifies a member of the gang and Jack sets out to find the rest of them and also deliver the horses. [35]

207

The eleventh serial in Columbia Pictures line-up was *Deadwood Dick*, consisting of fifteen chapters. In the Internet Movie Database, Helen is uncredited and unconfirmed in the role of a townswoman. This Western serial directed by an old acquaintance, James W. Horne from the Kalem Studio in 1915. Marin Sais, Helen's friend, plays Calamity Jane, while her stuntman friend, Yakima Canutt, has a bit part in chapter five. [36]

Helen found herself back at the Republic Pictures lot for another bit part. She played a relay station woman in *Young Bill Hickok* with Roy Rogers in the lead role.

Bill Hickok, assisted by Calamity Jane, is after a foreign agent and his guerrilla band, who are trying to take over some western territory just as the Civil War is coming to a close. [37]

Only a few weeks later Helen was back at the Republic Studio. It was for another bit part in the long running Western series, "The Three Mesquiteers". This film *The Trail Blazers* starred Robert Livingston (older brother of Jack Randall), Bob Steele, and Rufe Davis, as the trio. Helen's part was that of a woman at the ceremony.

The Continental Telegraph Company is putting in a telegraph line to the town and the fort. They know that the telegraph is needed to stop the activities of the outlaws, but only the outlaws can see the importance of the telegraph. They steal the supply wagons from the boys, which leaves only enough supplies to run a 30 mile line between Fort Dodd and Fort Jackson. But the outlaws attack the camp, killing everyone including Tom and Emily. The boys get more money and a new engineer to build the line between the forts. This time, they are not going to let the outlaws stop them and they will find the head outlaw. [38]

At the end of 1940, Helen was still getting work as a stunt double with the studios, both large and small. Clifton continued to work at Universal Studio as an electrician. However, change was coming to the Johnson household in 1941.

Jack Randall

CHAPTER 17

World War II, Stunt Doubling and More Bit Parts - 1941

The New Year, 1941, offered a seamless transition to Helen's random stunt work. She would be in two Republic Studio westerns with small parts during the year. Both films had a common theme. Hollywood westerns had taken on a new wrinkle, that of the singing cowboy, which were becoming very popular.

In early spring, Helen reported to the Andy Jaurequi Ranch on Placerita Canyon Road, Newhall, California, for her bit part, Emmy (uncredited). The film, *The Singing Hill* with Gene Autry. The singing from Gene and comedy from Smiley Burnette made up for the simple plot.

Gene Autry

> If a young lady gives up her inheritance, the local ranchers will lose their free grazing land. [1]

Shortly after her work was completed on this picture, Helen reported for work on the set of *Sheriff of Tombstone*. This time the singing cowboy was Roy Rogers, the comic relief provided by George "Gabby" Hayes. Helen's part was Liza Starr which was again uncredited.

> The Mayor has sent for a gunslinger who, though appearing to clean up the town, is really to be the mayor's means of taking the town over. When Roy and Gabby arrive in Tombstone, Roy is mistaken for the gunslinger. Just as Roy is ready to expose the mayor, the real gunslinger shows up. [2]

The remainder of the year Helen relied on just a few stunt double jobs.

Near the end of 1941, change would enter Helen and Clifton's life. After the December 7th bombing of Pearl Harbor, Clifton wanted to return to active duty. Helen said that he asked for active duty and got it. While he was serving in World War II, Helen continued working as a stunt double, took bit parts and added being an extra to her job credentials. [3]

The year 1942 was similar to the previous year except Helen only had bit parts in two films. Her first role was Mrs. Lane (uncredited) in Republic Pictures' *The Sombrero Kid* with Don "Red" Barry as the star player. He began using "Red" after playing in the 1940 Republic serial, *The Adventures of Red Ryder*.

Don "Red" Barry

> When Marshall Holden discovers gold, Martin tricks him into signing a deed and then has him killed. His natural son replaces him as Marshall, but his adopted son Jerry accidentally kills a man and is wrongly convicted of murder. However, Martin also has a son and he is the key to solving Jerry's problems. [4]

In between her first and second film, Helen got a few stunt double jobs. Then at year's end, Helen was called to Columbia Picture Corporation to play a bit part in an upcoming film production. Her part was Helen, townswoman (uncredited). It was *The Valley of Vanishing Men*, a fifteen chapter serial with Wild Bill Elliott as the lead actor.

Wild Bill Elliott

> Wild Bill Tolliver and Missouri Benson ride into the territory of New Mexico to search for Bill's father, Henry Tolliver, who disappeared while prospecting. They discover that a ruthless outlaw leader, Jonathan Kincaid, has joined forces with Carl Engler, a renegade European general, and Kincaid owns a giant gold mine and uses captured Mexican patriots, and others, to work as slaves on his property. Bill and Missouri become friendly with Consuelo Romeros, an agent for the Mexican government, and they learn that Bill's father is among the prisoner/slaves in the mine. After freeing his father, Bill sets out to smash both the slave-mine operation and Engler's attempts to overthrow Benito Juarez, the legal president of Mexico. [5]

The year 1943 was a very slim year for Helen in the bit part category. She did continue to get various stunt doubling through the year. She had a bit part in *The Blocked Trail*. It was a Western film from a popular series at Republic Studio.

> Everyone is looking for the three foot high horse called Brilliant that can lead them to a gold mine. Its owner has been killed and the Three Mesquiteers have been mistakenly arrested for the murder. [6]

After her role at Republic, Helen went back to her stunt double work along with an occasional job as an extra for the remainder of 1943. A high-point of that year was the homecoming of Clifton from the war. He returned to his old job at Universal Studio. Helen only had one bit part in 1944, which was an undetermined role in Universal Picture's *The Climax* with Boris Karloff.

> Dr. Hohner (Karloff), theater physician at the Vienna Royal Theater, murders his mistress, the star soprano, when his jealousy drives him to the point of mad obsession. Ten years later, another young singer reminds Hohner of the late diva, and his old mania kicks in. Hohner wants to prevent her from singing for anyone but him, even if it means silencing her forever. The singer's fiancée rushes to save her in the film's climax. [7]

The Three Mesquiteers

Another lean year, 1945, in bit parts for Helen. As in the past she did get occasional jobs as an extra or for a stunt doubling. Helen and Clifton took advantage of this as an opportunity to go fishing, which both liked to do. [8]

On January 22, 1946, Universal Pictures released *The Scarlet Horseman*, a thirteen chapter serial. Helen had an uncredited bit part as a townswoman. Each time the horseman played by Paul Guilfoyle appeared on the screen, a musical military charge is played on something that sounded like a kazoo. When the bad guys see the horseman and hear the charge, they flee. [9]

The Comanches are buying up rifles from unscrupulous gun smugglers in preparation for a wholesale uprising against settlers in Texas. Two undercover Texas Rangers discover the plot and set out to stop it. [10]

Universal was going to make a sequel, *The Scarlet Horseman Rides Again*, but it was cancelled when the studio stopped making serials in 1946. Anyone who saw the serial knows why it didn't have a sequel. [11]

The years 1947 and 1948 brought not one bit part or extra work for Helen. However, she did continue to get work as a stunt double for most of the Hollywood studios.

Early in 1949, Helen was contacted by Universal International to play a part in a western swing musical short. It was *Cheyenne Cowboy*, a 25 minute film with Tex Williams doing the singing. Helen's part was that of Cookie. [12]

Helen Gibson, who starred in many silent westerns and railroad pix at Universal 30 years ago, was set for a role in "Cheyenne Cowboy," second of U.I. Studio's series of three-reel westerns. [13]

In the latter part of 1949, Helen had a bit part in an upcoming western for Republic. It is *Outcasts of the Trail* with Monte Hale as the lead actor. Helen played the part of a woman with a boy.

Lavinia White and her younger brother, Chad, are shunned by the townspeople of Twin Wells because their father, Tom, is serving the last part of a long prison sentence for robbing the Rysen Company of $100,000. Their only friends are Doc Meadowlark and Pat Garrett, who is employed by the Rysen Transportation Company. When released, Tom is determined to return the money to its rightful owners over the objections of Jim Judd. Judd threatens to harm Chad and forces Lavinia to aid him, under the same threat against Chad, in the stick-up of the stage in which Tom is returning to Twin Wells with the money. Pat arrives and Judd and the girl escape without the money. The money is returned and Tom prepares to settle down and make amends for the past. Judd conspires with Elias Dunkenscold, the Rysen office manager, to steal the money and frame it on Tom. In a chase, Sheriff Wilson is shot but swears Pat in as a deputy before he dies. [14]

Reproduction Poster

With only a few weeks left in 1949, Helen continued to work with a variety of stunting to keep her busy.

CHAPTER 18

Helen in the 1950s – A Decade of Change

Helen didn't give up and found herself back in the bit role business halfway into 1950. Before taking on those roles, she was an extra in a prison film from Warner Brothers Studio. The film, *Caged,* with Eleanor Parker and Agnes Moorehead. [1]

> Helen Gibson, who used to be the cowboy's delight in Western pictures and was sort of a minor serial queen, wears the drab jeans of a prison inmate. Other actresses who once had billing and who greedily accepted the anonymous work of supernumeraries for "Caged," include Gertrude Michael, Leah Baird, Anne Luther and a favorite hoofer of the 1920's, Marjorie or Babe Kane. Nearly 100 extras were used in this prison drama. [2]

Helen's first two bit parts were those of the same character, Mrs. Ellison. She was hired by Lippert Pictures for *Crooked River*, (a.k.a. *The Last Bullet*, TV title). The film features two ex-sidekicks of Hopalong Cassidy, Jimmy "Shamrock" Ellison and Russell "Lucky" Hayden. The studio gave them this opportunity in lead roles.

Russell "Lucky" Hayden

> After Shamrock breaks up a stage robbery attempt by Kent and his men, he trails them to their hideout. Posing as an outlaw, he joins them and meets their leader, Lucky. But Kent and the others soon quit Lucky to go with the more famous outlaw, Gentry. Shamrock learns of their plans and organizes a posse to face them in a showdown. [3]

A couple of weeks later Helen traveled to the Jack Ingram Ranch in Woodland Hills, California, to again play Mrs. Ellison in *Fast on the Draw*, (a.k.a. *Sudden Death*, TV title).

When Shamrock was young, the Cat killed his parents. Now grown, Shamrock gets appointed Marshal when he breaks up a robbery attempt by Tex and his men. Tex works for the Cat and when he and his men rob the Express Office, Shamrock takes out after them hoping to get not only the gang, but also the Cat. [4]

A week and a day after this film's release Helen received very bad news. Her very old friend of thirty-five years, Helen Holmes, was gravely ill. Helen rushed to Holmes' San Fernando Valley home to be with her.

Hollywood old-timers were saddened yesterday by the death of Helen Holmes, 58, who, with Kathleen Williams, was the reigning serial queen in the silent days before Pearl White's "Perils of Pauline".

Helen Holmes   Kathleen Williams   Pearl White

Holmes died of a heart attack at her San Fernando Valley home.

Discovered by Mack Sennett in 1912, Helen later joined the old Kalem Company, where under the direction of J.P. McGowan, whom she later married, she specialized in hair-raising stunts that made her a favorite of millions of silent film fans.

Her series, "The Hazards of Helen", was a top thriller favorite of its day. During the past five years, she has been ailing from a heart condition.

Helen Gibson, the first wife of Cowboy Star, Hoot Gibson, who succeeded Helen Holmes as star of "The Hazards of Helen", remained her close friend for more than 30 years, and was at her bedside when she died. [5]

Shortly after the funeral Helen was called back to Republic for a minor role in *Lonely Heart Bandits*, released in August, 1950.

Two con artists join forces and pose as brother and sister. He then meets rich widows through the "personals" section of newspapers, marries them, and kills both the widows for their money.

Helen's last picture as a bit player came just before the end of 1950.

Hollywood – (UP) – Grant Withers plays his two hundredth screen part in "Hit Parade of 1951" and Helen Gibson celebrated her thirty-fifth year in movies by appearing with Audie Murphy in her two hundredth film, "Kansas Raiders" [6].

The Universal International film, *Kansas Raiders,* was filmed, in Technicolor in the Garner Valley of California.

Audie Murphy plays a young Jesse James falling under the Svengali-like spell of the outlaw William Quantrill, played by Brian Donlevy. Jesse and his youthful gang join the rebels to avenge the death of his parents only to become disillusioned with the senseless violence and looting of innocent civilians. Goaded by Quantrill's girl to leave, Jesse vacillates until the Yankees close in. Quantrill forces Jesse to leave and face the Yankees gunfire alone. Jesse rides off with his gang and the rest is history. [7]

It wasn't until February that Helen received an offer to be an extra in an upcoming Republic Picture.

Helen Gibson, first wife of Hoot Gibson and star of the silent thrillers, "The Hazards of Helen", is working in Republic's "The Fighting Coast Guard".

"I'm just an extra in this," she says, "but I get good bit parts every now and then. I have to laugh when I see the stuntmen today loaded up with harness and pads. I did all my stunts the hard way. Of course, I'm paying for it today." [8]

Audie Murphy

In May, 1951, Hollywood honored some of the silent film era for their contribution to the film industry.

Thirteen veterans of Hollywood's silent days today knew that the film capital remembered them.

Last night they were presented citations "for your help in making Hollywood the film capital of the world" at a ceremony in the Academy Award Theater.

Comedian Jack Benny presided over the program, sponsored by the Hollywood Chamber of Commerce. Chamber President, John B. Kingsley and Ronald Reagan, president of the Screen Actors Guild, also participated.

Many Hollywood notables were in the capacity audience.

Introduced by Benny and honored were:

Francis X. Bushman, who started in 1911 and became one of the screen's "great lovers," with a record of 400 pictures and 150 stage plays during his career.

Betty Blythe, one-time "siren" of the films.

Chester Conklin, mustached "Keystone Kop" character.

Heinie Conklin, who began with Mack Sennett in 1915.

William Farnum, stage and screen star, celebrating his 60th year in show business.

Julia Faye, who started in 1916 and is still active in pictures.

Pauline Garon, who starred in "Adam's Rib" in 1922.

215

Francis X. Bushman   Chester Conklin   William Farnum   Elmo Lincoln   Herbert Rawlinson

Helen Gibson, one of the first of the "serial" queens.

Elmo Lincoln, the original "Tarzan."

Hank Mann, another "Keystone Kop", now in his 40th year in the business.

Eddie Polo, flying trapeze artist who began in 1914.

Herbert Rawlinson, debonair leading man of the silent days. [9]

The Lon Davis Collection

Left to Right: Richard Conte, Francis X. Bushman, Helen Gibson, William Farnum and Betty Blythe at the gala party celebrating "The Hollywood Story."

216

The Gayla Johnson Collection
Betty Blythe (Left) and Helen Gibson (Right) are being escorted to the gala event by Tony Curtis.

At the same time as this ceremony took place, Helen was at Universal International Studio taking part in the making of *The Hollywood Story.* "She remembers that night very well".

In '51, Universal made "The Hollywood Story," which had Richard Conte, Julia Adams, Henry Hull and Fred Clark as the contemporary stars, and Francis X. Bushman, William Farnum, Betty Blythe and myself from the silent era.

217

The premiere was at the Academy Theater and Tony Curtis was assigned to escort me there. It was a gala night, and one I am not apt to forget for a long time. The Hollywood Chamber of Commerce gave each of us a plaque 'for your outstanding contribution to the art and science of motion pictures, for the pleasure you have brought to millions over the world, and for your help in making Hollywood the film capital of the world.'" [10]

The film, *The Hollywood Story,* was loosely based on the murder of William Desmond Taylor, a director during the silent era. That case was never officially solved.

Hollywood 1950: The successful producer, Larry O'Brian, arrives in Los Angeles to found a motion picture company. He buys an old studio which was unused since the days of silent movies. He's shown the office where the famous director, Franklin Farrara, was shot. The case hasn't been solved until now, although there were many suspects. O'Brian becomes fascinated by the subject and wants to shoot a movie about it. He investigates it himself and soon gets into danger himself. [11]

The Margaret Herrick Library Collection

The stars on stage at the gala event. Helen is eighth from the left.

Shortly after the release of *The Hollywood Story*, Helen was back at Republic in another uncredited bit part. She played a woman at a party in the film, *The Dakota Kid*.

The Dakota Kid is a young outlaw who joins a gang headed by Ace Crandall. Crandall's aim is to unseat Sheriff Tom White and then use his power to enrich himself at the community's expense. Dakota impersonates a long-lost nephew of the sheriff, and is made a marshal. Through his association with the sheriff's grandson, Red White, and his friend Judy, plus falling in love with Mary Lewis, the Kid gradually reforms. [12]

218

The Margaret Herrick Library Collection
Helen got her picture taken at the gala event.

From time to time, newspapers would report on Helen's current activities. The article that appeared on July 14, 1951 about her latest plan of employment was short and to the point. "Serial queen, Helen Gibson, is about to sign a contract to star in a TV film action series as a female sagebrush sheriff. She'll do all her own tricks, too." [13]

There is no documentation that this television action series ever happened.

In early 1952, Universal International hired Helen to play an uncredited bit part, that of a mother in *The Treasure of Lost Canyon*. The film was made on location at the McArthur-Burney Falls Memorial State Park – Highway 89, Burney, California.

> Young David, orphaned en route to California, falls into the hands of medicine-show rascal, Baltimore Dan. Years later, now a trained thief, he's adopted by eccentric 'Doc' Brown, retired miner and pharmacist. Doc and David become fast friends in their scenic outdoor rambles. But when they discover a hidden treasure, the idyllic interlude gives way to more troubles and a strange coincidence. [14]

In the Universal Pictures' *Ma and Pa Kettle at the Fair*, Helen had a minor role. It would not be the last time that Helen would see the set of the Kettle's series. [15]

Helen joined Universal International Studio six months later in another uncredited bit part. *Horizons West* starred Robert Ryan, Julie Adams and Rock Hudson. In addition, there were several other actors who in a few years would go into television. They were John McIntire, Raymond Burr, James Arness and Dennis Weaver. Helen Gibson played a townswoman.

> Home from the Civil War, young Neal Hammond is happy to return to Texas ranching, but brother Dan wants more. His attempts to enter business is thwarted when carpetbagger Cord Hardin beats and humiliates him in a poker

game. So Dan forms a rustling gang and parlays his ill-gotten gains into a land empire. But among the growing opposition to his gang is the new Marshal of Austin…brother Neal. [16]

The year 1953 didn't start very well for Helen. Especially in the first quarter of the year.

Silent star Helen Gibson, formerly wed to Hoot Gibson, has just recovered from a critical bout with blood poisoning. [17]

Helen got back to her old self in time to take an uncredited bit part in a Republic Picture, *City That Never Sleeps*. She plays the part of a woman in one scene.

Chicago cop, Johnny Kelly, dissatisfied with his job and marriage, would like to run away with his stripper girlfriend, Angel Face, but keeps getting cold feet. During one crowded night, Angel Face decides she has had enough vacillation, and crooked lawyer Biddel has an illegal mission for Johnny that could put him in a financial position to act. But other, conflicting schemes are also in progress. [18]

In mid-July 1953, Helen accepted an uncredited bit part of a woman on the train. The film, Universal International's *The Man from the Alamo*, with Glenn Ford and Julie Adams.

During the war for Texas independence, one man leaves the Alamo before the end (chosen by lot to help others' families) but it is too late to accomplish his mission, and he is branded a coward. Since he cannot now expose a gang of turncoats, he infiltrates them instead. Can he save a wagon train of refugees from Wade's Guerillas? [19]

Only a few newspapers carried Helen Gibson's film achievement and the announcement of her next film.

It's double milestones next month [August] for Helen Gibson, the former silent film serial queen – her 62nd birthday and her 40th year in pictures. She started her career in 1913, reached stardom two years later in the railroad thriller, "The Hazards of Helen", and married and divorced Hoot Gibson.

Glenn Ford

The latest Ma and Pa Kettle film is her 400th flicker. When she can't get lines to speak in pictures, she does extra work or doubles for other actresses. At 62, Helen can drive a buckboard, tumble from a horse and leap from a moving train. [20]

There was a follow-up to Helen's milestones a month later. A very short article hidden in a newspaper beyond the front page asked about her life story. It is not known if the response from Helen is serious or tongue-in-cheek.

Helen Gibson, an ex-wife of cowboy star, Hoot Gibson and a serial queen of railroad thrillers, still plays at U-I, Republic and other studios. She wants to see her life story filmed and recently talked to Judy Canova* about starring in it. [21]

Helen spent the first couple of months at Universal International working on *Ma and Pa Kettle at Home*. It was the sixth of seven in the series which started in 1949. The stars of the film were Marjorie Main and Percy Kilbride. Helen played a ranch wife in the film and also doubled for Marjorie Main.

Elwin Kettle might win a scholarship to an agricultural college. Essay contest judges Mannering and Crosby decide to choose between the two finalists by spending the weekend at the home of each. Pa makes numerous cosmetic improvements to his rundown home to impress the judges, but all wash away in a torrential rain storm. Will the judges still award the scholarship to Elwin? [22]

* Appendix B - Photograph of Judy Canova and Helen, page 254-255

Marjorie Main and Percy Kilbride as Ma and Pa Kettle

Shortly after completing the Ma and Pa Kettle film, Helen went into semi-retirement and she and Clifton moved to Diamond Springs, which is in El Dorado County, California.

"I did character parts and extra work until '54 when, for health reasons, my husband and I moved to Lake Tahoe, where I went into the real estate business. [23]

Helen Gibson, with Thailand Films in Hollywood, is making her home in Diamond Springs with her husband, Clifton L. Johnson, also from Hollywood. Her latest film was "Ma and Pa Kettle at Home," which was shown here several weeks ago. [24]

Mr. and Mrs. Clifton L. Johnson of Diamond Springs will celebrate their 21st wedding anniversary Sunday at a dinner in their home. Twenty-one friends have been invited to participate in their celebration. [25]

After a short retirement of three years, Helen found that her heart was not in the real estate business. So what do you do in a case like this?

Most of her activities in the Placerville [California] area were in the real estate business. Having been associated with the Stills' Real Estate business until a short time before her last trip to Southern California. [26]

The idle life was not for them and upon their return to the Valley where they had always resided previously, the Johnsons carefully selected Panorama City to settle down for the last time.

Mrs. Johnson suffered a slight stroke four days after they moved into their present abode, but is now up and around after a three week convalescence.

She expects to take life easy now, but recalls that just prior to her short-lived retirement period, she was doubling for film stars such as Marjorie Main and occasionally doing bits and parts to keep up with her career. [27]

While still living in El Dorado County, a reporter for the Sacramento Bee, Vernon E. Allen, came to write an article about her. His focus was on her years in the film business.

Diamond Springs, El Dorado County – "The heavies were always trying to kill me," says Helen Gibson Johnson in recalling her 40 years of work in motion pictures.

"I was always the girl at the railroad station, or the one they caught alone at the ranch house and believe me, it was pretty rugged."

"But I guess it was worth it. It gave me a chance to double for Marie Dressler in "Tugboat Annie" and I was never so sore in my life."

"I don't know which was the part I enjoyed the most. I was pretty wet and sore by the time they finished with me in "Tugboat Annie". I think the one I liked best was playing Calamity Jane in "Custer's Last Stand". But that's just one, you know."

Mrs. Johnson says she is frequently called on the telephone by neighbors or other friends who report one of the earlier pictures in which she appeared has been shown on television. [28]

During the year 1958, Helen was in two films possibly as an extra since she was not listed in the cast credits. The first film was a sixty-minute television drama for the *Suspicion* second season on NBC. The episode, *The Last Town Car*, aired on February 3, 1958. [29] The second film, *The Man Who Died Twice*, released by Republic Pictures on June 6, 1958, with Rod Cameron and Vera Ralston. [30]

On one of Helen's return visits to Diamond Springs, in El Dorado County, the local newspaper covered the event.

Mr. and Mrs. Cliff Johnson, former residents of Diamond Springs, now living in Panorama City, were in this area last Wednesday looking over their property on Pleasant Valley Road.

The Johnsons were in real estate in this county for several years but moved back to Southern California about a year and a half ago to resume their former professions there.

Mrs. Johnson, the former Mrs. "Hoot" Gibson and western actress, has appeared in minor roles in recent non-western movies and short television programs. To her former neighbor, Mrs. Jerry Conley, whom she visited while here, Mrs. Johnson named "The Man Who Died Twice" and Alfred Hitchcock's "Town Car" as two of the pictures in which she has appeared.

Johnson, again following his former profession, as an electrician at the studio of Republic Pictures. [31]

CHAPTER 19

Helen's Second Retirement Begins - 1962

Helen's stunting jobs continued in 1960 with no offers for bit parts or extra work. She did however, reach a milestone in 1961.

Helen Gibson, who came here with the Miller Brothers 101 Ranch Wild West Show in 1911 and remained to follow a film career, has just celebrated her 50th year on the screen. [1]

In 1962, Helen made her last film, *The Man Who Shot Liberty Valance*, with John Wayne and Jimmy Stewart. The Director was an old friend from her days at Universal Pictures, John Ford. [2]

Some of our older moviegoers may get a kick out of a yet-to-be-released motion picture called "The Man Who Shot Liberty Valance." Not only has it not been released, but filming of the picture continues in Hollywood.

It's directed by John Ford who for years has made sure that quite a few veteran performers kept working in his films. And by "veteran" I mean personalities who were the very latest thing in the Silent Screen era.

Here's the supporting cast of this "John Ford Stock Company:"

Gertrude Astor – Once famous in varied Hal Roach comedies, she moved up to heroine roles in such as David O. Selznick's "Rupert of Hentzau" and 1923's "Flaming Youth."

Helen Gibson – First wife of Nebraska's Hoot Gibson. Helen was featured in thriller movies of the serial variety.

Bill Henry – He became a child star in his first picture, "Lord Jim" in 1925, and continued to amuse American mothers for years thereafter.

Stuart Holmes – He is Theda Bara's romantic lead in many films, then got one of the top roles in the 1920 hit, "The Four Horsemen of the Apocalypse."

Eva Novak – She and her sister Jane (Jane was William S. Hart's long-time leading lady) made up a popular film sister team. No relation to Kim.

Buddy Roosevelt – Once a well-known western star.

John P. (Blackie) Whiteford – Mr. Whiteford is 92 and considered the oldest working actor in show business. He never reached stardom, though he appeared as the well-dressed heel and menace of many a silent feature. [3]

When Senator Ransom Stoddard [Stewart] returns home to Shinbone for the funeral of Tom Doniphon [Wayne], he recounts to a local newspaper editor the story behind it all. He had come to town many years before, a lawyer by profession. The stage was robbed on its way in by the local ruffian, Liberty Valance [Lee Marvin], and Stoddard has nothing to his name left save a few law books. He gets a job in the kitchen at the Ericson's restaurant and there meets his future wife, Hallie [Vera Miles]. The territory is vying for Statehood and Stoddard is selected as a representative over Valance, who continues terrorizing the town. When he destroys the local newspaper office and attacks the editor, Stoddard calls him out, though the conclusion is not as straightforward as legend would have it. [4]

BFI Collection

Gertrude Astor   Helen Gibson   Stuart Holmes   Eva Novak   Buddy Roosevelt

On August 23, 1962, Helen received word that her first husband, Edmund "Hoot" Gibson had died at the Motion Picture Country House and Hospital, in Woodland Hills. Helen did not attend the funeral.

Cowboy star, Hoot Gibson, who faced death with blazing sixguns in a generation of Western movies, died Thursday in bed, at 70, of cancer.

He made a fortune and spent it. He had survived horse spills and plane crashes with arrogance, enjoyed fame and suffered its loss, was married four times, and divorced thrice.

"Those were the days," he recalled in later, leaner, years, "when a big steak was 43 cents and a quart of good Bourbon was $1.25." His salary then: $14,500 a week.

His career lasted longer than that of any of those of his Western contemporaries. He retired from films in 1944 after making 200 silents and 75 talkies. He tried to break into television in 1950 and failed. [5]

Hollywood (AP) – Oldtime cowboy heroes who thrilled a generation of youngsters at Saturday matinees gathered Monday for the funeral of Hoot Gibson, one of the top western stars of yesteryear.

Present for the Masonic rites were Ken Maynard, Bob Steele, Tex Ritter, Wally Ford, Eddie Dean, Wild Bill Tucker and Iron Eyes Cody.

Ken Maynard

Bob Steele

Tex Ritter

There were other movieland greats, too – Buster Keaton, Reginald Denny and Sally Eilers, the second [third] of Gibson's three [four] wives.

On Gibson's coffin lay his 10-gallon Stetson and from a side room Eddie Dean sang the cowboy's lament "Empty Saddles".

As Dean sang, Keaton's famous frozen expression melted a little and tears filled the eyes of many a fearless fighter of Hollywood's old West. [6]

Several months after Helen's final on screen appearance, she gave a Los Angeles reporter a brief look into her future plans for her and husband Clifton.

Her last movie appearance, she said, was as an extra in "The Man That Shot Liberty Valance," in which she received $35 a day for driving a team of horses.

She is retired on a $200 monthly motion picture industry pension and admits "I don't know what to do with myself". She hopes to sell real estate part-time.

Diana Serra Cary Collection
Iron Eyes Cody

"I don't go to bars or places like that and my husband doesn't drink, either," she said.

She and her husband, Clifton Johnson, 64, have been married since 1935. They like to hunt and fish every season in Northern California and Oregon. [7]

After finishing her short scene in *The Man That Shot Liberty Valance*, Helen later felt that she would be on the cutting room floor if they needed to shorten the two-hour movie. However, her scene was left in. [8]

In 1963, Helen and Clifton moved to Roseburg, Oregon. This would be their final move.

Eddie Dean

Roseburg can now add a retired movie queen to its list of celebrities residing in the community. The couple has purchased a home at 1047 NE Lincoln.

Helen pulled the curtain on her acting career in 1961, and she's glad the movie days are over.

"I don't miss it [movie activity] at all," she reflected. "I thought I might, but I don't. Of course, I still think I hear the phone ringing. When you get involved in the movie business, they have you on the phone 24 hours a day."

Maybe that's one reason the Johnson residence on a quiet street in Roseburg doesn't have a telephone.

Roseburg caught Johnsons eye during visits here and last year when the couple stopped here during the Douglas County Fair, they decided Roseburg "would be a nice place to live". [9]

Kalton Lahue gave Helen an acknowledgment in his 1964 book, *Continued Next Week*. She helped with the era of silent serials in which she played a role. Lahue also noted that her seventy episodes of *The Hazards of Helen* must have made her an excellent telegraph operator.

The trade papers gave her profuse credit as being one of the best telegraph operators who ever pounded a key, but Helen told me herself that she has never been able to operate the infernal machine. [10]

In late 1967, Helen described her life to Mike Kornick from birth to Roseburg, Oregon. It was for an article in the January 1968 issue of *Film in Review*. This is what Helen said in the article's last three paragraphs.

The Gayla Johnson Collection
The leap in "A Girl's Grit.

"During my movie career, and since, I have been asked one question more often than any other: what do I consider my most dangerous stunt? My answer has always been the same: a leap from the roof of a [railroad] station onto the top of a moving train.

"I did it in *A Girl's Grit*, doubling for Helen Holmes. The distance between station roof and train top was accurately measured, and I practiced the jump with the train standing still. The train had to be moving on camera for about a quarter of a mile and its accelerating velocity was timed to the second. I was not nervous as the train approached, and leapt without hesitation. I landed right, but the train's motion made me roll toward the end of the car. I caught hold of an air vent [pipe] and hung on, allowing my body to dangle over the edge to increase the effect on the screen.

I suffered only a few bruises." [11]

In the book, *Stunting in the Cinema*, the authors explained why Helen Gibson was so successful in her stunt work. They used the railroad station leap as their example.

What one sees her doing on the screen she did in reality. Success depended entirely on her physical ability, her highly-developed sense of timing and her absolute conviction that the stunt, for her at least, was possible. The real difficulty of the stunt lay not in the leap itself, since she had practiced this with the train stationary and it clearly presented no difficulties, but in the timing. What such stunts require is an inbuilt awareness of the speed of the moving object. During the course of a leap, where a moving object is concerned, the special relationship between take-off point and landing point changes. Helen Gibson had this sensitivity to special relationships between objects in motion, but it is certainly not a gift shared by all stuntmen. [12]

226

CHAPTER 20

Life Far From the Silver Screen

After both Helen and Clifton retired, Helen for the second time, life got much simpler. Helen was in the Eastern Star and Clifton was involved with the Shriners for many years. Retirement didn't stop their activities.

Clifton had an extended family with his second marriage and enjoyed visiting them periodically. The two places of the family gatherings were Portland, Oregon and Lake Chelan, Washington. Helen's only living relative was a sister, Pearl, in Ohio.

Gayla Johnson remembers Cliff very well since he was her dad's brother. "I remember Cliff as a quiet guy from Spokane, Washington. When they retired and moved to Roseburg, Cliff and my dad, Vernon, would go fishing. They came to our house in Springfield and they would fish the McKenzie. My dad was a fly fisherman and I think Cliff was also. I think Helen fished with the guys. Helen had no hobbies, but she and Clifton loved to go fishing whenever possible. I can't remember her hanging around the house with us. My mom didn't care for her much (never knew why)."

"Their home at 1047 NE Lincoln Street in Roseburg was unpretentious, where Clifton did all the cooking. Helen wasn't a housewife. The home itself was very modest, but not their automobile. They bought a new Cadillac every two years, and immediately took the car to my dad's garage, Johnson Motor Company and had the 4-ply tires replaced with 6-ply tires. The October 1973 gasoline shortage became a problem for Helen. The speed limit was decreased to 55 miles per hour on most highways. This made Helen very angry since she liked to drive at least 70 miles per hour. 'My car wasn't made to go 55'. I guess you don't lose that daredevil spirit even at 82 years old."

"On several visits to Portland in the late 1960s, Helen was asked several times about her movie career and scrapbook. It was like pulling teeth to get her to talk about those things. She always looked nice, conservative dress, nails neat, no flashy jewelry, great sense of humor and happy with who she was. Aunt Helen had large hands and the knuckles of someone that has arthritis. She didn't talk about that either. She also appeared independent with no affinity for motherhood. Helen had a very thrifty approach to living, except for the Caddie. She never talked about her childhood. I've heard that articles were written about her father allowed her to join the Miller Brother 101 Ranch Wild West Show.* Gayla thinks she ran off to find her fortune.

"I did finally get to see the scrapbook. When I was in my twenties I got a phone call. "Hello, this is your Aunt Helen. Still want to see that scrapbook?" I said that I had always wanted to see it. "I'm in Portland at the Mallory Hotel, see you at 2 p.m." When I got there, we hugged, kissed and engaged in small talk for a few minutes. Then she got out the scrapbook. Aunt Helen didn't describe anything individually, instead she just answered my questions. I really didn't know what to ask." [1]

Robert Peterson of Spokane, Washington remembers one of the visits from his Aunt Helen and Uncle Clifton Johnson in Lake Chelan. Cliff's brother was Bob's stepfather.

When I told Bob what Gayla had said about their Aunt Helen, he agreed that it sounded like his aunt. Bob remembers a visit in which his Aunt Helen spoke of her stunting for Marjorie Main in *Ma and Pa Kettle at Home*. Among other things, he recalls hearing that Marjorie Main washed her hands constantly and kept to herself most of the time while off camera. After finishing her short anecdote, Helen said, "Okay, let's talk about something else now." Getting her to talk about those real interesting days in the movies was very hard to do. [2]

A short time after the visit to Lake Chelan, Helen was interviewed by a reporter from her hometown newspaper, *The News Review*. That story about Marjorie Main must have been on her mind. She told the reporter the same thing that Bob Peterson told me and more.

But during Mrs. Johnson's Hollywood days, she "doubled" in every one of the nine "Ma and Pa Kettle" films and in "Jackass Mail". As a double, Mrs. Johnson took over for Miss Main and was filmed in long shots driving a team or in a fist fight with other women, etc. "It wasn't very dangerous, but she [Marjorie Main] couldn't do it, and I didn't care," said Mrs. Johnson.

Marie Dressler   Ethel Barrymore   Irene Rich   Louise Fazenda

* Appendix B - Miller Brother 101 Ranch Comeback, page 253

In reminiscing about the well-known "Ma Kettle," Mrs. Johnson said that Miss Main was a rather quiet woman who "stayed by herself" all of the time and was afraid of germs. She was also allergic to dust and wouldn't allow the studio to turn on air conditioning when she was on the set.

She "doubled" for such well-known stars as Marie Dressler in "Tugboat Annie," Ethel Barrymore, Sally Eilers, Irene Rich and Louise Fazenda. In 'Tugboat Annie" she doubled for Miss Dressler on the tugboat in the storm. "I had to jump off a ship in San Pedro harbor," she said. "I couldn't swim, but I jumped anyway and they had someone right there off camera to rescue me," she laughed.

Does she miss Hollywood?

Not on your life. "Movies are too much of a racket now," she says. "They are just factories," she adds, a bit wistfully. [3]

Gayla pointed out, "After she had her stroke we stopped and saw her for the last time. She was in a hospital bed in the living room of her home. I pulled a chair up to her and she held my hand. I really liked her. She was still alert and funny."

Twenty-eight months after that interview, Helen Gibson Johnson passed away. Her fifty-one year career ended in 1962. Her death came just forty-four days after her 86th birthday, and 15 years since her retiring. [4]

The Roseburg, Oregon News-Review
May 15, 1975 - Page 8

229

Obituaries

Helen Johnson

JOHNSON, Helen Gibson passed away October 10, 1977 at a local hospital. She was born in Cleveland, Ohio. She had lived in the area since May of 1963 formerly of Studio City, California. She was a retired motion picture actress and a member of the Heritage Chapter of the Eastern Star, North Hollywood, California and the Episcopal Church of Cleveland, Ohio. Surviving is her husband; Clifton L. Johnson whom she married in 1935 in Burbank, California, 1 sister; Mrs. Pearl Thompson of Cleveland, Ohio and 3 nephews. Memorial services will be held in WILSON'S CHAPEL OF THE ROSES at 11 a.m. Thursday, October 13, 1977, with Rev. Robert Sheets, Minister of the First Christian Church officiating. Donations may be made in her memory to the Masonic and Eastern Star Home of Oregon. These may be left at the Chapel of the Roses.

Thanks for the ride Helen*.

It was a wonderful journey.

* Appendix A - Helen Gibson Johnson Death Certificate, page 239-240
  Appendix B - Clifton Johnson Obituary, page 256

APPENDIX A

Documentation

APPENDIX A

	IN CITIES.			of each person whose place of abode on June 1, 1900, was in this family. Enter surname first, then the given name and middle initial, if any. INCLUDE every person living on June 1, 1900. OMIT children born *since* June 1, 1900.	Relationship of each person to the head of the family.	Color or race.	Sex.	DATE OF BIRTH.		Age at last birthday.	Whether single, married, widowed, or divorced.	Number of years married.	Mother of how many children.	Number of these children living.
	Street.	House Number.	Number of dwelling-house, in the order of visitation.	Number of family, in the order of visitation.					Month.	Year.					
			1	2	3	4	5	6	7		8	9	10	11	12
51					Meyer Edward	Son	W	M	July	1894	5	S			
52		81	276	277	Wenger Fred	Head	W	M	July	1862	37	M	14		
53					— Annie	Wife	W	F	May	1865	35	M	14	5	4
54					— Lena	Daughter	W	F	Sep	1887	12	S			
55					— Frieda	Daughter	W	F	Nov	1889	10	S			
56					— Rose	Daughter	W	F	Aug	1891	8	S			
57					— Annie	Daughter	W	F	June	1893	6	S			

232

APPENDIX A

Pendleton Ore. Sep 6" 1913.

To whom it may concern:—

This is to certify that I am a legally licensed practitioner of Osteopathy in the state of Oregon,

That I have examined Edmund Richard Gibson and find him free from any disease, communicable, as specified under the laws relative to certificate for marriage license.

Signed;

G. S. Hoisington, D.O.

Subscribed and sworn to before me this 6th day of September 1913

L. O. Livermon

Notary Public for Oregon

233

APPENDIX A

PLACE OF MARRIAGE

RETURN OF MARRIAGE

County of
or
City of _Pendleton_

No. **19130124**

Registered No. _____

Street _____

Date of Marriage _Sept 6_, 191_3_

| | MONTH | | DAY | YEAR |

HUSBAND	WIFE
Full Name _Edmond Gibson_	Full Maiden Name _Rose Wenger_
Residence _Pendleton_	Residence _Pendleton Or_
Color _White_ ; Age _22_	Color _White_ ; Age _22_
YEARS MONTHS DAYS	YEARS MONTHS DAYS
Birthplace _Neb_	Birthplace _Ohio_
Occupation _Riding_	Occupation _Cow girl_
No. of Marriage _1st_	No. of Marriage _1st_
Father's Birthplace _Neb_	Father's Birthplace _Switzerland_
Mother's Birthplace _Indiana_	Mother's Birthplace _Germany_

By R J Brown Dpty (Signed) _Frank Saling_

County Clerk

234

APPENDIX A

Affidavit for Marriage License

Edmond Gibson

and

Rose Wenger

State of Oregon,
County of Umatilla } ss.

I, *B D Sherry* of *Pendliton Or*
being duly sworn, depose and say that I know *Rose Wenger* ;
that she is a resident of the County of Umatilla, State of Oregon, that she is over the age of *18*
years, to-wit: about *22* years; that there is no legal
impediments to the marriage of said *Rose Wenger* with
Edmond Gibson a resident of *Umatilla Co,*
Oregon, who is over the age of twenty-one years.

B D Sherry

Subscribed and sworn to before me this *6* day of *September* A.D. 191*3*

Frank Saling
County Clerk.

By *R T Brown* Deputy

235

APPENDIX A

State of Oregon,
County of Umatilla } ss.

This Is To Certify, That the undersigned, a _Justice of the Peace_ by authority of a license, bearing date the _6th_ day of _September_ A. D. 191_3_, and issued by the County Clerk of the County of Umatilla, did on the _6th_ day of _September_ A. D. 191_3_, at the _office of said Justice_ in the County and State aforesaid, join in lawful wedlock _Edmond Gibson_ of the County of _Umatilla_ and State of _Oregon_, and _Rose Wenger_ of the County of Umatilla and State of Oregon, with their mutual assent.

Witness my hand _Joe H. Parkes_
Justice of the Peace,
Pendleton District,

In presence of

T. D. Taylor
B. D. Sherry
Witnesses. _Umatilla Co. Oregon_

This certificate, properly filled out, to be returned to the Clerk of the County in which the marriage is solemnized, under penalty.

East Oregonian, Pub. Co., Pendleton, Ore.

APPENDIX A

COUNTY OF LOS ANGELES • REGISTRAR-RECORDER/COUNTY CLERK

DO NOT WRITE ON THIS SIDE
ALL BLANKS BELOW ARE FOR USE OF COUNTY RECORDER

PLACE OF MARRIAGE   California State Board of Health   State Index No.

County of Los Angeles

BUREAU OF VITAL STATISTICS

STANDARD CERTIFICATE OF MARRIAGE   Local Registered No.   11770

PERSONAL AND STATISTICAL PARTICULARS

GROOM	BRIDE
FULL NAME Clifton Lorenzo Johnson	FULL NAME Helen Rose Gibson
RESIDENCE 2746 W. 5th St., LA	RESIDENCE 212 S. Glenwood Pl., Burbank
COLOR OR RACE white AGE AT LAST BIRTHDAY 40	COLOR OR RACE white AGE AT LAST BIRTHDAY 41
SINGLE WIDOWED OR DIVORCED divorced NUMBER OF MARRIAGE 2nd	SINGLE WIDOWED OR DIVORCED divorced NUMBER OF MARRIAGE 2nd
BIRTHPLACE Wisc.	BIRTHPLACE Cleveland Ohio
OCCUPATION Ships Officer Marine	OCCUPATION Actress Motion Pictures
NAME OF FATHER John P. Johnson	NAME OF FATHER Fred Wenger
BIRTHPLACE OF FATHER Wisc.	BIRTHPLACE OF FATHER Switzerland
MAIDEN NAME OF MOTHER Clara Nelson	MAIDEN NAME OF MOTHER Anna Sigg
BIRTHPLACE OF MOTHER Wisc.	BIRTHPLACE OF MOTHER Ohio
	Helen Rose Wenger

MAIDEN NAME OF BRIDE, IF SHE WAS PREVIOUSLY MARRIED

We, the groom and bride in this Certificate, hereby certify that the information given hereon is correct to the best of our knowledge and belief.

Clifton L. Johnson   Groom   Helen Rose Gibson   Bride   M. Scharf

CERTIFICATE OF PERSON PERFORMING CEREMONY

I Hereby Certify that Clifton Lorenzo Johnson   and

Helen Rose Gibson   were joined in marriage by me

in accordance with the laws of the State of California, at   Burbank

this 5th day of August 1935

Signature of Witness to the Marriage
Gus H. Pulliam
Glendale, Calif.
Residence

Signature of Person Performing the Ceremony
Leroy O. Bostwick
Minister
Official position

August 7th 1935   C. L. LOGAN, Recorder, Registrar (County Recorder)   Residence 215 S. Pacific, Glendale

FILED   By A.O. Sagar Dep. 7th day of August 1935
at 9 A.M.   A full, true and correct copy of the original record filed this

C. L. LOGAN, Recorder,

By   L. Hellman   Deputy

DO NOT WRITE ON THIS PAGE
ALL BLANKS ABOVE ARE FOR USE OF RECORDER

APPENDIX A

U. S. SOCIAL SECURITY ACT Bur. 886 W
567-18-2943
APPLICATION FOR ACCOUNT NUMBER

PRINT NAME
HELEN   ROSE   GIBSON
(EMPLOYEE'S FIRST NAME)   (MIDDLE NAME)   (LAST NAME)
(MARRIED WOMEN: GIVE MAIDEN FIRST NAME, MAIDEN LAST NAME, AND HUSBAND'S LAST NAME)

212 So. Glenwood Place   3. Burbank   Calif
(STREET AND NUMBER)   (POST OFFICE)   (STATE)

Central Casting Corp   5. 5504 Hollywood Blvd
(BUSINESS NAME OF PRESENT EMPLOYER)   (BUSINESS ADDRESS OF PRESENT EMPLOYER)

44   7. 27 Aug 1892   8. Cleveland Ohio
(AGE AT LAST BIRTHDAY)   (DATE OF BIRTH. (MONTH)   (DAY)   (YEAR)   (SUBJECT TO LATER VERIFICATION))   (PLACE OF BIRTH)

Fred Wenger   10. Anna Routenberg
(FATHER'S FIRST NAME)   (MOTHER'S FULL MAIDEN NAME)

SEX: MALE   FEMALE ✓   12. COLOR: WHITE ✓   NEGRO   OTHER
(CHECK (✓) WHICH)   (CHECK (✓) WHICH)   (SPECIFY)

IF REGISTERED WITH THE U. S. EMPLOYMENT SERVICE, GIVE NUMBER OF REGISTRATION CARD

IF YOU HAVE PREVIOUSLY FILLED OUT A CARD LIKE THIS, STATE   Central Casting Corp   Dec-11-36
(PLACE)   (DATE)

16.   Helen Gibson
(DATE SIGNED)   (EMPLOYEE'S SIGNATURE, AS USUALLY WRITTEN)

DETACH ALONG THIS LINE

238

APPENDIX A

STATE OF OREGON — HEALTH DIVISION
Vital Statistics Section

CERTIFICATE OF DEATH

492
Local File Number

'77 015470

DECEASED—NAME
1. First: Helen Middle: Gibson Last: Johnson

DATE OF DEATH (month, day, year): October 10, 1977

3. RACE White, Negro, American Indian, etc. (specify): White
4. SEX: Female
5a. AGE—(last birthday (years)): 66
5b. Under 1 year mos. days
5c. Under 1 day hours min.
6. DATE OF BIRTH (month, day, year): August 27, 1891

7a. COUNTY OF DEATH: Douglas
7b. CITY, TOWN, OR LOCATION OF DEATH: Roseburg
7c. Inside City Limits (specify yes or no): Yes
7d. HOSPITAL OR OTHER INSTITUTION—NAME (if not in either, give street and number): Mercy Medical Center

8. STATE OF BIRTH (if not in U.S.A., name country): Ohio
9. CITIZEN OF WHAT COUNTRY: USA
10. MARRIED, NEVER MARRIED, WIDOWED, DIVORCED (specify): Married
11. NAME OF SPOUSE: Clifton L. Johnson

12. SOCIAL SECURITY NUMBER: 567-18-2943 - A
13. USUAL OCCUPATION (give kind of work done during most of working life, even if retired): Retired Motion Picture Actress
KIND OF BUSINESS OR INDUSTRY: Motion Pictures

14. RESIDENCE—STATE: Oregon
14b. COUNTY: Douglas
14c. CITY, TOWN, OR LOCATION: Roseburg
Inside City Limits (specify yes or no): Yes
14d. STREET AND NUMBER OR R.F.D.: 1047 N. E. Lincoln

15. FATHER—NAME first middle last: Gottfried Rangen
16. MOTHER—Maiden Name First middle last: Auguste (unknown)
17. INFORMANT—NAME and relationship to deceased: Clifton L. Johnson - Husband

PART I. DEATH WAS CAUSED BY: (ENTER ONLY ONE CAUSE PER LINE FOR (a), (b), and (c))
approximate interval between onset and death

18. Immediate cause (a): Cardiac arrest
due to, or as a consequence of:
Conditions, if any, which gave rise to immediate cause (a), stating the underlying cause last (b): Congestive heart failure
due to, or as a consequence of:
(c):

PART II. OTHER SIGNIFICANT CONDITIONS: conditions contributing to death but not related to cause given in Part I (a)
AUTOPSY (yes or no) 19a.: No
IF YES were findings considered in determining cause of death 19b.:

20a. ACCIDENT (specify yes or no):
20b. DATE OF INJURY (month, day, year):
20c. HOUR: M.
20d. HOW INJURY OCCURRED (enter nature of injury in part I or part II, item 18):
20e. INJURY AT WORK (specify yes or no):
20f. PLACE OF INJURY at home, farm, street, factory, office bldg., etc. (specify):
20g. LOCATION (street or R.F.D. No., city or town, county, state):

21. CERTIFICATION—PHYSICIAN: I attended the deceased from: 9-22-64 to 10-10-77
And Last Saw Him/Her Alive on: 10-10-77
I Did/Did Not view the body after death (specify): did
DEATH OCCURRED (hour): 6:56 a.m. at the place, on the date and, to the best of my knowledge, due to the cause(s) stated.

22a. PHYSICIAN—SIGNATURE: Fred Black M.D.
22b. NAME (type or print): Fred Black, M.D.
degree or Title:
22c. DATE SIGNED (month, day, year): 10-12-77

23. MAILING ADDRESS—PHYSICIAN: street: 1122 NW GardenValley Blvd. city or town: Roseburg, Oregon zip: 97470

24a. BURIAL, CREMATION, REMOVAL, etc. (specify): Cremation
24b. CEMETERY OR CREMATORY—NAME: Uniservice Crematory
24c. LOCATION city or town: Portland state: Oregon
24d. DATE (mo., day, year): Oct. 14, 1977

25a. FUNERAL DIRECTOR—SIGNATURE: James F. Keil
25b. FUNERAL HOME—NAME AND ADDRESS (street, city or town, state, zip): WILSON'S CHAPEL OF THE ROSES-PO BOX 358 ROSEBURG, OR 97470

26a. REGISTRAR—SIGNATURE: Arthur M. Locke
26b. DATE RECEIVED BY LOCAL REGISTRAR: Oct. 19, 1977
27. DATE RECEIVED BY STATE REGISTRAR: NOV 2 1977

28. RESERVED FOR REGISTRAR'S USE

VS-2 6-69

APPENDIX A

Wilson's Chapel of The Roses

This is all I could send to you. I hope it helps.

Fathers name; Gottfried Wenger

Mothers name; Auguste Cunknown

Date of Death; October 10, 1977

Date of Birth; August 27, 1891

Helen was cremated.

965 W. Harvard Blvd • Roseburg, Oregon 97471 • (541) 673-4455

APPENDIX B

Schedules
and
Other Material

APPENDIX B

MILLER BROTHERS AND ARLINGTON'S 101 RANCH SCHEDULE FOR 1910

April 1910

18-23 - St. Louis, Missouri
24 - Sunday
25 - Terre Haute, Indiana
26 - Indianapolis, Indiana
27 - Dayton, Ohio
28 - Springfield, Ohio
29 - Columbus, Ohio
30 - Cambridge, Ohio

May 1910

1 - Sunday
2 - Allegheny, Pennsylvania
3-4 - Pittsburgh, Pennsylvania
(East Liberty)
5 - Connellsville, Pennsylvania
6 - Greensburg, Pennsylvania
7 - Altoona, Pennsylvania
8 - Sunday
9-14 - Philadelphia, Pennsylvania
15 - Sunday
16-17 - Washington, DC
18-19 - Baltimore, Maryland
20 - Wilmington, Deleware
21 - Perth Amboy, New Jersey
22 - Sunday
23-25 - Brooklyn, New York
(Fifth Ave. & 3rd St.)
26 - 28 - Brooklyn, New York
(Halsey & Saratoga Ave.)
29 - Sunday
30 - Mt. Vernon, New York
31 - White Plains, New York

June 1910

1 - Bronx, New York City, NY
2 - Yonkers, New York
3 - Hudson, New York
4 - Gloversville, New York

5 - Sunday
6 - Albany, New York
7 - North Adams, Massachusetts
8 - Springfield, Massachusetts
9 - Holyoke, Massachusetts
10 - Worcester, Massachusetts
11 - Fitchburg, Massachusetts
12 - Sunday
13 - Bellows Falls, Vermont
14 - Keene, New Hampshire
15 - Lawrence, Massachusetts
16 - Gloucester, Massachusetts
17 - Cambridge, Massachusetts
18 - Haverhill, Massachusetts
19 - Sunday
20 - Portland, Maine
21 - Lewiston, Maine
22 - Watcrville, Maine
23 - Dover-Foxcroft, Maine
24 - Houlton, Maine
25 - Presque Isle, Maine
26 - Sunday
27 - Bangor, Maine
28 - Augusta, Maine
29 - Dover, New Hampshire
30 - Salem, Massachusetts

July 1910

1 - Lynn, Massachusetts
2 - Nashua, New Hampshire
3 - Sunday
4 - Manchester, New Hampshire
5 - Concord, New Hampshire
6 - Lowell, Massachusetts
7 - Woonsocket, Rhode Island
8 - Providence, Rhode Island
9 - Pawtucket, Rhode Island
10 - Sunday
11 - New Bedford, Massachusetts
12 - Fall River, Massachusetts
13 - Putnam, Connecticut

14 - Bristol, Connecticut
15 - Danbury, Connecticut
16 - Poughkeepsie, New York
17 - Sunday
18 - Kingston, New York
19 - Newburgh, New York
20-21 - Newark, New Jersey
22 - Elizabeth, New Jersey
23 - Long Branch, New Jersey
24 - Sunday
25 - Jersey City, New Jersey
26 - Plainfield, New Jersey
27 - Dover, New Jersey
28 - Somerville, New Jersey
29 - Camden, New Jersey
30 - Chester, Pennsylvania
31 - Sunday

August 1910

1 - Lancaster, Pennsylvania
2 - York, Pennsylvania
3 - Hanover, Pennsylvania
4 - Fredrick, Maryland
5 - Hagerstown, Maryland
6 - Cumberland, Maryland
7 - Sunday
8 - Fairmont, West Virginia
9 - Morgantown, West Virginia
10 - Mannington, West Virginia
11 - Clarksburg, West Virginia
12 - Sistersvile, West Virginia
13 - Marietta, Ohio
14 - Sunday
15 - Charleston, West Virginia
16 - Huntington, West Virginia
17 - Athens, Ohio
18 - Delaware, Ohio
19 - Toledo, Ohio
20 - LaPorte, Indiana

21-28 - Chicago, Illinois
(Riverview Exposition)
29 - Elgin, Illinois
30 - Racine, Wisconsin
31 - Manitowoc, Wisconsin

September 1910

1 - Oshkosh, Wisconsin
2 - Baraboo, Wisconsin
3 - LaCrosse, Wisconsin
4 - Sunday
5-10 - Hamline, MN
(Minnesota State Fair)
11 - Sunday
12 - Rochester, Minnesota
13 - Austin, Minnesota
14 - Fairmont, Minnesota
15 - Mason City, Iowa
16 - Spencer, Iowa
17 - Perry, Iowa
18 – Sunday
19 - Des Moines, Iowa
20 - Atlantic, Iowa
21 - Avoca, Iowa
22 - Omaha, Nebraska
23 - Lincoln, Nebraska
24 - Falls City, Nebraska
25 - Sunday
26-30 - St. Joseph, MO
(Interstate Live Stock Show)

October 1910

1-2 - Kansas City, Missouri
3 - Marshall, Missouri
4 - Roodhouse, Illinois
5 - Springfield, Illinois
6 - Carlinville, Illinois
7 - Alton, Illinois

October, 1910

8 - St. Louis, Missouri
9 - St. Louis, Missouri (Sunday)
10 - Anna, Illinois
11 - Cairo, Illinois
12 - Paducah, Kentucky
13 - Dyersburg, Tennessee
14 - Memphis, Tennessee
15 - Clarksdale, Mississippi
16 - Sunday
17 - Greenville, Mississippi
18 - Vicksburg, Mississippi
19 - Port Gibson, Mississippi
20 - Gloster, Mississippi
21 - Baton Rouge, Louisiana
22 - New Orleans, Louisiana
23 - New Orleans, Louisiana (Sunday)
24 - Brookhaven, Mississippi
25 - Jackson, Mississippi
26 - Keoskeon, Mississippi
27 - Aberdeen, Mississippi
28 - Birmingham, Alabama
29 - Cedartown, Georgia
30 - Sunday
31 - Atlanta, Georgia

November 1910

1 - Atlanta, Georgia
2-5 - Macon, Georgia
6 - Sunday
7 - Savannah, Georgia
8 - Cordelle, Georgia
9 - Amaericus, Georgia
10 - Columbus, Georgia

11 - Union Springs, Alabama
12 - Montgomery, Alabama
13 - Sunday
14 - Pensacola, Florida
15 - Mobile, Alabama
16 - Waynesboro, Mississippi
17 - Meridan, Mississippi
18 - Macon, Mississippi
19 - West Point, Mississippi

End of season

Winter quarters, Passiac, New Jersey.

Routes courtesy of Pfening collection.

(http://www.circushistory.org/Routes/MillerArlington.htm)

Joan Film Sales Co., Inc.
ANNOUNCES

—to State Right Buyers,—Independent Exchanges and Exhibitors throughout America and Canada, the early release of a new melodrama, a type of picture that never fails to draw crowds and get money for exhibitors. Using the words of the MOTION PICTURE NEWS—"A type of picture which is ever in demand." This picture is six reels in length, made in California, and stars Helen Gibson, Edward Coxen and splendid cast of players. The title—"NINE POINTS OF THE LAW" is dramatic in the extreme and a high powered Press Book is now being prepared to show exhibitors how to get big profits on this picture. Part of the territory was sold before the contract was even signed. Other territory already spoken for. If you are interested, write or wire Joan Film Sales Co., Inc., 33 W. 42nd St., New York, for complete details, territory and price, and keep in your mind this smashing Box Office title—

"Nine Points of the Law"

Ringling Bros. and Barnum & Bailey, 1924 Route

Charles and John Ringling, proprietors

March/April

Mar. 29 - Apr. 26 New York City,
Madison Square Garden
Apr. 28-30 Brooklyn, N.Y.

May

1-3 Brooklyn, N. Y.
5-10 Philadelphia, Pa.
12-14 Washington, D. C.
15-16 Baltimore, Md.
17 York, Pa.
19 Williamsport, Pa.
20 Harrisburg, Pa.
21 Reading, Pa.
22 Lancaster, Pa.
23 Camden, N. J.
24 Norristown, Pa.
26-27 Newark, N. J.
28 Allentown, Pa.
29 Wilkes-Barre, Pa.
30 Scranton, Pa.
31 Middletown, N.Y.

June

2 Waterbury, Conn.
3 Bridgeport, Conn.
4 New Haven, Conn.
5 New London, Conn.
6-7 Providence, R.I.
9 Portland, Me.
10 Salem, Mass.
11 Worcester, Mass.
12 Hartford, Conn.
13 Springfield, Mass.
14 Albany, N. Y.
16 Utica, N. Y.
17 Syracuse, N. Y.
18 Rochester, N. Y.
19 Niagara Falls, N. Y.

20 Buffalo, N. Y.
21 Erie, Pa.
23-24 Cleveland, O.
25 Akron, O.
26 Canton, O.
27 Youngstown, O.
28 New Castle, Pa.
30 Pittsburgh, Pa.

July

1 Pittsburgh, Pa.
2 Wheeling, W. Va.
3 Parkersburg, W. Va.
4 Huntington, W. Va.
5 Charleston, W.Va.
7 Columbus, O.
8 Springfield, O.
9 Dayton, O.
10 Lima, O.
11 Mansfield, O.
12 Toledo, O.
14-15 Detroit, Mich.
16 Flint, Mich.
17 Grand Rapids, Mich.
18 Kalamazoo, Mich.
19 South Bend, Ind.
21 Aurora, Ill.
22 Kewanee, Ill.
23 Davenport, Ia.
24 Cedar Rapids, Ia.
25 Waterloo, Ia.
26 Iowa Falls, Ia.
28 Des Moines, Ia.
29 Fort Dodge, Ia.
30 Mason City, Ia.
31 Sheldon, Ia.

August

1 Sioux City, Ia,
2 Sioux Falls, S. D.
4 Fairmont, Minn.
5 Owatonna, Minn.
6-7 Minneapolis, Minn.
8 St. Paul, Minn.
9 Duluth, Minn.
11 Stevens Point, Wis.
12 Oshkosh, Wis.
13 Madison, Wis.
14 Milwaukee, Wis.
15-24 Chicago (Grant Park), Ill.
25 Danville, Ill.
26 Indianapolis, Ind.
27 Terre Haute, Ind.
28 Evansville, Ind.
29 Mattoon, Ill.
30-31 St. Louis, Mo.

September

1 St. Louis, Mo.
2 Springfield, Ill.
3 Decatur, Ill.
4 Peoria, Ill.
5 Macomb, Ill.
6 Quincy, Ill.
8 Kansas City, Mo.
9 Emporia, Kan.
10 Hutchinson, Kan.
11 Great Bend, Kan.
12 Salina, Kan.
13 Concordia, Kan.
15 Wichita, Kan.
16 Arkansas City, Kan.
17 Coffeyville, Kan.
18 Chanute, Kan.
19 Pittsburg, Kan.
20 Springfield, Mo.

September 1924

22 Okmulgee, Okla.
23 Tulsa, Okla.
24 Enid, Okla.
25 Clinton, Okla.
26 Chickasha, Okla.
27 Lawton, Okla.
29 Dallas, Tex.
30 Fort Worth, Tex.

October

1 Cleburne, Tex.
2 Waco, Tex.
3 Austin, Tex.
4 San Antonio, Tex.
6 Sherman, Tex.
7 Greenville, Tex.
8 Paris, Tex.
9 Terrell, Tex.
10 Marshall, Tex.
11 Texarkana, Tex.
13 Mt. Pleasant, Tex.
14 Tyler, Tex.
15 Corsicana, Tex.
16 Mexia, Tex.
17 Hillsboro, Tex.
18 Temple, Tex.
20 Ardmore, Okla.
21 Oklahoma City, Okla.
22 Shawnee, Okla.
23 Ada, Okla.
24 Muskogee, Okla.
25 Fort Smith, Ark.
27 Jonesboro, Ark.
28 Memphis, Tenn.
29 Sheffield, Ala.
30 Birmingham, Ala.
31 Anniston, Ala.

November

1 Atlanta, Ga.
3 Greensboro, N. C.
End of season

1925 Route

Charles & John Ringling,
proprietors

March/April
Mar. 28 - May 2 New York City,
Madison Square Garden

May

4-9 Philadelphia, Pa.
11-13 Baltimore, Md.
14-16 Washington, D. C.
18-19 Newark, N. J.
20 Wilmington, Del.
21 Harrisburg, Pa.
22 Altoona, Pa.
23 Johnstown, Pa.
25-26 Pittsburgh, Pa.
27 Youngstown, O.
28 Akron, O.
29-30 Cleveland, O.

June

1 Buffalo, N. Y.
2 Rochester, N. Y.
3 Olean, N. Y.
4 Elmira, N. Y.
5 Scranton, Pa.
6 Wilkes-Barre, Pa.
8-13 Boston, Mass.
15 Worcester, Mass.
16-17 Providence, R. I.

June

18 Hartford, Conn.
19 Waterbury, Conn.
20 Bridgeport, Conn.
22 New Haven, Conn.
23 Springfield, Mass.
24 Albany, N. Y.
25 Utica, N. Y.
26 Syracuse, N. Y.
27 Auburn, N. Y.
29-30 Montreal, Can.

July

1 Ottawa, Can.
2 Belleville, Can.
3 Toronto, Can.
4 Kitchener, Can.
6 London, Can.
7 Port Huron, Mich.
8 Saginaw, Mich.
9 Alma, Mich.
10 Grand Rapids, Mich.
11 Muskegon, Mich.
13-14 Detroit, Mich.
15 Lansing, Mich.
16 South Bend, Ind.

July

17-26 Chicago (Grant Park), Ill.
27 Racine, Wis.
28 Milwatikee, Wis.
29 Appleton, Wis.
30 Wausau, Wis.
31 Eau Claire, Wis.

August

1 Duluth, Minn.
3-4 Minneapolis, Minn.

August 1925

5 St. Paul, Minn.
6 Mankato, Minn.
7 Sioux Falls, S. D.
8 Yankton, S. D.
10 Watertown, S. D.

11 Aberdeen, S. D.
12 Jamestown, N. D.
13 Fargo, N. D.
14 Devils Lake, N. D.
15 Minot, N. D.
17 Great Falls, Mont.
18 Helena, Mont.
19 Butte, Mont.
20 Missoula, Mont.
21 Spokane, Wash.
22 Wenatchee, Wash.
24-25 Seattle, Wash.
26 Tacoma, Wash.
27-28 Portland, Ore.
29 Salem, Ore.
31 Redding, Cal.

September

1 Chico, Cal.
2 Sacramento, Cal.
3-4 Oakland, Cal.
5-7 San Francisco, Cal.
8-9 San Jose, Cal.
9 Salinas, Cal.
10 San Luis Obispo, Cal.
11 Santa Barbara, Cal.
12-15 Los Angeles, Cal.
16 San Diego, Cal.
17 Santa Ana, Cal.
18 Long Beach, Cal.
19 San Bernardino, Cal.
21 Phoenix, Ariz.
23 El Paso, Tex.
24 Albuquerque, N. M.
25 Clovis, N. M.
26 Amarillo, Tex.

28 Wichita Falls, Tex.
29 Fort Worth, Tex.
30 Dallas, Tex.

October

1 Dallas, Tex.
2 Sulphur Springs, Tex.
3 Shreveport, La.
5 Clarksdale, Miss.
6 Greenville, Miss.
7 Greenwood, Miss.
8 Columbus, Miss.
9 Meridian, Miss.
10 Mobile, Ala.
12 Tuscaloosa, Ala.
13 Gadsden, Ala.
14 Chattanooga, Tenn.
15 Knoxville, Tenn.
16 Asheville, N. C.
17 Greenville, S. C.
19 Charlotte, N. C.
20 Winston-Salem, N. C.
21 Raleigh, N. C.
22 Goldsboro, N. C.
23 Rocky Mount, N. C.
24 Durham, N. C.
26 Salisbury, N. C.

End of season

1926 Route

Charles and John Ringling, proprietors

March/April
Mar. 31 - May 1
New York City,
Madison Square Garden

May

3-8 Philadelphia, Pa.
10-11 Washington, D. C.
12-13 Baltimore Md.

14 Wilmington, Del.
15 Lancaster, Pa.
17-18 Newark N. J.
19 Allentown, Pa.
20 Reading, Pa.
21 Williamsport, Pa.
22 Clearfield, Pa.
24-25 Pittsburgh Pa.
26 Canton, O.
27 Columbus, O.
28 Dayton, O.
29 Cincinnati, O.
31 Cleveland, O.

June

1 Cleveland, O.
2 Erie, Pa.
3 Buffalo, N. Y.
4 Rochester, N. Y.
5 Syracuse, N. Y.
7-12 Boston, Mass.
14 Providence, R. I.
15 New Bedford, Mass.
16 Lowell, Mass.
17 Marblehead, Mass.
18 Manchester, N. H.
19 Portland, Me.
21-22 Montreal, Ont.
23 Ottawa, Ont.
24 Belleville, Ont.
25 Peterboro, Ont.
26 Hamilton, Ont.
28 London Ont.
29 Brantford Ont.
30 Toronto, Ont.

July

1 Niagara Falls, N. Y.
2 Jamestown, N. Y.
3 Youngstown, O.
5 Akron, O.
6 Mansfield O.

July 1926

7 Toledo, O.
8 Adrian, Mich.
9-10 Detroit, Mich.
12 Flint, Mich.
13 Lansing, Mich.
14 Jackson, Mich.
15 Fort Wayne, Ind
16 South Bend, Ind.
17-25 Chicago (Grant Park), Ill.
26 Milwaukee, Wis.
27 Sheboygan, Wis.
28 Fond du Lac, Wis.
29 Madison. Wis.
30 Janesville, Wis.
31 Rockford, Ill.

August

2 Davenport, Ia.
3 Newton, Ia.
4 Des Moines, Ia.
5 Fort Dodge, Ia.
6 Waterloo, Ia.
7 Cedar Rapids, Ia.
9 Mason City, Ia.
10 Albert Lea, Minn.
11-12 Minneapolis, Minn.
13 St. Paul, Minn.
14 Duluth, Minn.
16 Winona, Minn.
17 Rochester, Minn.
18 New Ulm, Minn.
19 Algona, Ia.
20 Boone, Ia.
21 Carroll Ia.
23 Sioux City, Ia.
24 Norfolk, Neb.
25 Grand Island, Neb.
26 York, Neb.
27 Omaha, Neb.

28 Red Oak, Ia.
30 Ottumwa, Ia.
31 Trenton, Mo
.

September

1 St. Joseph, Mo.
2 Kansas City, Mo.
3 Topeka, Kan.
4 Manhattan, Kan.
6 Concordia, Kan.
7 Salina, Kan.
8 Emporia, Kan.
9 Wichita, Kan.
10 Alva, Okla.
ll Woodward, Okla.
13 Enid, Okla.
14 Oklahoma City, Okla.
15 Ponca City, Okla.
16 Independence, Kan.
17 Pittsburg, Kan.
18 Springfield, Mo.
20 Joplin, Mo.
21 Miami, Okla.
22 Tulsa, Okla.
23 Okmulgee, Okla.
24 Ada, Okla.
25 Durant, Okla.
27 Dallas, Tex.
28 Fort Worth, Tex.
29 Wichita Falls, Tex.
30 Altus, Okla.

October

1 Clinton, Okla.
2 Lawton, Okla.
4 Shawnee, Okla.
5 Ardmore, Okla.
6 Paris, Tex.
7 Greenville, Tex.
8 Waxahachie, Tex.

9 Corsicana, Tex.
11 Waco, Tex.
12 Temple, Tex.
13 Taylor, Tex.
14 Austin, Tex.
15 San Antonio, Tex.
16 Cuero, Tex.
18 Galveston, Tex.
19-20 Houston, Tex.
21 Beaumont, Tex.
22 Baton Rouge, La.
23-24 New Orleans, La.
25 Brookhaven, Miss.
26 Jackson, Miss.
27 Greenwood, Miss.
28 Memphis, Tenn.
29 Tupelo, Miss.
30 Birmingham, Ala.

November

1 Atlanta, Ga.

End of season

From Ringling Bros. and Barnum & Bailey Circus 1954 Route Book. Provided by John Polacek.

http://www.circushistory.org/Routes/Ringling19.htm)

HOPI ARTICLES

Uncle Ray's CORNER

THE SNAKE DANCE

In cities where college football games are held, the students often take part in "snake dances." With arm linked in arm, rows of students prance from side to side of the street or the athletic field. There is a movement forward, as well as sideways, and someone watching from above might be reminded of a snake winding its way ahead.

The Hopi Indians of Arizona have a snake dance of a different kind. It

The Hopi dancers held snakes in their mouths while they danced about the plaza.

is a feature of a festival held every two years.

Before the festival begins, men are sent north, east, south and west to gather snakes—real, live snakes. These are placed in a pen, and are fed and cared for until the time for the snake dance arrives.

On the morning of a late August day, the snakes are washed in the presence of the tribe, and a sand altar is built. In the afternoon a number of Hopi men climb out of a "kiva," or large round hole in their pueblo. They are painted, and wear kilts, moccasins, necklaces, bracelets, armlets and anklets.

These men are the snake dancers. They march to the plaza and circle around four times. Each man passes over a board set in the ground and stamps on it. This stamping is to tell the beings of the lower world that the snake dance is about to commence.

The dancers form in groups of three and dance with a hopping step to a place where there is an opening in the plaza. A man leans down to the opening, and a snake is handed up. He takes it in his mouth, holding it by the middle of the body, then dances four times around the plaza. Other men do the same thing, and while they dance, they are sprinkled with sacred meal by Hopi women and girls.

Some of the snakes are poisonous, but strangely enough the dancers are seldom bitten. They know how to handle the snakes carefully.

After the dancing is over, the snakes are set free.

Uncle Ray

(Copyright, 1926, Publishers Syndicate)

Newburgh (PA) News. 10-11-1926. n.p.

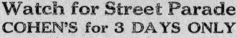

San Diego Evening Tribune. 12-07-1926. p. 8.

250

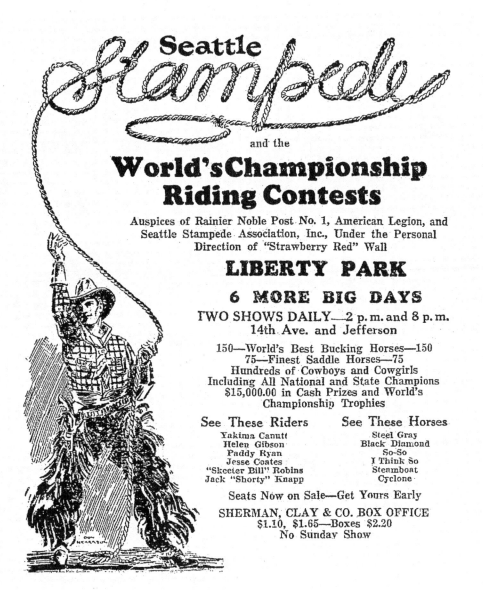

Seattle Stampede

and the

World's Championship Riding Contests

Auspices of Rainier Noble Post No. 1, American Legion, and Seattle Stampede Association, Inc., Under the Personal Direction of "Strawberry Red" Wall

LIBERTY PARK

6 MORE BIG DAYS

TWO SHOWS DAILY—2 p. m. and 8 p. m.
14th Ave. and Jefferson

150—World's Best Bucking Horses—150
75—Finest Saddle Horses—75
Hundreds of Cowboys and Cowgirls
Including All National and State Champions
$15,000.00 in Cash Prizes and World's
Championship Trophies

See These Riders	See These Horses
Yakima Canutt	Steel Gray
Helen Gibson	Black Diamond
Paddy Ryan	So-So
Jesse Coates	I Think So
"Skeeter Bill" Robins	Steamboat
Jack "Shorty" Knapp	Cyclone

Seats Now on Sale—Get Yours Early

SHERMAN, CLAY & CO. BOX OFFICE
$1.10, $1.65—Boxes $2.20
No Sunday Show

Seattle Daily Times. 07-03-1927. p. 4.

1 WILD WEST SHOW
AND
1 RODEO, BOTH IN 1932

THURSDAY, NOVEMBER 10, 1932

IN BENEFIT SHOW—Helen Gibson is shown with horse she will ride in Frontier Wild West show to be staged November 18-20 for benefit of Parent-Teachers milk fund. Dramatic episodes in life of old west will be reproduced under direction of old cattlemen.

THURSDAY, DECEMBER 8, 1932

Helen Gibson, famous Rodeo star, is to be one of the feature attractions at Cy Toosie's Farm on December 17 and 18. The former Encino Country club is being transformed into the famous farm.

Helen Gibson Scrapbook. December 8, 1932. Page 39

Famed 101 Wild West Show
Scores on Comeback Trail

COL. ZACK T. MILLER
Organizes wild west show

LAWTON, Okla., Nov. 2 (AP) The old timer in that front row wiped away a reminiscent tear as he watched a man on a white horse ride into the glare of a spotlight and slowly raise his gleaming ten-gallon hat.

"That's just the way Buffalo Bill used to do it," sighed the old timer. "Old Colonel Zack hasn't lost his touch."

The old timer was talking about Col. Zack T. Miller, last ramrod of the once world-renowned 101 ranch wild west show, who hit the comeback trail this year.

Colonel Zack shrugged off years of reverses during which he lost the famed 101 ranch—so named because it once spanned 101,000 acres—and organized his new show venture.

Show Full of Thrills

The show is complete with howling Indians, chuck wagons, roundup scenes, including branding and an attack on a covered wagon train by a band of painted redskins as its whooping finale.

The biggest thrill comes,

however, when Colonel Zack rides into the spotlight and dramatically poses with a white Stetson in his outthrust hand just as Buffalo Bill Cody did when the 101 ranch show played the capitals of Europe at the turn of the century.

Ranch House Razed

The doughty colonel lost the famous 101 ranch in 1930 when mortgage holders foreclosed. He fought a protracted legal battle until 1937, but Miller had no success and even the ranch's famed white house was razed.

During the days of the Miller brothers' control, the door of the white house never was closed.

Famous people from the world over, most of whom the Millers met on their travels with their show, visited the ranch house.

There was a parade of stage and screen stars through the years—headed by Tom Mix, who got his start with the 101 ranch show.

Will Rogers Often Guest

William S. Hart was a frequent visitor, Helen Gibson, Richard Bennett and Jack Mulhall often were there. Will Rogers sang cowboy songs in the living room for other guests and twirled his famous rope.

"He always was the life of any party," Colonel Zack sighs as he recalls Will's visits.

Mrs. Gordon Lillie, wife of the famous Pawnee Bill, often accompanied Rogers as he sang.

Irvin S. Cobb sat long hours in the ranch house regaling guests with his famous stories; Publisher Fred Bonfils of Denver came to see a terrapin derby; Sidney Smith, creator of "Andy Gump," drew pictures of his comic strip character on the walls.

Famous Names Sign

William Randolph Hearst, Edna Ferber, Rex Beach, William Jennings Bryan, President Theodore Roosevelt and many other noted persons signed the ranch house guest register.

Miller's original show, beset by losses, went when the big ranch passed from his control.

After the big ranch folded, Colonel Zack tried his hand at ranching on a smaller scale and took part in other ventures but all the time, he admits, his mind was set on reopening the old wild west show.

He hit bottom in 1933, when a judge sentenced him to jail in Kay county, Oklahoma, for failure to pay alimony.

His old friend, William H. "Alfalfa Bill" Murray, then governor, rescued him with an unprecedented order giving him a military pardon.

Guard Releases Zack

A national guardsman was dispatched with orders to release Miller even if he found it necessary to break down the jail door.

Miller was freed and started his long, uphill fight toward his goal—his new show.

Oregonian, November 3, 1946. Page 9

253

Judy Canova (November 20, 1913 – August 5, 1983)

Helen Gibson, Capital Film Company (1920). Any resemblance to Judy Canova?

Clifton Johnson remarried after Helen's death.
He lived 15 years after her passing.

Clifton L. Johnson

JOHNSON, Clifton L. — Age 90 a resident of Roseburg, passed away April 3, 1992. Born September 6, 1901 in Star Prairie, Wisconsin. Mr. Johnson served in the U.S. Navy during WWII and the Korean Conflict as a Lt. Commander. Clifton retired from Universal Studio after 35 years as a Electrician Technician. He was a life member of Laurel Masonic Lodge #13 of Roseburg, Scotish Rite, Eastern Star and Shriners. Mr. Johnson moved to Roseburg in 1963 from Los Angles, California. Survivors include his wife Kathleen Johnson of Roseburg; son Wayne Ramsey and grandchildren Donald, Michael and Kathleen all of Roseburg; sisters Burnetta Mellom, Viola Dixon, Marcella Madden and Lila Bailey all of Washington. At his request no services will be held. Memorial contributions may be made in memory of Clifton L. Johnson to the Shriners Hospital for Crippled Children, 3101 S.W. Sam Jackson Park Rd, Portland, Oregon 97201. WILSON'S CHAPEL OF THE ROSES is in charge of arrangements.

ACKNOWLEDGEMENTS

Juvanne Martin, CG - The Research Network
P.O. Box 9065 - Nampa, Idaho 83652
www.researchnetwork.com
208-461-8866

Consultant: Lon Davis
Consultant: Christopher Snowden
Consultant: David Shepard
Consultant and Contributor: Robert S. Birchard
Consultant and Contributor: Marc Wanamaker
Consultant and Contributor: Sam Gill
Consultant and Contributor: Shirley Freitas
(Helen Holmes Great-granddaughter)

Dr. Geoff Mayer
Reader and Associate Professor - Head of School
School of Communication, Arts & Critical Enquiry
La Trobe University - Victoria 3086 Australia
Ph +61 (0)3 94792042
g.mayer@latrobe.edu.au

Heidi Stringham, Reference Staff
Research Center of the Utah State Archives & Utah
State History
300 S. Rio Grande - Salt Lake City, UT 84101
http://historyresearch.utah.gov
historyresearch@utah.gov

Jason D Stratman, Assistant Librarian, Reference
Missouri History Museum

Winnipeg Public Library
251 Donald Street - Winnipeg, MB R3C-3P5
Webpage: http://wpl.winnipeg.ca/
E-mail: eref@winnipeg.ca

Laura Hoff, Library Assistant
Bostonian Society • Old State House
206 Washington Street - Boston, MA 02109
517-720-1713 ext 13
Fax 617-720-3289
library@bostonhistory.org   www.bostonhistory.org

Reference and Information Services
Boston Public Library

700 Boylston St. Boston, MA 02216
ask@bpl.org
617-859-2270
http://www.bpl.org/questions/question.htm

Keith Petersen
State Historian/Associate Director
Idaho State Historical Society - North Idaho Office
112 West 4th Street, Ste 7 - Moscow, ID 83843
Phone: 208-882-1540
Fax: 208-882-1763
keith.petersen@ishs.idaho.gov

Cecile W. Gardner
Reference Librarian, Microtext Department
Boston Public Library
700 Boylston Street - Boston, MA 02116
(617) 859-2018
microtextref@bpl.org

Scott Daniels
Reference Librarian, Oregon Historical Society
1200 SW Park Avenue - Portland, OR 97205
scott.daniels@ohs.org
503-306-5240

National Film Information Service
Fairbanks Center for Motion Picture Study
333 S. La Cienega Blvd.
Beverly Hills CA 90211
Telephone : (310) 247-3000
Fax: (310) 657-5597
Email: nfis@oscars.org

New-York Historical Society
170 Central Park West
New York, New York 10024-5194
1-(212)-485-9225

Anne Richardson
(Oregon Movies, A to Z) www.talltalestruetales.com
www.melblancproject.wordpress.com
www.oregoncartooninstitute.com

Kristine Krueger
National Film Information Service
Margaret Herrick Library
Academy of Motion Picture Arts and Sciences
Tel 310-247-3000 x2275
Fax 310-657-5597
www.oscars.org
kkrueger@oscars.org

Dave McCall, BFI Commercial Manager
British Film Institute
21 Stephen Street - London W1T 1LN
Tel. 00 44 (0)20 7957 4840
Fax. 00 44 (0)20 7436 7950
e-mail: dave.mccall@bfi.org.uk

Virginia Roberts, President
Round-Up and Happy Canyon Hall of Fame
Pendleton, Oregon

Lauren Williams, Research Manager
National Cowgirl Museum and Hall of Fame
1720 Gendy Street - Fort Worth, Texas 76107
(817) 336-4475
(817) 509-8665 direct
www.cowgirl.net

Sophie Hyde - Producer/Director
Adelaide Studios - 226 Fullarton Road - Glenside 5065,
South Australia
Sophhyde@CloserProductions.com.au
Phone: +61 414 574 584
Kent Town Business Centre
P.O. Box 636 - Kent Town, South Australia 5071
Phone: +618 8394 2535
www.CloserProductions.com.au

Annie and Judy Solomon
The Seattle Public Library
Business, Science and Technology

Sherry Bullard, Reference Clerk
Paula Dasher, Interlibrary Loan
Coeur d'Alene Public Library
702 E Front Avenue - Coeur d'Alene, ID 83814
Phone: 208-769-2315
Fax: 208-769-2381
email: info@cdalibrary.org
http://www.cdalibrary.org/

Judy Griffin, Circus Historical Society

Chicago History Museum Research Center
http://www.chicagohistory.org

Mary K. Huelsbeck, WHS
Wisconsin Center for Film and Theater Research
412 Historical Society - 816 State Street - Madison, WI
53706
(608) 264-6466

Pete Shrake, Archivist - Circus World Museum
415 Lynn St. Baraboo, WI 53913
Email: pshrake@circusworldmuseum.com
Phone: 608-356-8341

Robert L. Parkinson Library and Research Center
Circus World Museum, Baraboo, Wisconsin.
http://circusworld.wisconsinhistory.org/About/Re-
searchCenter.aspx
Phone number: 608-356-8341.
email address: on website.

Photofest, New York

Antoinette Watson (Delmar)

Barbara Hollace - Editor and Author.
BarbaraHollace.com

Mary Langer Smith - Editor and Author. The one who
kept me focused during the entire writing process.

Anna and Ron Goodwin - The Error Detectives who
took the final look at this manuscript before the publisher got it.

Jeffery Jeske (Fellow writer) - The eyes of an eagle.

FILMOGRAPHY

Ranch Girls on a Rampage (May 15, 1912), Kalem Film Company. One reel. **Cast:** Edward Coxen, Ruth Roland, Marshall Neilan, Rose Wenger, Phyllis Daniels, Jane Hoskins.

The Girl of the Range (February 19, 1913) Frontier Film Company. One reel. **Cast:** Helen Gibson (Rosaline).

Old Moddington's Daughters (September 9, 1913), Vitagraph Company of America.
One reel. **Producer:** W.J. Bauman, **Story:** William Lisenhee, **Cast:** George Stanley, Otto Lederer, Helen Gibson, Patricia Palmer, Earle Williams, Fred Mace, Harry Mann, Jane Bernoudy.

Hazards of Helen (#049) A Test of Courage (October 16, 1915), Kalem Company. One reel. **Cast:** Helen Gibson, Robyn Adair and Charles Murchison.

Hazards of Helen (#050) A Mile a Minute (October 23, 1915), Kalem Company. One reel. **Cast:** Helen Gibson, Robyn Adair, E.Z. Roberts and Charles Murchison.

Hazards of Helen (#051) The Rescue of the Brakeman's Children (October 30, 1915), Kalem Company. One reel. **Scenario:** W.H. Baugh. **Cast:** Helen Gibson, Franklin Hall, Jennie Antibus, Norma Antibus, Bobbie Antibus, Robyn Adair and Clarence Burton.

Hazards of Helen (#052) Danger Ahead! (November 6, 1915), Kalem Company. One reel. **Cast:** Helen Gibson, Clarence Burton, Robyn Adair, Franklin Hall and Jack Messick.

Hazards of Helen (#053) The Girl and the Special (November 13, 1915), Kalem Company. One reel. **Cast:** Helen Gibson, Betty Hartigan, Clarence Burton, Franklin Hall and Robyn Adair.

Hazards of Helen (#054) The Girl on the Bridge (November 20, 1915), Kalem Company. One reel. **Cast:** Helen Gibson, Clarence Burton and Franklin Hall.

Hazards of Helen (#055) The Dynamite Train (November 27, 1915), Kalem Company. One reel. **Scenario:** E. W. Matlack. **Cast:** Helen Gibson, Robyn Adair, Thomas Means, Frank Henderson and Clarence Burton.

Hazards of Helen (#056) The Tramp Telegrapher (December 4, 1915), Kalem Company. One reel. **Cast:** Helen Gibson, Robyn Adair, Edward Greer, Franklin Hall and Clarence Burton.

Hazards of Helen (#057) Crossed Wires (December 11, 1915), Kalem Company. One reel. **Cast:** Helen Gibson, Robyn Adair, Clarence Burton, Franklin Hall and Hi Sing.

Hazards of Helen (#058) The Wrong Train Order (December 18, 1915), Kalem Company. One reel. **Producer:** James Davis. **Story:** E. W. Matlack. **Cast:** Helen Gibson (Operator at Lone Point), Robyn Adair (Savage), Clarence Burton (Macker), Franklin Hall (Torney) and True Boardman Jr. (Billie Boy).

Hazards of Helen (#059) A Boy at the Throttle (December 25, 1915), Kalem Company. One reel. **Scenario:** E. W. Matlack. **Cast:** Helen Gibson (Operator at Lone Point), Franklin Hall (Odell, an engineer), Clement Graw (Pinture, his fireman), Clarence Burton (Layson) and True Boardman Jr. (Bobbie).

Hazards of Helen (#060) At the Risk of her Life (January 1, 1916), Kalem Company. One reel. **Cast:** Helen Gibson (Operator at Lone Point), Franklin Hall and Robyn Adair. .

Hazards of Helen (#061) When Seconds Count (January 8, 1916), Kalem Company. One reel. **Cast:** Helen Gibson (Operator at Lone Point), Franklin Hall (Toney, a half-breed Mexican) and Robyn Adair (Jim, a cowboy).

Hazards of Helen (#062) The Haunted Station (January 15, 1916), Kalem Company. One reel. **Producer:** James Davis. **Story:** E. W. Matlack **Cast:** Helen Gibson (Operator at "Haunted Station"), Robyn Adair (Joe Wood), Clarence Burton (Chief Dispatcher).

Hazards of Helen (#063) The Open Track (January 22, 1916), Kalem Company. One reel. **Producer:** James Davis. **Story:** E. W. Matlack **Cast:** Helen Gibson (Operator at "Haunted Station"), R. Adams and Clarence Burton (Railroad detectives), Franklin Hall, George Robinson and Glen Gano (Counterfeiters).

Hazards of Helen (#064) Tapped Wires (January 29, 1916), Kalem Company. One reel. **Producer:** James Davis. **Cast:** Helen Gibson (Operator at Lone Point), Robyn Adair (Relief operator), George Robinson, Glen Gano and Franklin Hall (Crooks).

Hazards of Helen (#065) The Broken Wire (February 5, 1916), Kalem Company. One reel. **Producer:** James Davis. **Story:** E. W. Matlack **Cast:** Helen Gibson (Operator at Lone Point), Robyn Adair and Franklin Hall (Crooks), Clarence Burton (Conductor).

Hazards of Helen (#066) The Peril of the Rails (February 12, 1916), Kalem Company. One reel. **Producer:** James Davis. **Story:** E. W. Matlack **Cast:** Helen Gibson (Operator at Lone Point), Robyn Adair (Conductor Lawton), Clarence Burton (Engineer), Franklin Hall (Leader of the Crooks).

Hazards of Helen (#067) The Perilous Swing (February 19, 1916), Kalem Company. One reel. **Producer:** James Davis. **Story:** C. Doty Hobart. **Cast:** Helen Gibson (Operator at Lone Point), Clarence Burton (The Sheriff), Franklin Hall ("Red" Purdy).

Hazards of Helen (#068) The Switchman's Story (February 26, 1916), Kalem Company. One reel. **Cast:** Helen Gibson (Operator at Lone Point), Clarence Burton and Franklin Hall.

Hazards of Helen (#069) The Girl Telegrapher's Nerve (March 4, 1916), Kalem Company. One reel. **Cast:** Helen Gibson (Helen, the operator), Hal Clements (Steve Nelson), Guy Coombs (Dick Pearse) and Henry Hallam (James Ogden, sheriff).

Hazards of Helen (#070) A Race for a Life (March 11, 1916), Kalem Company. One reel. **Producer:** James Davis. **Story:** Herman A. Blackman. **Cast:** Helen Gibson (The operator), Robyn Adair (Helen's friend), Charles Mulgro (President of the Road) and Percy Pembroke (His Son).

Hazards of Helen (#071) The Girl Who Dared (March 18, 1916), Kalem Company. One reel. **Producer:** James Davis. **Cast:** Helen Gibson (Operator at Lone Point), Franklin Hall (The Smuggler), Percy Pembroke (The Wireless Operator), Clarence Burton and Robyn Adair (Detectives).

Hazards of Helen (#072) The Detective's Peril (March 25, 1916), Kalem Company. One reel. **Producer:** James Davis. **Cast:** Helen Gibson (Operator at Lone Point), Clarence Burton (The Paymaster) and Robyn Adair (The Detective).

Hazards of Helen (#073) The Trapping of "Peeler" White (April 1, 1916), Kalem Company. One reel. **Producer:** James Davis. **Story:** Herman A. Blackman. **Cast:** Helen Gibson (Helen, the Operator), True Boardman ("Peeler" White), Percy Pembroke (Dick Benton), Roy Watson ("Diamond Joe") and Henry Schum (Burns).

Hazards of Helen (#074) The Record Run (April 8, 1916), Kalem Company. One reel. **Producer:** James Davis. **Cast:** Helen Gibson (The Operator), True Boardman (Engineer of the Mail Train), George Williams (President Benton), Roy Watson (The Rival Road's President) and Percy Pembroke (Leader of the Road's Agents).

Hazards of Helen (#075) The Race for a Siding (April 15, 1916), Kalem Company. One reel. **Producer:** James Davis. **Story:** S.A. Van Petten. **Cast:** Helen Gibson (The Operator at Lone Point), True Boardman (The Detective), Percy Pembroke (His Assistant).

Hazards of Helen (#076) The Governor's Special (April 22, 1916), Kalem Company. One reel. **Cast:** Helen Gibson (The Operator at Lone Point), P.S. Pembroke (Tom Arnold), True Boardman (Detective Stanton), George Williams (The Governor), Roy Watson (Glen Nash), Harry Schum and Ed Gibson (His Aides).

Hazards of Helen (#077) The Trail of Danger (April 29, 1916), Kalem Company. One reel. **Director:** James Davis. **Cast:** Helen Gibson (The Operator), George Williams (Train Dispatcher), Roy Watson (Detective Burton), P. Pembroke, Harry Schum and Ray Lincoln (The Conspirators).

Hazards of Helen (#078) The Human Telegram (May 6, 1916), Kalem Company. One reel. **Director:** James Davis. **Cast:** Helen Gibson (The Operator at Lone Point), P. Pembroke (Superintendent Purdy), H. Schum (The Discharged Operator), G. A. Williams (President of the Western Railway) and Roy Watson (Mine Foreman).

Hazards of Helen (#079) The Bridge of Danger (May 13, 1916), Kalem Company. One reel. **Director:** James Davis. **Story:** Herman A. Blackman. **Cast:** Helen Gibson (The Operator at Lone Point), Percy. Pembroke, G. A. Williams and Roy Watson.

Hazards of Helen (#080) One Chance in a Hundred (May 20, 1916), Kalem Company. One reel. **Director:** James Davis. **Scenario:** Edward Matlack. **Cast:** Helen Gibson (Helen, the Operator), P.S. Pembroke (Billy Warren), Harry Schum (Brent), Roy Watson (Easton), and G. A. Williams (The Construction Boss).

Hazards of Helen (#081) The Capture of Red Stanley (May 27, 1916), Kalem Company. One reel. **Director:** James Davis. **Cast:** Helen Gibson, P.S. Pembroke, Harry Schum, Roy Watson, Edmund Gibson, O. Fillippi and G. A. Williams.

Hazards of Helen (#082) The Spiked Switch (June 3, 1916), Kalem Company. One reel. **Director:** James Davis. **Scenario:** Edward W. Matlack. **Cast:** Helen Gibson (Helen, the Operator), G.A. Williams (Engineer Trent), Pearl Anibus (His Daughter), P.S. Pembroke (Hume, the Fireman) and Roy Watson (Chief Dispatcher).

Hazards of Helen (#083) The Treasure Train (June 10, 1916), Kalem Company. One reel. **Producer:** James Davis. **Scenario:** S.A. Van Patten. **Cast:** Helen Gibson (Helen, the Operator), P.S. Pembroke (Jim Spencer, the Guard), Harry Schum ("Red" Byrd), O. Phillippi and Edmund Gibson (His Aides).

Hazards of Helen (#084) A Race Through the Air (June 17, 1916), Kalem Company. One reel. **Producer:** James Davis. **Scenario:** Herman A. Blackman. **Cast:** Helen Gibson, P.S. Pembroke, G. A. Williams and Roy Watson.

Hazards of Helen (#085) The Mysterious Cipher (June 24, 1916), Kalem Company. One reel. **Director:** James Davis. **Scenario:** Homer Von Flindt. **Cast:** Helen Gibson (Helen, the Operator), G.A. Williams (Chilton, dealer in Antiques), P.S. Pembroke (His Partner), Ed. Gibson (Blanding, their Tool).

Hazards of Helen (#086) The Engineer's Honor (July 1, 1916), Kalem Company. One reel. **Producer:** James Davis. **Scenario:** Herman A. Blackman. **Cast:** Helen Gibson (Helen, the Operator), O. Phillippi (Gypsy Joe), G.A. Williams (Auditor Blake), and P.S. Pembroke (His Son).

Notch Number Nine (July 5, 1916), Kalem Company. One reel. **Producer:** James Davis. **Cast:** Helen Gibson,

Hazards of Helen (#087) To Save the Road (July 8, 1916), Kalem Company. One reel. **Producer:** James Davis. **Scenario:** Homer Von Flindt. **Cast:** Helen Gibson (Helen), G.A. Williams (Senator Brown), and P.S. Pembroke (Road Superintendent).

Hazards of Helen (#088) The Broken Brake (July 15, 1916), Kalem Company. One reel. **Producer:** James Davis. **Scenario:** E.W. Matlack. **Cast:** Helen Gibson (Helen, the Operator at Lone Point), George Routh (Johnson, Construction Foreman), P.S. Pembroke (His Assistant) and G.A. Williams (The Doctor).

Hazards of Helen (#089) In Death's Pathway (July 22, 1916), Kalem Company. One reel. **Producer:** James Davis. **Scenario:** S.A. Van Petten. **Cast:** Helen Gibson (Helen, Lone Point Operator), P.S. Pembroke (Dick Benton), Pearl Anibus (Eleanor Burkett), G.A. Williams (Her Father) and George Routh (Guy Warren)...

Hazards of Helen (#090) A Plunge From the Sky (July 29, 1916), Kalem Company. One reel. **Producer:** James Davis. **Scenario:** E.W. Matlack. **Cast:** Helen Gibson (The Lone Point Operator), P.S. Pembroke (Dick Benton), G.A. Williams, George Routh and George Robinson (The Foreign Agents).

Hazards of Helen (#091) A Mystery of the Rails (August 5, 1916), Kalem Company. One reel. **Director:** James Davis. **Scenario:** Herman E. Blackman. **Cast:** Helen Gibson (The Lone Point Operator), P.S. Pembroke (Tom Ransom), George Routh Jud Hendricks), G.A. Williams (The Sheriff) and O. Phillippi (Gypsy Joe).

Hazards of Helen (#092) Hurled Through the Drawbridge (August 12, 1916), Kalem Company. One reel. **Director:** James Davis. **Cast:** Helen Gibson (The Lone Point Operator), P.S. Pembroke (Gordon), G.A. Williams (Sinton), Glen Gano and Jack Messick (His Aides) and George Routh (Naroche).

Hazards of Helen (#093) With the Aid of the Wrecker (August 19, 1916), Kalem Company. One reel. **Director:** James Davis. **Scenario:** E.W. Matlack. **Cast:** Helen Gibson (The Lone Point Operator), G.A. Williams (Greggs, Diamond Dealer), P.S. Pembroke (Gentleman Joe) and George Routh (His Accomplice).

Hazards of Helen (#094) At Danger's Call (August 26, 1916), Kalem Company. One reel. **Director:** James Davis. **Story:** Frank Howard Clark. **Cast:** Helen Gibson (The Operator at Lone Point), G.A. Williams (Superintendent Waller), P.S. Pembroke (Bob, the Foreman) George Routh (The Camp Bully) and True Boardman Jr. (Waller's Son).

Hazards of Helen (#095) The Secret of the Box Car (September 2, 1916), Kalem Company. One reel. **Director:** James Davis. **Scenario:** E.W. Matlack. **Cast:** Helen Gibson (Operator at Lone Point), G.A. Williams (Bank Official), P.S. Pembroke (Gentleman Joe) and George Routh (His Pal).

Hazards of Helen (#096) Ablaze on the Rails (September 9, 1916), Kalem Company. One reel. **Producer:** James Davis. **Scenario:** E.W. Matlack. **Cast:** Helen Gibson (Operator at Lone Point), P.S. Pembroke (Construction Superintendent), George Routh (Foreman), Jack Messick (Detective Kent), Gladys Blue (His Sweetheart) and G.A. Williams (Benton).

Hazards of Helen (#097) The Hoodoo of Division B (September 16, 1916), Kalem Company. One reel. **Director:** James Davis. **Scenario:** E.W. Matlack. **Cast:** Helen Gibson (The Operator at Lone Point), G.A. Williams (Kent, A Veteran Engineer), P.S. Pembroke (Benton, Just Breaking in) and George Routh (The New Superintendent).

Hazards of Helen (#098) Defying Death (September 23, 1916), Kalem Company. One reel. **Director:** James Davis. **Cast:** Helen Gibson (The Operator at Lone Point), G.A. Williams (President of the Road), P.S. Pembroke (Dick Benton) and George Routh (Riggs, the Rival Lawyer).

Hazards of Helen (#099) The Death Swing (September 30, 1916), Kalem Company. One reel. **Director:** James Davis. **Cast:** Helen Gibson (Helen, Day Operator at Lone Point), P.S. Pembroke (Dick Benton, Night Operator), G.A. Williams (His Father) and George Routh (Stallings).

Hazards of Helen (#100) The Blocked Track (October 7, 1916), Kalem Company. One reel. **Director:** James Davis. **Scenario:** E.W. Matlack. **Cast:** Helen Gibson (Operator at Lone Point), P.S. Pembroke (Superintendent Melvin), G.A. Williams (Butler, Ex-Telegrapher) and George Routh (Stang, an Ex-Convict).

Hazards of Helen (#101) To Save the Special (October 14, 1916), Kalem Company. One reel. **Director:** James Davis. **Scenario:** E.W. Matlack. **Cast:** Helen Gibson (Operator at Lone Point), P.S. Pembroke (Dick Benton), George Routh (Strang).and G.A. Williams (The Railroad President).

Hazards of Helen (#102) A Daring Chance (October 21, 1916), Kalem Company. One reel. **Director:** James Davis. **Scenario:** E.W. Matlack. **Cast:** Helen Gibson (Helen, Day Operator), George Routh (The Night Operator), True Boardman Jr. (His Son), P.S. Pembroke (Dick Benton, Lineman), and G.A. Williams (President of the Road).

Hazards of Helen (#103) The Lost Messenger (October 28, 1916), Kalem Company. One reel. **Director:** James Davis. **Scenario:** E.W. Matlack. **Cast:** Helen Gibson (Operator at Lone Point), P.S. Pembroke (Benton, Express Messenger), G.A. Williams (President Lanfers) and George Routh (Express Agent).

Hazards of Helen (#104) The Gate of Death (November 4, 1916), Kalem Company. One reel. **Director:** James Davis. **Cast:** Helen Gibson (The Operator at Lone Point), P.S. Pembroke (Paymaster Benton), G.A. Williams (Superintendent Purdy) and George Routh (The Crook).

Hazards of Helen (#105) The Lone Point Mystery (November 11, 1916), Kalem Company. One reel. **Director:** Walter Morton. **Cast:** Helen Gibson (Operator at Lone Point), George Routh (Arnold), P.S. Pembroke (Dick Benton), and G.A. Williams (The Railroad President).

Hazards of Helen (#106) The Runaway Sleeper (November 18, 1916), Kalem Company. One reel. **Director:** Walter Morton. **Scenario:** E.W. Matlack. **Cast:** Helen Gibson (Operator at Lone Point), G.A. Williams (Mr. Greyson), P.S. Pembroke (The Lineman) and George Routh (Spug).

Hazards of Helen (#107) The Forgotten Train Order (November 25, 1916), Kalem Company. One reel. **Director:** Walter Morton. **Scenario:** E.W. Matlack. **Cast:** Helen Gibson (The Operator at Lone Point), P.S. Pembroke (Dick Benton), George Routh ("Red" Byrd) and G.A. Williams (Mr. Purdy).

Hazards of Helen (#108) The Trial Run (December 2, 1916), Kalem Company. One reel. **Director:** Walter Morton. **Scenario:** S.A. Van Petten. **Cast:** Helen Gibson (Operator at Lone Point), P.S. Pembroke (Arthur Lane), G.A. Williams (Morton, of the United), and George Routh (Superintendent Purdy).

Hazards of Helen (#109) The Lineman's Peril (December 9, 1916), Kalem Company. One reel. **Director:** Walter Morton. **Cast:** Helen Gibson (Operator at Lone Point), P.S. Pembroke (Dick Benton, Lineman), G.A. Williams (Superintendent of the Road), and George Routh (His Assistant).

Hazards of Helen (#110) The Midnight Express (December 16, 1916), Kalem Company. One reel. **Director:** Walter Morton. **Cast:** Helen Gibson (Operator at Lone Point), P.S. Pembroke (The Express Messenger), George Routh (Gentleman Joe) and G.A. Williams (Banker Randall).

Hazards of Helen (#111) The Vanishing Box Car (December 23, 1916), Kalem Company. One reel. **Director:** Walter Morton. **Cast:** Helen Gibson (Operator at Lone Point), P.S. Pembroke (Dick Benton), Juanita Sponsler (Edith), G.A. Williams (Hedley) and.George Routh (Powden, His Henchman).

Hazards of Helen (#112) The Race With Death (December 30, 1916), Kalem Company. One reel. **Director:** Walter Morton. **Cast:** Helen Gibson (Operator at Lone Point), P.S. Pembroke (The Night Operator), George Routh (Ranch Foreman) G.A. Williams (Purdy, a Rancher) and Juanita Sponsler (His Daughter, Edith).

Hazards of Helen (#113) The Mogul Mountain Mystery (January 6, 1917), Kalem Company. One reel. **Director:** Walter Morton. **Scenario:** S.A. Van Petten. **Cast:** Helen Gibson (Helen, operator at Lone Point), P.S. Pembroke (Bert Morgan), George Routh (Squirt Booth), William Burns and Gus Pullian (his accomplices), W. Foster ("Lefty") and G.A. Williams (division superintendent).

Hazards of Helen (#114) The Fireman's Nemesis (January 13, 1917), Kalem Company. One reel. **Director:** Walter Morton. **Scenario:** Frank Howard Clark. **Cast:** Helen Gibson (Helen, operator at Lone Point), Richard Johnson (Joe Cordona, the fireman), George Routh (Scarlotta, an Italian) and G.A. Williams (chief dispatcher).

Hazards of Helen (#115) The Wrecked Station (January 20, 1917), Kalem Company. One reel. **Director:** Walter Morton. **Scenario:** Samuel J. Taylor. **Cast:** Helen Gibson (Helen, operator at Lone Point), George Routh (Sydney Wayne, superintendent gravel plant), George Williams (Stanton Grey), Babe Crisman (his daughter Edith) and Richard Johnson (Cole, a gambler).

Hazards of Helen (#116) The Railroad Claim Intrigue (January 27, 1917), Kalem Company. One reel. **Director:** Walter Morton. **Cast:** Helen Gibson (Helen), G.A. Williams (Fleming), G.A. Routh (Barstow) and Richard Johnson (Duncan).

Hazards of Helen (#117) The Death Siding (February 3, 1917), Kalem Company. One reel. **Director:** Walter Morton. **Scenario:** E.W. Matlack. **Cast:** Helen Gibson (Helen, operator at Lone Point), G.A. Williams (the sheriff) and Richard Johnson (Migel, a Greaser).

Hazards of Helen (#118) The Prima Donna's Special (February 10, 1917), Kalem Company. One reel. **Director:** Walter Morton. **Scenario:** Herman A. Blackman. **Cast:** Helen Gibson (Helen), G.A. Williams ("Dad" Morley) and Lillian Lorraine (Mlle. Gazle).

Hazards of Helen (#119) The Sidetracked Sleeper (February 17, 1917), Kalem Company. One reel. **Director:** Walter Morton. **Scenario:** E.W. Matlack. **Cast:** Helen Gibson (Helen), George Routh (Rupert Winslow) and G.A. Williams (George Summers).

A Daughter of Daring (#1) In the Path of Peril (March 17, 1917), Kalem Company. One reel. **Director:** Walter Morton. **Scenario:** Herman A. Blackman. **Cast:** Helen Gibson (Helen), L.T. Whitlock (Engineer Compton), George Routh (Gypsy Joe), Lillian Clark (Anita, Gypsy Queen) and G.A. Williams (The sheriff).

A Daughter of Daring (#2) The Registered Pouch (March 24, 1917), Kalem Company. One reel. **Director:** Walter Morton. **Scenario:** E.W. Matlack **Cast:** Helen Gibson (Helen), G.A. Williams (Kinney), Marion Emmons (Jimmy) and George Routh (Jose, a track hand).

A Daughter of Daring (#3) The Borrowed Engine (March 31, 1917), Kalem Company. One reel. **Director:** Walter Morton. **Scenario:** E.W. Matlack **Cast:** Helen Gibson (Helen), L.T. Whitlock (Dick Patterson), G.A. Williams (John Cummings), Lillian Clark (Grace, his daughter) and George Routh (Jason Graves).

A Daughter of Daring (#4) The College Boys' Special (April 7, 1917), Kalem Company. One reel. **Director:** Scott Sidney. **Cast:** Helen Gibson (Helen), L.T. Whitlock, G.A. Williams.

A Daughter of Daring (#5) The Mystery of the Burning Freight (April 14, 1917), Kalem Company. One reel. **Director:** Scott Sidney. **Scenario:** Herman A. Blackman. **Cast:** Helen Gibson (Helen), L.T. Whitlock (Victor Brown), G.A. Williams (Amos Brown) and George Routh (Jim Selby).

A Daughter of Daring (#6) The Lone Point Feud (April 21, 1917), Kalem Company. One reel. **Director:** Scott Sidney. **Cast:** Helen Gibson (Helen), G.A. Williams (Squire Briggs), Gladys Blue (Grace, his daughter) and L.T. Whitlock (Benton).

The Wrong Man (July 4, 1917), Bison/Universal. Two reel. **Producer:** Fred Kelsey. **Story:** N.P. Oaks. **Scenario:** J.L. Cunningham. **Cast:** Harry Carey (Jack Wilson), George Berrell (Ben Bostwick), Fritzi Ridgeway (Alice Malone), Bill Gettinger (Larry Malone), Vester Pegg ("Chip" Stevens), Hoot Gibson ("Chip's" Pal) and Helen Gibson (Un-credited).

The Perilous Leap (September 10, 1917), Gold Seal/Universal. Three reel. **Director:** James Davis. **Story:** T. Shelley Sutton. **Scenario:** George Hively. **Cast:** O.C. Jackson (Joe Mead), George Williams ("Dad" Shannon), George Routh (Pete Larkins), Helen Gibson (Effie) and Val Paul (Ned Donnely).

The Dynamite Special (September 29, 1917), Bison/Universal. Two reel. **Director:** J. D. Davis. **Scenario:** George Hively. **Cast:** George Williams (David Carleton), M.K. Wilson (Ralph Carleton), Marc Fenton (Bill Manville), Helen Gibson (Ruth Manville), Val Paul (Joe Brooks) and Al Harris (Jimmy Thurman).

Saving the Fast Mail (October 9, 1917), Bison/Universal. Two reel. **Director:** James D. Davis. **Scenario:** James D. Davis. **Cast:** Helen Gibson (Helen), Jack Dill (Dan, the engineer), M.K. Wilson (Jim Hardy), Marc Fenton (President Hardy) and Harry Timbrook (Jack Day).

The End of the Run (October 22, 1917), Gold Seal/Universal. Three reel. **Producer:** James Davis. **Story:** T. Shelley Sutton. **Scenario:** George Hively. **Cast:** O.C. Jackson (Giles Stafford), George Williams (Jim Durman), George Routh (Portland Pete), Val Paul (William Craig), Helen Gibson (Nona Durman) and George Berrell (Sheriff).

A Daughter of Daring (#7) A Race to the Drawbridge (November 7, 1917), Kalem Company. One reel. **Director:** James Davis. **Assistant Director**: A.C. Gage. **Cameraman:** O. Zangrelli. **Cast:** Helen Gibson (Helen), G. Routh (Johnson) and G. A. Williams (Brandon).

A Daughter of Daring (#8) The Munitions Plot (November 14, 1917), Kalem Company. One reel. **Director:** James Davis. **Assistant Director**: A.C. Gage. **Cameraman:** O. Zangrelli. **Cast:** Helen Gibson (Helen), George A. Williams (Belding), George Routh (Steele), G. Pullium (Wertz) and L.T. Whitlock (Merkel).

A Daughter of Daring (#9) The Detective's Danger (November 21, 1917), Kalem Company. One reel. **Director:** James Davis. **Assistant Director**: A.C. Gage. **Cameraman:** O. Zangrelli. **Cast:** Helen Gibson (Helen), L.T. Whitlock (Norman Brown), George Routh (Sam Duvall) and G. A. Williams ("Bummer Bill").

A Daughter of Daring (#10) The Railroad Smugglers (November 28, 1917), Kalem Company. One reel. **Director:** James Davis. **Assistant Director**: A.C. Gage. **Cameraman:** O. Zangrelli. **Cast:** Helen Gibson (Helen), G. A. Williams (Julius Hecker), George Routh (John, his son), Hal Clements (A Mexican) and L.T. Whitlock (Harry Holmes).

Fighting Mad – aka: The Man of God (December 3, 1917), Butterfly/Universal. Five reel. **Director:** Edward J. LeSaint. **Story:** J.G. Alexander and Fred Myton. **Cast:** William Stowell ("Doc" Lambert), Helen Gibson (his wife), Hector Dion (the gambler), Betty Schade (Faro Fanny), Alfred Allen, Mildred Davis and Millard K. Wilson.

A Daughter of Daring (#11) The Deserted Engine (December 5, 1917), Kalem Company. One reel. **Director:** James Davis. **Assistant Director**: A.C. Gage. **Cameraman:** O. Zangrelli. **Cast:** Helen Gibson (Helen), R. Ryan (Jack Forney), George Routh (Bob Ashton), Tom Walsh (mail clerk) and G. A. Williams (Superintendent).

The Lion's Claw (April 6, 1918), Universal Film Company. Eighteen serial. **Directors:** Harry Harvey, Jacques Jaccard. **Scenario:** Jacques Jaccard. **Story:** W.B. Pearson. **Cast:** Marie Walcamp (Beth Johnson), Ray Hanford (Buck Masterson), Near Hart (Captain Harris), Frank Lanning (Musa), Thomas G. Lingham (Captain Johnson), Alfred Allen (Colonel Leighton), Gertrude Astor (Lady Mary Leighton), Edwin August (Roger Hammond), Helen Gibson (Guest appearance, chapter 10).

CH. 1: *A Woman's Honor* (4/6/18), two reels
CH. 2: *Beasts of the Jungle* (4/13/18), two reels
CH. 3: *Net of Terror* (4/20/18), two reels
CH. 4: *A Woman's Scream* (4/27/18), two reels
CH. 5: *The Secret Document* (5/4/18), two reels
CH. 6: *The Dungeon of Terror* (5/11/18), two reels
CH. 7: *Quicksand* (5/18/18), two reels
CH. 8: *Into the Harem* (5/25/18), two reels
CH. 9: *The Human Pendulum* (6/1/18), two reels
CH. 10: *Escape Through the Flames* (6/8/18), two reels
CH. 11: *Caught in the Tolls* (6/15/18), two reels
CH. 12: *The Spies' Cave* (6/22/18), two reels
CH. 13: *In Disguise* (6/29/18), two reels
CH. 14: *Hell Let Loose* (7/6/18), two reels
CH. 15: *Bridge of the Beast* (7/13/18), two reels
CH. 16: *The Jungle Pool* (7/20/18), two reels
CH. 17: *The Well of Horror* (7/27/18), two reels
CH. 18: *The Doom of Rej Hari* (8/3/18), two reels

Play Straight or Fight (June 15, 1918), Universal Film Company. Two reel. **Director:** Paul Hurst. **Story:** Leon De Mothe. **Scenario:** Karl K. Coolidge. **Cast:** Helen Gibson, G. Raymond Nye, Hoot Gibson, Millard K. Wilson and Noble Johnson.

Quick Triggers (June 22, 1918), Universal Film Company. Two reel. **Director:** George Marshall. **Story:** George Marshall. **Screenplay:** George Marshall. **Cast:** Neal Hart, Eileen Sedgwick, Dick La Reno, Gypsy Hart, Joe Rickson, Buck Connors, Helen Gibson.

The Midnight Flyer (June 29, 1918), Universal Film Company. Two reel. **Director:** George Marshall. **Cast:** Hoot Gibson, Violet Mersereau, Helen Gibson, G. Raymond Nye.

The Branded Man (July 13, 1918), Universal Film Company. Two reel. **Cast:** Hoot Gibson (Sheriff), Donna Kee (John Ewing), Helen Gibson (Helen Ewing), Millard K. Wilson (Jim Calvert), G. Raymond Nye (Val Heywood), Noble Johnson (Trovio Valdez).

The Shooting Party (July 20, 1918), Universal Film Company. Two reel. **Cast:** Helen Gibson, Mignon Anderson.

The Payroll Express (July 27, 1918), Universal Film Company. Two reel. **Cast:** Helen Gibson.

Bawled Out (August 14, 1918), Century Comedy. Two reel. **Director:** James D. Davis. **Cast:** Alice Howell, Hughie Mack, Vin Moore and Helen Gibson.

Beating the Limited (August 24, 1918), Universal Film Company. Two reel. **Director:** George Marshall. **Scenario:** Tom Gibson, **Story:** George Marshall. **Cast:** Neal Hart, Janet Eastman, Howard Crampton, Joe Rickson, George Brooks, George Marshall, Helen Gibson.

Danger Ahead (September 14, 1918), Universal Film Company. Two reel. **Director:** James D. Davis. **Scenario:** L. Caulfield. **Cast:** Helen Gibson, Millard K. Wilson and Orin Jackson.

Under False Pretenses (September 28, 1918), Universal Film Company. Two reel. **Director:** James D. Davis. **Scenario:** George Hively. **Cast:** Helen Gibson, Millard K. Wilson, Wilbur Higby, Albert MacQuarrie and Orin Jackson.

The Fast Mail (October 12, 1918), Universal Film Company. Three reel. **Director:** George Marshall. **Story:** Frank H. Spearman. **Scenario:** Robert Dillon. **Cast:** Helen Gibson, Val Paul, Buck Connors and G. Raymond Nye.

The Dead Shot (October 26, 1918), Universal Film Company. Two reel. **Director:** Harry Harvey. **Story:** Alan James. **Cast:** Helen Gibson, Frank Whitson, Mark Fenton and Frank Lee.

The Silent Sentinel (October 28, 1918), Universal Film Company. Two reel. **Director:** Harry Harvey. **Story:** Alan James. **Scenario:** Harry Wulze. **Cast:** Helen Gibson and L.C. Shumway.

Captured Alive (December 14, 1918), Universal Film Company. Two reel. **Director:** Harry Harvey. **Story:** Leon De Mothe. **Cast:** Helen Gibson, Edward Pell Sr., Louis Fitzroy and Leon D. Kent. Film re-released in 1925 by Mustang.

The Robber (December 21, 1918), Universal Film Company. Two reel. **Director:** Harry Harvey. **Story:** Leon De Mothe. **Cast:** Helen Gibson, Edward Pell Sr., and Yvette Mitchell.

Wolves of the Range (December 28, 1918), Universal Film Company. Two reel. **Director:** Harry Harvey. **Story:** Alan James. **Scenario:** Alan James. **Cast:** Leo D. Maloney, Helen Gibson, Lee Hill and Louis Fitzroy.

The Girl Sheriff (January 1, 1919), Universal Film Company. Two reel. **Cast:** Helen Gibson.

The Secret Peril (January 5, 1919), Universal Film Company. Two reel. **Director:** Alan James. **Story:** Alan James. **Cast:** Leo D. Maloney, Helen Gibson, Mignon Anderson, Millard K. Wilson and Rex De Rosselli.

The Canyon Mystery (February 2, 1919), Universal Film Company. Two reel. **Director:** Jack Ford. **Scenario:** George Hively. **Scenario:** George Hively. **Cast:** Pete Morrison, Helen Gibson, Buck Connors, Vester Pegg and Harry De More.

The Black Horse Bandit (March 15, 1919), Universal Film Company. Two reel. **Director:** Jack Ford. **Scenario:** George Hively **Cast:** Pete Morrison, Helen Gibson, Hoot Gibson, Vester Pegg and Buck Connors.

Riding Wild (March 23, 1919), Universal Film Company. Two reel. **Director:** Harry Harvey. **Story:** Alan James. **Cast:** Helen Gibson, Leo D. Maloney, Helen Gibson and Pete Morrison.

The Rustlers (April 22, 1919), Universal Film Company. Two reel. **Director:** Reginald Barker. **Story:** George Hively. **Scenario**: George Hively. **Cast:** Pete Morrison, Hoot Gibson, Helen Gibson and Jack Woods.

Rustlers (April 26, 1919), Universal Film Company. Two reel. **Director:** John Ford. **Cast:** Pete Morrison, Hoot Gibson, Helen Gibson and Jack Woods.

Gun Law (May 10, 1919), *aka The Posse's Prey*. Universal Film Company. Two reel. **Director:** John Ford. **Story:** H. Tipton Steck. **Scenario**: H. Tipton Steck. **Cast:** Pete Morrison, Hoot Gibson, Jack Woods, Helen Gibson, Otto Meyer, Harry Chambers and Ed Jones.

Ace High (June 7, 1919), Universal Film Company. Two reel. **Director:** George Holt. **Story:** William Pigott. **Scenario:** Karl R. Coolidge. **Cast:** Pete Morrison, Madga Lane, Hoot Gibson, Helene Rosson, Jack Walters, Martha Mattox and Helen Gibson.

Down But Not Out (June 30, 1919), Universal Film Company. Two reel. **Director:** Jacques Jaccard. **Story:** George Hively. **Scenario**: George Hively. **Cast:** Eddie Polo, Charles Brinley and Helen Gibson. Episode #8 of 10 in the *Cyclone Smith* series.

Loot (October 6, 1919), Universal Film Company. Six reel. **Director:** William C. Dowlan. **Story:** Arthur Somers Roche. **Scenario:** Violet Clark. **Cast:** Darrell Foss (Hildreth), Ora Carew (Morn Light), Joseph W. Girard (Pete Fielding), Frank Thompson (Williams), Alfred Allen (Lark Ashby), Wadsworth Harris (Arabin), Arthur Mackley (Detective Tyron), Gertrude Astor (Lady Gwendolyn), Frank McQuarrie (Jacques) and Helen Gibson (Maid).

The Opium Runners (November 13, 1919), Capital Film Company. Two reel. **Director:** George Holt. **Story:** William Pigott. **Scenario:** Karl R. Coolidge. **Cast:** Helen Gibson.

The Trail of the Rails (November 15, 1919), Capital Film Company. Two reel. **Director:** George Holt. **Story:** William Pigott. **Scenario:** Karl R. Coolidge. **Cast:** Helen Gibson.

Daring Danger (December 12, 1919), Capital Film Company. Two reel. **Director:** George Holt. **Story:** William Pigott. **Scenario:** Karl R. Coolidge. **Cast:** Helen Gibson.

Flirting With Terror (December 24, 1919), Capital Film Company. Two reel. **Director:** George Holt. **Story:** William Pigott. **Scenario:** Karl R. Coolidge. **Cast:** Helen Gibson.

The Clutch of the Law (January 23, 1920), Capital Film Company. Five reel. **Director:** George Holt. **Story:** William Pigott. **Scenario:** Karl R. Coolidge. **Cast:** Helen Gibson.

The Broken Trestle (February 6, 1920), Capital Film Company. Two reel. **Director:** George Holt. **Story:** William Pigott. **Scenario:** Karl R. Coolidge. **Cast:** Helen Gibson, William Gettinger.

The Golden Star Bandits (February 12, 1920), Capital Film Company. Two reel. **Director:** George Holt. **Story:** William Pigott. **Scenario:** Karl R. Coolidge. **Cast:** Helen Gibson.

Border Watch Dogs (February 20, 1920), Capital Film Company. Two reel. **Director:** George Holt. **Story:** William Pigott. **Scenario:** Karl R. Coolidge. **Cast:** Helen Gibson.

The Ghost of the Canyon (March 20, 1920), Capital Film Company. Two reel. **Director:** George Holt. **Story:** William Pigott. **Scenario:** Karl R. Coolidge. **Cast:** Helen Gibson (Helen), S.D. Wilcox (J.F. Mortimer), Millard Wilson (Tom Forrest), Bert Law (Peter Wells).

The Overland Express (March 31, 1920), Capital Film Company. Two reel. **Director:** George Holt. **Story:** William Pigott. **Scenario:** Karl R. Coolidge. **Cast:** Helen Gibson.

The Payroll Pirates (April 30, 1920), Capital Film Company. Two reel. **Director:** George Holt. **Story:** William Pigott. **Scenario:** Karl R. Coolidge. **Cast:** Helen Gibson.

Winning the Franchise (May 3, 1920), Capital Film Company. Two reel. **Director:** Robert Myles. **Story:** R.A. Dillion. **Scenario:** R.A. Dillion. **Cameraman:** Carl Widen. **Cast:** Helen Gibson (Helen), Leo Maloney (Bob Ferris), Roy Coulson (Valentine Dunton), M. McCormick (Haye's Private Secretary).

Wires Down (May 15, 1920), Capital Film Company. Two reel. **Director:** George Holt. **Story:** William Pigott. **Scenario:** Karl R. Coolidge. **Cast:** Helen Gibson.

Terror of the Rails (May 22, 1920), Capital Film Company. Two reel. **Director:** George Holt. **Story:** William Pigott. **Scenario:** Karl R. Coolidge. **Cast:** Helen Gibson.

The Danger Signal (June 4, 1920), Capital Film Company. Two reel. **Director:** George Holt. **Story:** William Pigott. **Scenario:** Karl R. Coolidge. **Cast:** Helen Gibson.

The Broken Brake (June 26, 1920), Capital Film Company. Two reel. **Director:** Norbert Myles. **Story:** Norbert Myles. **Scenario:** Norbert Myles. **Cast:** Helen Gibson (Helen Sutton), William Gettinger (Jim Wharton)..

Running Wild (August 6, 1920), Capital Film Company. Two reel. **Director:** George Holt. **Story:** William Pigott. **Scenario:** Karl R. Coolidge. **Cast:** Helen Gibson.

No Man's Woman (February 5, 1921), Helen Gibson Productions/Associated Photoplays. Xxx reel. **Director:** Wayne Mack, Leo D. Maloney. **Story:** L.V. Jefferson. **Scenario:** Ford Beebe. **Cast:** Helen Gibson (The Girl), Edward Coxen (The Man), Leo D. Maloney (Cullen), Aggie Herring, Estelle Allen, Charles Smiley, Al Cody, Mrs. R.T. Curry, Little Margareta Curry and Duncan Pulliam. Re-released as *Nine Points of the Law* in March 1922 by Rainbow Film Company.

The Wolverine (September 23, 1921), Spencer Productions. Xxx reel. **Director:** William Bertram. **Story:** Bertha Muzzy Sinclair. **Scenario:** Helen Van Upp. **Cast:** Helen Gibson (Billy Louise), Jack Connolly (Ward Warren), Leo D. Maloney (Charlie Fox), Ivor McFadden (Buck Olney), Anne Schaefer (Martha Mellke), Gus Saville (Jase Mellke), Martha Mattox and Doris Race.

Nine Points of the Law (March 22, 1922), **aka A Girl's Decision**. Rainbow Film Company/Joan Film Sales Company Inc. Xxx reel. **Director:** Wayne Mack, Leo D. Maloney. **Story:** L.V. Jefferson. **Scenario:** Ford Beebe. **Cast:** Helen Gibson (Cherie Du Bois), Edward Coxen (Bruce McLeod), Leo D. Maloney (Fred Cullen), Aggie Herring (Mrs. Prouty), Estelle Allen, Charles Smiley, Al Cody, Mrs. R.T. Curry, Little Margareta Curry and Duncan Pulliam.

Thorobred (August 1, 1922), Clark-Cornelius Corporation. Five reel. **Director:** George Halligan. **Scenario:** George Halligan. **Cast:** Helen Gibson (Helen), Bob Burns (Ben Grey) Otto Nelson (Pop Martin) and Jack Ganzhorn (Blackie Wells).

Heroes of the Wild (November 1, 1927), Mascot Pictures. Ten-chapter serial. **Producer:** Nat Levine. **Director:** Harry S. Webb. **Scenario:** Carl Krusada. **Cast:** Jack Hoxie (Jack Hale), Josephine Hill (Selma Sanderson), Joe Bonomo (John Kemp), Tornado the Dog (Tornado), White Fury the Horse (White Fury), Linda Loredo (Carmen), Jay J. Bryan (Winslow), Emily Gerdes (Myra), Helen Gibson (Julia) and Roy Craft.

CH. 1: *Heroes of the Wild* (11/1/27), two reels
CH. 2: *Sword to Sword* (11/8/27), two reels
CH. 3: *The Plunge of Peril* (11/15/27, two reels
CH. 4: *The Slide of Life* (11/22/27), two reels
CH. 5: *The Trap of Death* (11/29/27), two reels
CH. 6: *The Flaming Fiend* (12/6/27), two reels
CH. 7: *The Clutching Hand* (12/13/27), two reels
CH. 8: *The Broken Cable* (12/20/27), two reels
CH. 9: *The Fatal Arrow* (12/27/27), two reels
CH. 10: *The Crown of the Incas* (1/3/28), two reels

The Chinatown Mystery (September 1, 1928), Syndicate Pictures. Ten-chapter serial. **Producer:** Trem Carr. **Director:** J.P. McGowen. **Story:** Francis Ford. **Scenario:** J.P. McGowan. **Cast:** Joe Bonomo (Joe Masters), Ruth Hiatt (Sally Warren), Paul Malvern, Francis Ford, Paul Panzer, Sheldon Lewis, Harry Myers, Rosemary Theby, Grace Cunard, George Cheseboro, Helen Gibson, Jack Richardson, Billy Ford, William Clifford, Sybil Grove, Al Baffert, J.P. McGowan, Spencer Bell, Duke Green, Carl Sepulveda, Tom Curran, Rolfe Sedan, Ernest Shields, Peggy O'Day, Harry Moran, Duke Worne and James Leong.

CH. 1: *The Chinatown Mystery* (9/1/28), two reels
CH. 2: *The Clutching Claw* (9/8/28), two reels
CH. 3: *The Devil's Dice* (9/15/28), two reels
CH. 4: *The Mysterious 13* (9/22/28), two reels
CH. 5: *Galloping Fury* (9/29/28), two reels
CH. 6: *The Depth of Danger* (10/6/28), two reels
CH. 7: *The Invisible Hand* (10/13/28), two reels
CH. 8: *The Wreck* (10/20/28), two reels
CH. 9: *Broken Jade* (10/27/28), two reels
CH. 10: *The Thirteenth Hour* (11/3/28), two reels

The Vanishing West (October 15, 1928), Mascot Pictures. Ten-chapter serial. **Producer:** Nat Levine. **Director:** Richard Thorpe. **Story:** Wyndham Gittens. **Cast:** Jack Perrin (Jack Marvin), Eileen Sedgwick (Betty Kincaid), Jim Dougherty (Jack Marvin), Yakima Canutt (Steve Marvin), Leo D. Maloney (Jack Trent), William Fairbanks (Long Collins), Mickey Bennett (Wally Lee), Helen Gibson (Mrs. Kincaid), Bob Burns (Robert Lee), Fred Church, Harry Lorraine, Aaron Edwards, Tom Bay and Ed Waldon.

CH. 1: *The Trail to Yesterday* (10/15/28), two reels
CH. 2: *The Flaming Trap* (10/22/28), two reels
CH. 3: *Thundering Hoofs* (10/29/28), two reels
CH. 4: *The Balance of Fate* (11/5/28), two reels
CH. 5: *The Chasm of Danger* (11/12/28), two reels
CH. 6: *Roaring Wheels* (11/19/28), two reels
CH. 7: *The Phantom Roper* (11/26/28), two reels
CH. 8: *The Tunnel of Terror* (12/3/28), two reels
CH. 9: *The Final Second* (12/10/28), two reels
CH. 10: *The End of the Trail* (12/17/28), two reels

The Lightning Warrior (December 1, 1931), Mascot Pictures. Twelve-chapter serial. **Producer:** Nat Levine. **Director:** Benjamin H. Kline, Armand Schaefer. **Story:** Ford Beebe. **Scenario:** Wyndham Gittens. **Cast:** Rin Tin Tin (Rinty), Frankie Darro (Jimmy Carter), Georgia Hale (Dianne La Farge), George Brent (Alan Scott), Hayden Stevenson (Carter), Pat O'Mailey (Sheriff A.W. Brown), Theodore Lorch (Pierre La Farge), Lafe McGee (John Hayden), Frank Brownlee (Angus MacDonald), Bob Kortman (Henchman Wells), Dick Dickinson (Adams), Yakima Canutt (Ken Davis/Deputy), Frank Lanning (Indian George/Jim), Helen Gibson (Pioneer Woman).

CH. 1: *Drums of Doom* (12/1/31), two reels
CH. 2: *The Wolf Man* (12/8/31), two reels
CH. 3: *Empty Saddles* (12/15/31), two reels
CH. 4: *Flaming Arrows* (12/22/31), two reels
CH. 5: *The Invisible Enemy* (12/29/31), two reels
CH. 6: *The Fatal Name* (1/5/32), two reels
CH. 7: *The Ordeal of Fire* (1/12/32), two reels
CH. 8: *The Man Who Knew* (1/19/32), two reels
CH. 9: *Traitor's Hour* (1/26/32), two reels
CH. 10: *Secret of the Cavel* (2/2/32), two reels
CH. 11: *Red Shadows* (2/9/32), two reels
CH. 12: *Painted Faces* (2/16/32), two reels

The Cheyenne Cyclone (January 10, 1932), *aka Rustlers' Ranch*. Willis Kent Productions. 57 Minutes. **Director:** Armand Schaefer. **Story:** Oliver Drake. **Scenario:** Oliver Drake. **Cast:** Lane Chandler (Bob Carleton), Marie Quillan (Patsy O'Brien), Frankie Darro ('Orphan' McGuire), Jay Hunt (Patrick O'Brien), J. Frank Glendon (Dan Fanning), Connie Lamont (Genevieve – the actress), Edward Hearn (J.C. 'Flash' Corbin), Henry Roguemore (Harrison – the actor), Slim Whitaker (Hank), Yakima Canutt (Ed Brady), Raven the Horse (Raven – Bob's Horse), Helen Gibson (Uncredited).

Human Targets (January 10, 1932), Big 4 Film. 56 Minutes. **Director:** J.P. McGowen. **Story:** George Morgan. **Cast:** Buzz Barton (Buzz Dale), Pauline Parker (Nellie Dale), Ralph Bushman (Bart Travis), Edmund Cobb (Duke Remsden), Helen Gibson (Mrs. Dale), Franklyn Farnum (Sheriff), Ted Adams (Deputy), Nanci Price (Marjorie), John Ince (The Doctor), Fred 'Snowflake' Toones (Snowflake).

Single-Handed Sanders (February 10, 1932), *aka Wyoming*. Monogram Pictures. 61 Minutes. **Director:** Charles A. Post. **Story:** Adele S. Buffington. **Cast:** Tom Tyler (Matt Sanders), Robert Selter (Phillip Sanders), Margaret Morris (Alice Parker), John Wlliott (Senator Graham), Gordon De Main (Judge Parker), Fred 'Snowflake' Toones (Snowflake), Helen Gibson (Judd's Wife), Loie Bridge (Mrs. Perkins), Hank Bell (Hank Perkins).

The Silver Lining (April 16, 1932), *aka Big House for Girls*. Alan Grosland Production. 59 Minutes. **Director:** Alan Grosland. **Story:** Hal Conklin. . **Scenario:** Claire Corvalho. **Cast:** Maureen O'Sullivan (Joyce Moore), Betty Compson (Kate Flynn), John Warburton (Larry Clark), Montagu Love (Michael Moore), Mary Doran (Doris Lee), Cornelius Keefe (Jerry), Martha Mattox (Matron), Wally Allbright (Bobby O'Brien), Grace Valentine (Mrs. O'Brien), J. Frank Glendon (Judge), Jane Kerr (Matron), Mildred Golden (Ella Preston), Marion Stokes (Edna Joyce), Helen Gibson (Dorothy Dent), Willfred Lucas (Yacht Captain).

Law and Lawless (November 30, 1932), Western Star Productions, Majestic Pictures. 59 Minutes. **Director:** Armand Schaefer. **Story:** Oliver Drake. **Cast:** Jack Hoxie ('Montana'), Hilda Moreno (Rosita Lopez), Julian Rivero (Pancho Gonzales), Yakima Canutt (Tex Barnes), Jack Mower (Don Roberto Lopez), Hal Taliaferro (Buck Daggett), J. Frank Glendon ('Cash' Hopton), Edith Fellows (Betty Kelley), Bob Burns (Mr. Kelley), Helen Gibson (Mrs. Kelley), Dynamite the Horse (Dynamite, Montana's Horse).

King of the Arena (June 1, 1933), Universal Pictures. 59 Minutes. **Director:** Alan James. **Story:** Hal Berger. **Scenario:** Ray Bouk. **Cast:** Ken Maynard (Captain Ken Kenton), Lucile Browne (Mary Hiller), John St. Polis (Governor), Bob Kortman (Bargoff), Michael Visaroff (Baron Petroff), James A. Marcus (Colonel Hiller), Jack Rockwell (Ranger Jack Saunders), Frank Rice (Tin Star), Bobby Nelson (Jimmy Hiller) Helen Gibson (Circus Cowgirl), Tarzan (Tarzan – Ken's Horse).

Tugboat Annie (August 4, 1933), Metro-Goldwyn-Mayer. 86 Minutes. **Director:** Mervyn LeRoy. **Story:** Norman Reilly Raine, Zelda Sears. **Cast:** Marie Dressler (Annie Brennan), Wallace Beery (Terry Brennan), Robert Young (Alexander Brennan), Maurine O'Sullivan (Patricia Severn), Willard Robertson (Red Severn), Frankie Darro (Alexander as a child) and Helen Gibson (Stunt double for Marie Dressler).

Wheels of Destiny (March 1, 1934), Ken Maynars Productions, Inc. 64 Minutes. **Director:** Alan James. **Story:** Nate Gatzert. **Cast:** Ken Maynard (Ken Manning), Dorothy Dix (Mary Collins), Philo McCullough (Rocky), Frank Rice (Pinwheel), Jay Wilsey (Bill Collins), Edward Coxen (Dad Collins), Fred Sales Jr. (Freddie Collins), Fred MacKaye (Henchman Red), Jack Rockwell (Ed), William Gould (Deacon), Nelson McDowell (Trapper), Chief John Big Tree (Chief War Eagle), Helen Gibson (Settler's Wife), Tarzan (Tarzan – Ken's Horse).

Rocky Rhodes (September 24, 1934), Buck Jones Productions, Universal Pictures. 64 Minutes. **Director:** Alfred Raboch. **Story:** W.C. Tuttle. **Scenario:** Edward Churchill. **Cast:** Buck Jones ('Rocky' Rhodes), Sheila Terry (Nan Street), Stanley Fields (Harp Haverty), Walter Miller (Dan Murtch), Alfred P. James (John Street, Nan's Father), Paul Fix (Joe Hilton), Lydia Knott (Mrs. Rhodes, "Rocky's" Mother), Lee Shumway (Henchman Stark), Jack Rockwell (Sheriff Reed), Carl Stockdale (Lawyer Bowles), Monte Montague (Henchman Jake), Bud Osborne (Henchman 'Red'), Harry Semels (Dick Boggs), Helen Gibson (Townswoman), Silver (Silver – 'Rocky's' Horse).

The Way of the West (October 15, 1934), Superior Talking Pictures. 55 Minutes. **Director:** Robert Emmett Tansey. **Story:** Barry Barringer. **Dialogue:** Robert Emmett Tansey. **Cast:** Hal Taliaferro (Wally Gordon), Bobby Nelson (Bobby Parker), Myria Bratton ('Firey'). Fred Parker ('Dad'), James Sheridan ('Skipy'), William Desmond ('Cash' Horton), Art Mix (Tim), Bill Pattor (Buck), Jack Jones (Sheriff #2 – Jed Hampton), Harry Beery (Older Cowhand), Helen Gibson (Townswoman), Tiny Skeltor (Tiny), Gene Layman (Jeff Thompson) and Jimmy Aubrey (Sheriff #1 – Bartender Jim).

365 Nights in Hollywood (December 10, 1934), Fox Film Corporation. 77 Minutes. **Director:** George Marshall. **Story:** William H. Conselman, Henry Johnson. **Cast:** James Dunn (James 'Jimmy' Dale), Alice Faye (Alice Perkins), Frank Mitchell (Percy), Jack Durant (Clarence), John Bradford (Adrian Almont), Grant Mitchell (J. Walter Delmar), Frank Melton (Frank Young), John Qualen (Prof. Herman Ellenbogen), Helen Gibson (Student Actress).

Cyclone of the Saddle (April 3, 1935), Argosy Production Coroporation, Weiss Productions. 53 Minutes. **Director:** Elmer Clifton. **Story:** Elmer Clifton, George M. Merrick. **Cast:** Rex Lease (Andy Thomas), Janet Chandler (Suzanne 'Sue' Carter), Bobby Nelson (Dickie Carter), Helen Gibson ('Ma' Carter), Yakima Canutt (Snake), Milburn Morante (Bison – the old timer), Chief Thunderbird (Thundercloud), George Cheseboro (Cherokee Charlie), Art Mix (Wagon Train Member), William Desmond (Wagon Master Blaine), Black Fox (Black Fox – Dickie's Horse).

Bride of Frankenstein (April 22, 1935), Universal Pictures. 75 Minutes. **Director:** James Whale. **Story:** Mary Shelley. **Scenario:** William Hurlbut. **Cast:** RBoris Karloff (The Monster), Colin Clive (Henry Frankenstein), Valerie Hobson (Elizabeth), Ernst Thesiger (Doctor Pretorius), Elsa Lanchester (The Monster's Bride), Gavin Gordon (Lord Byron), Douglas Walton (Percy Bysshe Shelley), Una O'Connor (Minnie), E.E. Clive (Burgomaster), Lucien Prival (Butler), O.P. Heggie (Hermit), Dwight Frye (Karl), Reginald Barlow (Hans), Mary Gordon (Han's Wife), Helen Gibson (Uncredited Villager), Anne Darling (Shepherdess).

Fighting Caballero (May 5, 1935), Weiss Productions. 65 Minutes. **Director:** Elmer Clifton. **Story:** Elmer Clifton, George M. Merrick. **Cast:** Rex Lease (Joaquin Florenz), Dorothy Gulliver (Pat), Earl Douglas (Pedro), George Cheseboro ('Devil' Jackson), Robert Walker (Henchman Bull), Hal Taliaferro (Henchman Wildcat), Milburn Morante (Alkall Potts), George Morrell (Mayor Si Jenkins), Pinky Barnes (Beetle – Mine Watchman), Carl Mathews (Jose Rodriquez), Barney Furey (Sheriff), Helen Gibson (Drusella Jenkins), Franklyn Farnum (Bartender).

The Drunkard (September 2, 1935), Weiss Productions. 63 Minutes. **Director:** Albert Herman. **Story:** Al Martin. **Screenplay:** William H. Smith. **Cast:** James Murray (Edward Middleton), Clara Kimball Young (Mrs. Karns), Janet Chandler (Mary Wilson), Bryant Washburn (Mr. Karns), Theodore Lorch (Lawyer Squire Gibbs), 'Snub' Pollard (Property Man), Rosemary Theby (Mrs. Jackson), Pat O'Malley (First Drunk), Vera Stedman (Telephone Operator), Gertrude Astor (Peggy), Eric Mayne)Artie Rencelaw), George Stewart (William Dowton), Victor Potel (Farmer Gates), Joseph De Grasse (Mr. Miller), Jerome Storm (Second Drunk), Helen Gibson (Uncredited).

Custer's Last Stand (January 2, 1936), Weiss Productions. Fifteen-chapter serial. **Director:** Elmer Clifton. **Story:** George Arthur Durlam, Eddie Granemann. **Cast:** Rex Lease (Kit Cardigan – John C. Cardigan), Lona Andre (Belle Meade), William Farnum (James Fitzpatrick), Ruth Mix (Elizabeth Custer), Jack Mulhall (Lt. Cook), Nancy Caswell (Barbara Trent), George Cheseboro (Lt. Frank Roberts), Dorothy Gulliver (Red Fawn), Frank McGlynn Jr. (General George Custer), Helen Gibson (Calamity Jane), Josef Swickard (Major Henry Trent MD), Chief Thundercloud (Young Wolf), Reed Howes (Tom 'Keen' Blade), Bobby Nelson (Bobby Trent).

CH. 1: *Perils of the Plains* (1/2/36), two reels
CH. 2: *Thundering Hoofs* (1/9/36), two reels
CH. 3: *Fires of Vengeance* (1/16/36), two reels
CH. 4: *The Ghosts Dancers* (1/23/36), two reels
CH. 5: *Trapped* (1/30/36), two reels
CH. 6: *Human Wolves* (2/6/36), two reels
CH. 7: *Demons of Disaster* (2/13/36), two reels
CH. 8: *White Treachery* (2/20/36), two reels
CH. 9: *Circle of Death* (2/27/36), two reels
CH. 10: *Flaming Arrow* (3/6/36), two reels
CH. 11: *Warpath* (3/13/36), two reels
CH. 12: *Firing Squad* (3/20/36), two reels
CH. 13: *Red Panthers* (3/27/36), two reels
CH. 14: *Custer's Last Ride* (4/3/36), two reels
CH. 15: *The Last Stand* (4/10/36), two reels

The Lawless Nineties (February 15, 1936), Republic Pictures. 55 Minutes. **Director:** Joseph Kane. **Screenplay:** Joseph F. Poland. **Cast:** John Wayne (John Tipton), Ann Rutherford (Janet Carter), Harry Woods (Charles K. Plummer), George 'Gabby' Hayes (Major Carter), Al Bridge (Steele), Fred 'Snowflake' Toones (Moses), Etta McDaniel (Mandy Lou Schaefer), Tom Brower (Marshal Bowen), Lane Chandler (Bridger), Cliff Lyons (Davis), Jack Rockwell (Smith), Al Taylor (Red), Charles King (Hartley), George Cheseboro (Green), Tracy Layne (Belden), Helen Gibson (Townswoman).

Lady of Secrets (February 21, 1936), Columbia Pictures Corporations.. 73 Minutes. **Director:** Marion Gering. **Story:** Zoe Akins, Joseph Anthony. **Cast:** Ruth Chatterton (Celia Whittaker), Otto Kruger (David), Lionel Atwill (Mr. Whittaker), Marian Marsh (Joan), Lloyd Nolan (Michael), Robert Allen (Richard Terrance), Dorothy Appleby (Erma), Wade Boteler (Steamship Employment Manager), Nana Bryant (Aunt Harriet), Esther Dale (Miss Eccles), Ann Doran (Reporter), Jessie McAllister (Mother), Ivan Miller (Real Estate Agent), Elisabeth Risdon (Mrs. Emily Whittaker), Paul Weigel (Dr Claudel), Helen Gibson (Nurse).

Last of the Warrens (May 10, 1936), Supreme Pictures. 60 Minutes. **Director:** Robert N. Bradbury. **Story:** Robert N. Bradbury. **Cast:** Bob Steele (Ted Warren), Margaret Marquis (Mary Burns), Charles King (Kent), Horace Murphy (Grizzly), Lafe McKee (Sheriff Bates), Charles K. French (Bruce Warren), Helen Gibson (Mrs. Burns), Blackie Whiteford (Slip Gerns), Steve Clark (Spike).

Winds of the Wasteland (July 6, 1936), Republic Pictures. 54 Minutes. **Director:** Mack V. Wright. **Screenplay:** Joseph F. Poland. **Cast:** John Wayne (John Blair), Phyllis Cerf (Barbara Forsythe), Lew Kelly (Rocky O'Brien), Douglas Cosgrove (Cal Drake), Lane Chandler (Larry Adams), Sam Flint (Dr. William Forsythe), Bob Kortman (Cherokee Joe), Ed Cassidy (Mr. Dodge), Jon Hall (Jim – Pony Express Rider), Merrill McCormack (Henchman Pete), Christian J. Frank (Telegraph Crew Chief), Jack Rockwell (Buchanan City Marshal), Arthur Millett (Buchanan City Postmaster) Tracy Layne (Reed), Helen Gibson (Settler's Wife).

Jungle Jim (January 18, 1937), Universal Pictures. Twelve-chapter serial. **Director:** Ford Beebe, Clifford Smith. **Story:** Alex Raymond. **Screenplay:** Wyndham Gittens, Norman S. Hall and Ray Trampe. **Cast:** Grant Withers ('Jungle Jim' Bradley), Betty Jane Rhodes (Joan Redmond), Raymond Hatton (Malay Mike), Evelyn Brent (Shanghai Lil), Henry Brandon (The Cobra), Bryant Washburn (Bruce Redmond), Claude King (Territorial Consul Gilbert), Selmer Jackson (Attorney Tyler), Al Bridge (Slade), Paul Sutton (LaBat), Al Duvall (Kolu), Frank Mayo (Tom Redmond), J.P. McGowan (Ship Captain J.S. Robinson), Frank McGlynn Jr. (Red Hallihan), Helen Gibson (Mrs. Raymond).

CH. 1: *Into the Lion's Den* (1/18/37), two reels
CH. 2: *The Cobra Strikes* (1/25/37), two reels
CH. 3: *The Menacing Herd* (2/1/37), two reels
CH. 4: *The Killer's Trail* (2/8/37), two reels
CH. 5: *The Bridge of Terror* (2/15/37), two reels
CH. 6: *Drums of Doom* (2/22/37), two reels
CH. 7: *The Earth Trembles* (3/1/37), two reels
CH. 8: *The Killer Lion* (3/8/37), two reels
CH. 9: *The Devil Bird* (3/15/37), two reels
CH. 10: *Descending Doom* (3/22/37), two reels
CH. 11: *In the Cobra's Coils* (3/29/37), two reels
CH. 12: *The Last Safari* (4/5/37), two reels

High, Wide, and Handsome (October 24, 1937), Paramount Pictures. 110 Minutes. **Director:** Rouben Mamoulian. **Story:** Oscar Hammerstein II, George O'Nell. **Cast:** Irene Dunne (Sally Watterson), Randolph Scott (Peter Cortlandt), Dorothy Lamour (Molly Fuller), Elizabeth Patterson (Grandma Cortlandt), Raymond Walburn (Doc Watterson), Charles Bickford (Red Scanlon), Akim Tamiroff (Joe Varese), Ben Blue (Zeke), William Frawley (Mac), Alan Hale (Walt Brennan), Irving Pichel (Mr. Stark), Stanley Andrews (Lem Moulton), James Burke (Stackpole), Roger Imhof (Pop Bowers), Lucien Littlefield (Mr. Lippincott), Helen Gibson (Uncredited).

Danger Valley (November 3, 1937), Monogram Pictures. 58 Minutes. **Director:** Robert N. Bradbury. **Story and Screenplay:** Robert Emmett Tansey. **Cast:** Addison Randall, (Jack Bruce), Lois Wilde (Mickey Temple), Hal Price (Sidekick Lucky), Charles King (Dana), Earl Dwire (Hardrock), Earnie Adams (Soapy), Jimmy Aubrey (Australia), Ed Brady (Jake Reed), Frank LaRue (Pappy Temple), Chick Hannon (Joe), Helen Gibson (Nana Temple), Merrill McCormick (Henchman).

The Old Barn Dance (January 29, 1938), Republic Pictures. 54 Minutes. **Director:** Joseph Kane. **Screenplay:** Bernard McCo-nville and Charles F. Royal. **Cast:** Gene Autry (Gene Autry), Smiley Burnette (Frog Millhouse), Joan Valerie (Sally Dawson), Sammy McKim (Johnny Dawson), Walt Shrum and his Colorado Hillbillies (Musicians), The Stafford Sisters (Comic Singing Trio), Maple City Four (Comic Singers), Roy Rogers (Singer), Ivan Miller (Mr. Thornton), Earl Dwire (Clem Handley), Hooper Atchley (Maxwell), Ray Bennett (Buck), Carleton Young (Peabody), Frankie Marvin (Cowboy), Earl Hodgins (Terwilliger), Helen Gibson (Woman at Dance).

Condemned Women (March 18, 1938), RKO Radio Pictures. 77 Minutes. **Producer:** Robert Sisk. **Director:** Lew Landers. **Story and Screenplay:** Lionel Houser. **Cast:** Sally Ellers (Linda Wilson), Louis Hayward (Dr. Phillip Duncan), Anne Shirley (Millie Anson), Esther Dale (Mrs. Clara Glover, Head Matron), Lee Patrick ('Big Annie' Barry), Leona Roberts (Kate Holt), George Irving (Warden Edmund Miller), Richard Bond (David), Netta Packer (Sarah Norton), Rita La Roy (Cora), Florence Lake (Prisoner), Helen Gibson (Matron).

Flaming Frontiers (July 5, 1938), Universal Pictures. Fifteen-chapter serial. **Director:** Alan James. **Story:** Peter B. Kyne. **Screenplay:** Wyndham Gittens. **Cast:** Johnny Mack Brown (Tex Houston), Eleanor Hansen (Mary Grant), John Archer (Tom Grant), William Royle (Henchman Jim Crosby), Charles Middleton (Ace Daggett), James Blaine (Bart Eaton), Charles Stevens (Henchman Breed), Jack Rutherford (Buffalo Bill Cody), Eddy Waller (Andy Grant), Ed Cassidy (Henchman Joe), Karl Hackett (Jake), Jim Farley (Hawkins), Horace Murphy (Sheriff), Pat J. O'Brien (Henchman) Helen Gibson (Uncredited – Chapter 9).

CH. 1: *The River Runs Red* (7/5/38), two reels
CH. 2: *Death Rides the Wind* (7/12/38), two reels
CH. 3: *Treachery at Eagle Pass* (7/19/38), two reels
CH. 4: *A Night of Terror* (7/26/38), two reels
CH. 5: *Blood and Gold* (8/2/38), two reels
CH. 6: *Trapped by Fire* (8/9/38), two reels
CH. 7: *A Human Target* (8/16/38), two reels
CH. 8: *The Savage Horde* (8/23/38), two reels
CH. 9: *Toll of the Torrent* (8/30/38), two reels
CH. 10: *In the Claws of the Cougar* (9/6/38), two reels
CH. 11: *The Half-Breed's Revenge* (9/13/38), two reels
CH. 12: *The Indians are Coming* (9/20/38), two reels
CH. 13: *The Fatal Plunge* (9/27/38), two reels
CH. 14: *Dynamite* (10/4/38), two reels
CH. 15: *A Duel to Death* (10/11/38), two reels

Stagecoach (March 2, 1939), Walter Wanger Productions. 96 Minutes. **Director:** John Ford. **Story:** Ernst Haycox. **Screenplay:** Dudley Nichols. **Cast:** John Wayne (Ringo Kid), Claire Trevor (Dallas), Andy Devine (Buck), John Carradine (Hatfield), Thomas Mitchell (Doc Boone), Louis Pratt (Lucy Mallory), George Bancroft (Curley), Donald Meek (Peacock), Berton Churchill (Gatewood), Tim Holt (Lieutenant), Tom Tyler (Luke Plummer), Helen Gibson (Girl in Saloon).

Southward Ho (March 19, 1939), Republic Pictures. 58 Minutes.. **Director:** Joseph Kane. **Story:** Gerald Geraghty and Jack Natteford. **Cast:** Roy Rogers (Roy), Lynne Roberts (Ellen Denbigh), George 'Gabby' Hayes (Gabby Whitaker), Wade Boteler (Colonel Denbigh), Arthur Loft (Captain Jeffries), Lane Chandler (Jim Crawford), Tom London (Union Sergeant), Charles R. Moore (Skeeter), Ed Brady (Mears), Helen Gibson (Mrs. Crawford).

The Oregon Trail (July 4, 1939), Universal Pictures. Fifteen-chapter serial. **Director:** Ford Beebe, Saul A. Goodkind. **Story:** George H. Plympton. **Screenplay:** Basil Dickey. **Cast:** Johnny Mack Brown (Jeff Scott), Louise Stanley (Margaret Mason), Fuzzy Knight (Deadwood Hawkins), Bill Cody Jr. (Jimmie Clark), Edward LeSaint (John Mason), James Blaine (Sam Morgan), Charles Stevens (Breed), Jack C. Smith (Bull Bragg), Roy Barcroft (Colonel Custer), Charles Murphy (Tompkins), Colin Kenny (Slade), Forrest Taylor (Daggett), Charles King (Dirk), Jim Toney (Idaho Ike), Helen Gibson (Wagon Train Pioneer – Chapter 6).

CH. 1: *The Renegade's Revenge* (7/4/39), two reels
CH. 2: *The Flaming Forest* (7/11/39), two reels
CH. 3: *The Brink of Disaster* (7/18/39), two reels

CH. 4: *Thundering Doom* (7/25/39), two reels
CH. 5: *Stampede* (8/1/39), two reels
CH. 6: *Indian Vengeance* (8/8/39), two reels
CH. 7: *Trail of Treachery* (8/15/39), two reels
CH. 8: *Redskin's Revenge* (8/22/39), two reels
CH. 9: *The Avalanche of Doom* (8/29/39), two reels
CH. 10: *The Plunge of Peril* (9/5/39), two reels
CH. 11: *Trapped in the Flames* (9/12/39), two reels
CH. 12: *The Bated Trap* (9/19/39), two reels
CH. 13: *Crashing Timbers* (9/26/39), two reels
CH. 14: *Death in the Night* (10/3/39), two reels
CH. 15: *The End of the Trail* (10/10/39), two reels

New Frontier (August 10, 1939), Republic Pictures. 57 Minutes.. **Director:** George Sherman. **Screenplay:** Betty Burbridge and Luci Ward. **Cast:** John Wayne (Stoney Brooke), Ray Corrigan (Tucson Smith), Raymond Hatton (Rusty Joslin), Jennifer Jones (Celia Braddock), Eddy Waller (Major Steven Braddock), Sammy McKim (Stevie Braddock), LeRoy Mason (M.C. Gilbert), Harrison Greene (William Proctor), Reginald Barlow (Judge Bill Lawson), Burr Caruth (Doctor William Hall), Dave O'Brien (Jason Braddock), Hal Price (Sheriff), Jack Ingram (Harmon), Bud Osborne (Dickson), Slim Whitaker (Jed Turner), Helen Gibson (Jed's Wife).

The Marshal of Mesa City (November 3, 1939), RKO Radio Pictures. 62 Minutes.. **Director:** David Howard. **Screenplay:** Jack Lait Jr. **Cast:** George O'Brien (Cliff Mason), Virginia Vale (Virginia King), Leon Ames (Sheriff Jud Cronin), Henry Brandon (Duke Allison), Lloyd Ingraham (Mayor Sam Bentley), Helen Gibson (Mrs. Bentley), Slim Whitaker (Jake Morris), Joe McGuinn (Pete Henderson), Mary Gordon (Mrs. Dudley), Frank Ellis (Slim Walker).

Saga of Death Valley (November 17, 1939), Republic Pictures. 58 Minutes.. **Director:** Joseph Kane. **Screenplay:** Karen De-Wolf and Stuart Anthony. **Cast:** Roy Rogers (Roy Rogers), George 'Gbby' Hayes (Gabby Whittaker), Don 'Red' Barry (Jerry), Doris day (Ann Meredith), Frank M. Thomas (Ed Tasker), Jack Ingram (Brace), Hal Taliaferro (Rex), Lew Kelly (Meredith), Fern Emmett (Miss Minnie), Tommy baker (Roy as a Boy), Helen Gibson (Woman at Party).

Cowboys from Texas (November 29, 1939), Republic Pictures. 54 Minutes. **Director:** George Sherman. **Story:** William Colt MacDonald. **Screenplay:** Oliver Drake. **Cast:** Robert Livingston (Stony Brooke), Raymond Hatton (Rusty Joslin), Duncan Renaldo (Renaldo), Carole Landis (June Jones), Charles Middleton (Kansas Jones), Ivan Miller (Clay Allison), Betty Compson (Belle Starkey), Ethan Laidlaw (Duke Plummer), Yakima Canutt (Tex Dawson), Walter Wills (Jeff Morgan), Ed Cassidy (Jed Tyler), Helen Gibson (Settler).

Covered Wagon Trails (April 10, 1940), Monogram Pictures. 52 Minutes. **Director:** Bernard B. Ray. **Story:** Tom Gibson. **Screenplay:** Tom Gibson. **Cast:** Addison Randall (Jack Cameron), Sally Cairns (Carol Bradford), David Sharpe (Ed Cameron), Lafe McKee (John Bradford), Budd Buster (Sidekick Manny), Glen Strange (Fletcher), Kenne Duncan (Blaine), George Cheseboro (Carter), Carl Mathews (Nixon), Jimmy Aubrey (Denton), Frank Ellis (J.P. Allen), John Elliott (Rancher Beaumont), Tex Terry (Friend of Fletcher), Hank Bell (Sheriff), Helen Gibson (Woman in Wagon Train).

Deadwood Dick (July 19, 1940), Columbia Pictures Corporation. Fifteen-chapter serial. **Director:** James W. Horne. **Screenplay:** Wyndham Gittens and Morgan Cox.. **Cast:** Donald Douglas Dick Stanley – aka Deadwood Dick), Lorna Gray (Anne Butler), Harry Harvey (Dave Miller), Marin Sais (Calamity Jane), Lane Chandler (Wild Bill Hickok), Jack Ingram (Buzz Ricketts), Charles King (Tex), Ed Cassidy (Tennison Drew), Robert Fiske (Ashton), Lee Shumway (Bentley), Helen Gibson (Uncredited)

CH. 1: *A Wild West Empire* (7/19/40), two reels
CH. 2: *Who Is the Skull* (7/26/40), two reels
CH. 3: *Pirates of the Plains* (8/2/40), two reels
CH. 4: *The Skull Baits a Trap* (8/9/40), two reels
CH. 5: *Win, Lose or Draw* (8/16/40), two reels
CH. 6: *Buried Alive* (8/23/40), two reels
CH. 7: *The Chariot of Doom* (8/30/40), two reels

CH. 8: *The Secret of Number Ten* (9/6/40), two reels
CH. 9: *The Fatal Warning* (9/13/40), two reels
CH. 10: *Framed for Murder* (9/20/40), two reels
CH. 11: *The Bucket of Death* (9/27/40), two reels
CH. 12: *A Race Against Time* (10/4/40), two reels
CH. 13: *The Arsenal of Revolt* (10/11/40), two reels
CH. 14: *Holding the Fort* (10/18/40), two reels
CH. 15: *The Deadwood Express* (10/25/40), two reels

Young Bill Hickok (October 21, 1940), Republic Pictures. 59 Minutes.. **Director:** Joseph Kane. **Screenplay:** Norton S. Parker and Olive Cooper. **Cast:** Roy Rogers (Wild Bill Hickok), George 'Gabby' Hayes (Gabby Whitaker), Julie Bishop (Louise Mason), John Miljan (Nicholas Tower), Sally Payne (Calamity Jane), Archie Twitchell (Phillip), Monte Blur (Marshal Evans), Hal Taliaferro (Morrell), Ethel Wales (Mrs. Stout), Jack Ingram (Red Burke), Helen Gibson (Relay Station Woman).

The Trail Blazers (November 11, 1940), Republic Pictures. 58 Minutes. **Director:** George Sherman. **Story:** William Colt MacDonald. **Screenplay:** Barry Shipman. **Cast:** Robert Livingston (Stony Brooke), Bob Steele (Tucson Smith), Rufe Davis (Lullaby Joslin), Pauline Moore (Marcia Kelton), Weldon Heyburn (Jeff Bradley), Carol Nye (Jim Chapman), Tom Chatterton (Major R.C. Kelton), Si Jenks (T.L. Johnson), Mary Field (Alice Chapman), John Merton (Mason), Rex Lease (Reynolds), Robert Blair (Stage Passenger), Helen Gibson (Woman at Ceremony).

The Sing Hill (April 26, 1941), Republic Pictures. 54 Minutes. **Director:** Lew Landers. **Story:** Jesse Lasky Jr. and Richard Murphy. **Cast:** Gene Autry (Gene Autry), Smiley Burnette (Frog), Virginia Dale (Jo Adams), Mary Lee (Patsy), Spencer Charters (Judge Henry Starrbottle), Gerald Oliver Smith ('Dada' the Butler), George Meeker (John R. Ramsey), Wade Boteler (Pop Sloan), Henry Stubbs (James Morgan), Cactus Mack (Cactus Mack), Jack Kirk (Flint), Helen Gibson (Emmy).

Sheriff of Tombstone (May 2, 1941), Republic Pictures. 54 Minutes. **Director:** Joseph Kane. **Story:** James Webb and Oliver Cooper. **Cast:** Roy Rogers (Brett Starr), George 'Gabby' Hayes (Judge Gabby Whitaker), Elyse Knox (Mary Carson), Addison Richards (Major Luke Keeler), Sally Payne (Queenie Whitaker), Harry Woods (Shotgun Cassidy), Zeffie Tilbury (Granny Carson), Hal Taliaferro (A.J. Slade), Jay Novello (John Anderson), Jack Ingram (Bill Starr), Helen Gibson (Liza Starr).

Jackass Mail (July 1, 1942), Metro Goldwyn Mayer. 78 Minutes. **Director:** Norman Z. McLeod. **Story:** C. Gardner Sullivan. **Screenplay:** Lawrence Hazard. **Cast:** Wallace Beery (Marmaduke 'Just' Baggot)**,** Marjorie Main (Clementine 'Tina' Tucker)**,** J. Carrol Naish (Signor Michel O'Sullivan), Darryl Hickman (Tommy Gargan), William Haade (Red Gargan), Dick Curtis (Jim Swade) and Helen Gibson (Stunt double for Marjorie Main).

The Sombrero Kid (July 31, 1942), Republic Pictures. 56 Minutes. **Director:** George Sherman. **Story:** Norman S. Hall. **Cast:** Don 'Red' Barry (Jerry Holden), Lynn Merrick (Dorothy Russell), Robert Homans (Marshal Thomas Holden), John James (Tommy Holden), Joel Friedkin (Uriah Martin), Stuart Hamblen (Smoke Denton), Robert McKenzie (Judge tater), Slim Andrews (Panamint), Anne O'Neal (Mrs. Barnett), Helen Gibson (Mrs. Lane).

The Valley of Vanishing Men (December 17, 1942), Columbia Pictures Corporation. Fifteen-chapter serial. **Director:** Spencer Gordon Bennet. **Screenplay:** Harry L. Fraser and Lewis Clay. **Cast:** Bill Elliott (Wild Bill Tolliver), Slim Summerville (Missouri Benson), Carmen Morales (Consuelo Ramirez), Kenneth MacDonald (Jonathan Kincaid), Jack Ingram (Butler), George Cheseboro (Taggart), John Shay (Mullins), Tom London (Slater), Arno Frey (Colonel Engler), Lane Chandler (Major Stacy Roberts), Roy Barcroft (Deputy Luke Lucas), Helen Gibson (Townswoman).

CH. 1: *Trouble in Canyon City* (12/17/42), two reels
CH. 2: *The Mystery of Ghost City* (12/24/42), two reels
CH. 3: *Danger Walks by Night* (12/31/42), two reels
CH. 4: *Hillside Horror* (1/7/43), two reels
CH. 5: *Guns in the Night* (1/15/43), two reels
CH. 6: *The Bottomless Well* (1/22/43), two reels
CH. 7: *The Man in the Gold Mask* (1/29/43), two reels
CH. 8: *When the Devil Drives* (2/5/43), two reels

CH. 9: *The Traitor's Shroud* (2/12/43), two reels
CH. 10: *Death Strikes at Seven* (2/19/43), two reels
CH. 11: *Satan in the Saddle* (2/26/43), two reels
CH. 12: *The Mine of Missing Men* (3/5/43), two reels
CH. 13: *Danger on Dome Rock* (3/12/43), two reels
CH. 14: *The Door that Has No Key* (3/19/43), two reels
CH. 15: *Empire's End* (3/26/43), two reels

The Blocked Trail (March 12, 1943), Republic Pictures. 55 Minutes. **Director:** Elmer Clifton. **Story:** John K. Butler and Jacquin Frank. **Cast:** Bob Steele (Tucson Smith), Tom Tyler (Stony Brooke), Jimmy Dodd (Lullaby Joslin), Helen Deverell (Ann Martin), George G. Lewis (Freddy), Walter Soderling ('Mad' Martin), Charles Miller (Frank Nolan), Kermit Maynard (Reese), Pierce Lyden (Rankin), Carl Mathews (Lon), Hal Price (Sheriff Pillsbury), Budd Buster (Deputy McGee), Helen Gibson (Townswoman), Brillant (Brillant – Martin's Horse).

The Climax (October 22, 1944), Universal Pictures. 86 Minutes. **Director:** George Waggner. **Story:** Edward Locke. **Screenplay:** Curt Slodmak. **Cast:** Boris Karloff (Dr. Friedrich Hohner), Susanna Foster (Angela Klatt), Turhan Bey (Franz Munzer), Gale Sondergaard (Luise), Thomas Gomez (Count Seebruck), June Vincent (Marcellina), George Dolenz (Amato Roselli), Ludwig Stossel (Carl Baumann), Jane Farrar (Jarmila Vadek), Erno Verebes (Brunn), Lotte Stein (mama Hinzi), Scotty Beckett (The King), William Edmunds (Leon), Helen Ginson (Role Undetermined).

The Scarlet Horseman (January 22, 1946), Universal Pictures. Thirteen-chapter serial. **Director:** Lewis D, Collins, Ray Taylor. **Story:** Tom Gibson and Patricia Harper. **Opening Narration**: Milburn Stone. **Cast:** Peter Cookson (Kirk Norris), Paul Guilfoyle (Jim Bannion), Janet Shaw (Elise Halliday), Virginia Christine (Carla Marguette), Victoria Horne (Loma), Cy Kendall (Amigo Manana), Edward Howard (Zero Quick), Harold Goodman (Idaho Jones), Danny Morton (Ballou), Helen Bennett (Mrs Ruth Halliday), Jack Ingram (Tragg), Edmund Cobb (Kyle), Guy Wilkerson (Panhandle), Al Woods (Senator Mark Halliday), Fred Coby (Tioga), Helen Gibson (Townswoman).

CH. 1: *Scarlet for a Champion* (1/22/46), two reels
CH. 2: *Dry Grass Danger* (1/29/46), two reels
CH. 3: *Railroad Rescue* (2/5/46), two reels
CH. 4: *Staked Plains Stampede* (2/12/46), two reels
CH. 5: *Death Shifts Passengers* (2/19/46), two reels
CH. 6: *Stop that Stage* (2/26/46), two reels
CH. 7: *Blunderbuss Broadside* (3/5/46), two reels
CH. 8: *Scarlet Doublecross* (3/12/46), two reels
CH. 9: *Doom Beyond the Door* (3/19/46), two reels
CH. 10: *The Edge of Danger* (3/26/46), two reels
CH. 11: *Comanche Avalanche* (4/2/46), two reels
CH. 12: *Staked Plains Massacre* (4/9/46), two reels
CH. 13: *Scarlet Showdown* (4/16/46), two reels

Cheyenne Cowboy (February 2, 1949), Universal International Pictures. 25 Minutes. **Director:** Nate Watt. **Story:** Luci Ward. **Cast:** Tex Williams (Buck McCloud), Lina Romay (Kate Harman), Smokey Rogers (Smokey), Deuce Spriggins (Deuce), Stanley Andrews (Ace Harmon), Riley Hill (Jud Keller), Helen Gibson (Cookie).

Outcasts of the Trail (June 8, 1949), Republic Pictures. 59 Minutes. **Director:** Phillip Ford. **Story:** Olive Cooper. **Cast:** Monte Hale (Pat Garrett), Paul Hurst (Doc Meadowlark), Jeff Donnell (Vinnie White), Roy Barcroft (Jin Judd), John Gallaudet (Ivory White), Milton Parsons (Ellas Dunkenscold), Tommy Ivo (Chad White), Minerva Urecal (Abbie Rysen), Ted Mapes (Fred Smith), George Lloyd (Horace Rysen), Steve Darrell (Sheriff Wilson), Helen Gibson (Woman with Boy).

Crooked River (June 9, 1950), Lippert Pictures. 56 Minutes. **Director:** Thomas Carr. **Story:** Ron Ormond. **Screenplay:** Maurice Tombragel. **Cast:** James Ellison (Shamrock Ellison), Russell Hayden (Lucky Hayden), Raymond Hatton (Colonel), Fuzzy Knight (Deacon), Julie Adams (Ann Hayden), Tom Tyler (Weston), George J. Lewis (Gentry), John L. Cason (Kent), Stanley Price (Sheriff), Stephen Carr (Butch), Dennis Moore (Bob), George Cheseboro (Dad Ellison), Bud Osborne (Bud), Helen Gibson (Mrs. Ellison).

Fast on the Draw (June 30, 1950), *aka **Sudden Death***. Lippert Pictures. 55 Minutes. **Director:** Thomas Carr. **Story:** Ron Ormond. **Screenplay:** Maurice Tombragel. **Cast:** James Ellison (Shamrock Ellison), Russell Hayden (Lucky Hayden), Raymond Hatton (Colonel), Fuzzy Knight (Deacon), Julie Adams (Ann), Tom Tyler (Outlaw Leader), George J. Lewis (Pedro), John L. Cason (Tex), Stanley Price (Carter), Stephen Carr (Posse Member), Dennis Moore (Dick), George Cheseboro (Sam Ellison), Bud Osborne (Stage Driver), Helen Gibson (Mrs. Ellison).

Lonely Heart Bandits (August 29, 1950), Republic Pictures. 60 Minutes. **Director:** George Blair. **Story:** Gene Lewis. **Cast:** Dorothy Patrick (Louise Curtis), John Eldredge (Tony Morell), Barbara Fuller (Laurel Vernon), Robert Rockwell (Police Lt. Carroll), Ann Doran (Nancy Crane), Richard Travis (Aaron Hunt), Dorothy Granger (Duchess Belle), Eric Sinclair (Bobby Crane), Kathleen Freeman (Bertha Martin), Frank Kreig (Cal), Harry Cheshire (Sheriff Polk), William Schallert (Dave Clark), Howard Negley (Elmer Jayson), John Crawford (Stevedore), Eddie Dunn (Sheriff York), Helen Gibson (Minor Role).

Kansas Raiders (November 15, 1950), Universal International Pictures. 80 Minutes. **Director:** Ray Enright. **Story:** Robert L. Richards. **Cast:** Audie Murphy (Jesse James), Brian Donlevy (Colonel William Clark Quantrill), Marguerite Chapman (Kate Clarke), Scott Brady (Bill Anderson), Tony Curtis (Kit Dalton), Richard Arlen (Union Captain), Richard Long (Frank James), James Best (Cole Younger), John Kellogg (Red Leg Leader), Dewey Martin (James Younger), George Chandler (Willie), Charles Delaney (Pell), Richard Egan (First Lieutenant), David Wolfe (Rudolph Tate), Helen Gibson (Bit Role).

Fighting Coast Guard (June 1, 1951), Republic Pictures. 86 Minutes.. **Director:** Joseph Kane. **Story:** Charles Marquis Warren. **Screenplay:** Kenneth Gamet. **Cast:** Brian Donlevy (Commander McFarland), Forest Tucker (Bill Rourk), Ella Raines (Louise Ryan), John Russell (Barney Walker), Richard Jaeckel (Tony Jessup), William Murphy (Sandy Jessup), Martin Milner (Al Prescott), Steve Brody ('Red' Toon), Hugh O'Brian (Tom Peterson), Tom Powers (Admiral Ryan), Jack Pennick (Guardsman), Olin Howard (Clerk), Damian O'Flynn (Captain Adair), Morris Ankum (Navy Captain), James Flavin (Commander Rogers), Helen Gibson (Extra).

Hollywood Story (June 1, 1951), Universal International Pictures. 76 Minutes. **Director:** William Castle. **Story:** Frederick Kohner and Frederick Brady. **Cast:** Richard Conte (Larry O'Brien), Julie Adams (Sally Rousseau), Richard Egan (Police Lieutenant Bud Lennox), Henry Hull (Phillip Ferrara), Fred Clark (Sam Collyer), Jim Backus (Mitch Davis), Houseley Stevenson (Miller, Studio Guard), Francis X. Bushman (Himself as Old-time Movie Star), Betty Blythe (Herself as Old-time Movie Star), William Farnum (Himself as Old-time Movie Star), Helen Gibson (Herself as Old-time Movie Star) and Joel McCrea (Himself as Movie Star of Today).

The Dakota Kid (July 1, 1951), Republic Pictures. 60 Minutes. **Director:** Phillip Ford. **Story:** William Lively. **Screenplay:** Michael Chapin, Eilene Janssen and James Bell. **Cast:** Michael Chapin (Red), Eilene Janssen (Judy Dawson), James Bell (Sheriff White), Danny Morton (Dakota Kid), Margaret Field (Mary Lewis), Robert Shayne (Ace Crandall), Roy Barcroft (Turk Smith), Mauritz Hugo (Squire Mason), House Peters Jr. (Sam Dawson), Lee Bennett (Cole White), Holly Bane (Messenger), Helen Gibson (Woman at Party).

The Treasure of Lost Canyon (March 1, 1952), Universal International Pictures. 82 Minutes. **Director:** Ted Tetzlaff. **Story:** Brainerd Duffield. **Screenplay:** Charles Drake. **Cast:** William Powell ('Doc' Brown), Julie Adams (Myra Wade), Charles Drake (Jim Anderson), Rosemary DeCamp (Samuella), Tommy Ivo (David), Henry Hull (Lucas Cooke), Chubby Johnson (Baltimore Dan), John Doucette (Gyppo), Marvin Press (Pappy), Griff Barnett (Judge Wade), Helen Gibson (Mother).

Ma and Pa Kettle at Home (July 11, 1952), Universal International Pictures. 78 Minutes. **Director:** Charles Barton. **Story:** John Grant and Jack Henley. **Cast:** Marjorie Main (Phoebe 'Ma' Kettle), Percy Kilbride (Frank 'Pa' Kettle), James Best (Marvin Johnson), Lori Nelson (Rosie Kettle), Esther Dale (Birdie Hicks), Emory Parnell (Billy Reed), Oliver Blake (Geoduck), Russell Simpson (Clem Johnson), Rex Lease (Sheriff), Helen Gibson (Minor Role).

Horizons West (October 11, 1952), Universal International Pictures. 81 Minutes. **Director:** Budd Boetticher. **Story:** Louis Stevens. **Cast:** Robert Ryan (Dan Hammond), Julie Adams (Lorna Hardin), Rock Hudson (Neil Hammond), Judith Braun (Sally Eaton), John McIntire (Ira Hammond), Raymond Burr (Cord Hammond), James Arness (Tiny McGilligan), Dennis Weaver (Dandy Taylor), Frances Bavier (Martha Hammond), Tom Powers (Frank Tarleton), John Hubbard (Sam Hunter), Rodoifo Acosta (General Jose Escobar Lopez), Douglas Fowley (Ed Tompkins), Walter Reed (Layton), Raymond Greenleaf (Ed Dodson), Helen Gibson (Townswoman).

City That Never Sleeps (June 12, 1953), Republic Pictures. 90 Minutes. **Director:** John H. Auer. **Story:** Steve Fisher. **Cast:** Gig Young (Johnny Kelly), Mala Powers ('Angel Face' Connors), William Talman (Hayes Stewart), Edward Arnold (Penrod Biddel), Chill Wills (Sgt. Joe), Marie Windsor (Lydia Biddel), Paula Raymond (Kathy Kelly), Otto Hulett (Sgt. 'Pop' Kelly Sr.), Wally Cassell (Gregg Warren), Ron Hagerthy (Stubby Kelly), James Andelin (Lt. Parker), Tom Poston (Detective), Bunny Kacher (Agnes DuBois), Phillip L. Boddy (Maltre d'Hotel), Thomas Jones (Fancy Dan), Helen Gibson (Woman).

The Man From The Alamo (August 7, 1952), Universal International Pictures. 79 Minutes. **Director:** Budd Boetticher. **Story:** Steve Fisher. **Screenplay:** D.D. Beauchamp. **Cast:** Glenn Ford (John Stroud), Julie Adams (Beth Anders), Chill Wills (John Gage), Hugh O'Brien (Lt. Lamar), Victor Jory (Jess Wade), Neville Brand (Dawes), John Daheim (Cavish), Myra Marsh (Ma Anders), Jeanne Cooper (Kate Lamar), Marc Cavell (Carlos), Edward Norris (Mapes), Guy Williams (Sergeant), Helen Gibson (Woman on Train).

Ma and Pa Kettle at Home (March 10, 1954), Universal International Pictures. 80 Minutes. **Director:** Charles Lamont. **Story:** Kay Lenard. **Screenplay:** Kay Lenard. **Cast:** Marjorie Main (Phoebe 'Ma' Kettle), Percy Kilbride (Frank 'Pa' Kettle), Alan Mowbray (Alphonsus Mannering), Alice Kelley (Sally Maddocks), Brett Halsey (Elwin Kettle), Ross Elliott (Pete Crosby), Mary Wickes (Miss Wetter), Oliver Blake (Geoduck), Stan Ross (Crowbar), Emory Parnell (Billy Reed), Irving Bacon (John Maddocks), Virginia Brissac (Martha Maddocks), Richard Eyer (Billy Kettle), Helen Gibson (Ranch Wife).

The Man Who Shot Liberty Valance (April 22, 1962), Paramount Pictures, John Ford Productions. 123 Minutes. **Director:** John Ford. **Story:** James Warner Beliah. **Screenplay:** Willis Goldbeck. **Cast: John Wayne (Tom Doniphon), James Stewart (Ransom Stoddard), Vera Miles (Hallie Stoddard), Lee Marvin (Liberty Valance), Edmond O'Brien (Dutton Peabody), Andy Devine (Marshal Link Appleyard), Ken Murray (Doc Willoughby), John Carradine (Major Casslus Starbuckle), Jeanette Nolan (Nora Ericson), John Qualen (Peter Ericson), Willis Bouchey (Jason Tully), Carleton Young (Maxwell Scott), Woody Strode (Pompey), Denver Pyle (Amos Carruthers), Strother Martin (Floyd), Helen Gibson (Woman Driving the Wagon).**

Chapter Notes

Chapter One: Those Early Years 1891-1910

1. "101 Ranch Show Today," *St. Louis Republic*, April 16, 1910, p. 5.
2. "Mike Kornick, Helen Gibson, "In Very Early Days," *Films in Review*, January 1968, p. 28.
3. "Cleveland Girl Rides Steer Daily at Wild West Show," *Cleveland Plain Dealer*, June 25, 1911, p. 10.
4. Mike Kornick, Helen Gibson, "In Very Early Days," *Films in Review*, January 1968, p. 28.
5. "Twinkle, Twinkle, Buckeye Film Stars," *Cleveland Plain Dealer*, August 27, 1916, n.p.
6. Mike Kornick, Helen Gibson, "In Very Early Days," *Films in Review*, January 1968, p. 28.
7. "101 Ranch Show Today," *St. Louis Republic*, April 16, 1910, p. 5.
8. "Miller Bros Big 101 Ranch Show," *The Daily Courier*, May 5, 1910, p. 1.
9. "Wild West Thrills," *Baltimore Sun* [MD]," May 19, 1910, p. 14.
10. "Great Minnesota State Fair," *Austin Daily Herald* [TX], August 25, 1910, n.p.
11. "Mike Kornick, Helen Gibson, "In Very Early Days," *Films in Review*, January 1968, p. 28.

Chapter Two: Rose Meets Richard Edmund Gibson 1911 – 1913

1. "Escaped Steer is Proof Show is Here," *Boston Journal*, April 6, 1911, p. 11.
2. "Cleveland Girl Rides Steer Daily at Wild West Show," *Plain Dealer*, June 25, 1911, p. 10.
3. "Cowgirls With the Wild West Show," October 1911, Helen Gibson Scrapbook, from the Helen Gibson collection, Vancouver, Washington, p. 7.
4. Mike Kornick, Helen Gibson, "In Very Early Days," *Films in Review*, January 1968, p. 28.
5. Michael Wallis, "The Real Wild West," N.Y., St. Martin Griffin, 1998, p. 362.
6. Mike Kornick, Helen Gibson, "In Very Early Days," *Films in Review*, January 1968, p. 28.
7. "Wild West Show Leaves Winter Quarters," 1912, Helen Gibson Scrapbook, from the Helen Gibson collection, Vancouver, Washington, p. 8.
8. Mike Kornick, Helen Gibson, "In Very Early Days," *Films in Review*, January 1968, p. 28.
9. Mike Kornick, Helen Gibson, "In Very Early Days," *Films in Review*, January 1968, p. 28.
10. "The Isis Theater," *Idaho Statesman*, June 9, 1912, p. 6.
11. Mike Kornick, Helen Gibson, "In Very Early Days," *Films in Review*, January 1968, p. 28.
12. "The Girl of the Range," Moving Picture World, February 15, 1913, p. 710.
13. Mike Kornick, Helen Gibson, "In Very Early Days," *Films in Review*, January 1968, p. 29.
14. Mario DeMarco, Hoot Gibson: The Photostory of "The Dean of Cowboy Stars," DeMarco Publishing, p. 22.
15. Mario DeMarco, Hoot Gibson: The Photostory of "The Dean of Cowboy Stars," DeMarco Publishing, p. 18.
16. Mike Kornick, Helen Gibson, "In Very Early Days," *Films in Review*, January 1968, p. 29.
17. "Eastern Utah Advocate," *Stampede That Was a Stampede*, July 17, 1913, p. 2.
18. "Injured Rider Wins Bride," *Oregonian*, July 29, 1913, p. 3.
19. "Saturday's Round-Up at the Stampede," *Manitoba Free Press*, August 11, 1913, p. 10.
20. Mike Kornick, Helen Gibson, "In Very Early Days," *Films in Review*, January 1968, p. 29.
21. Gibsons Win New Honors at Boise, unknown newspaper, September 1913, Helen Gibson Scrapbook, from the Helen Gibson collection, Vancouver, Washington.
22. "Sunshine Puts Rainmakers in Clover," *Idaho Statesman*, September 24, 1913, p. 6.
23. "Cupid Ropes Ed "Hoot" Gibson," *East Oregonian*, September 8, 1913, p. 1.
24. Mike Kornick, Helen Gibson, "In Very Early Days," *Films in Review*, January 1968, p. 29.

Chapter Three: Rose Becomes Helen 1913 – 1915

1. Mike Kornick, Helen Gibson, "In Very Early Days," *Films in Review*, January 1968, p. 29.
2. "Opening Day Rodeo Events Make Hit with Large Crowd," *Dalles Weekly Chronicle*, October 16, 1913, n.p.

3. "Gibsons Win New Honors at Boise," unknown newspaper, September 1913, Helen Gibson Scrapbook, from the Helen Gibson collection Vancouver, Washington, n.p.

4. Mike Kornick, Helen Gibson, "In Very Early Days," *Films in Review*, January 1968, p. 29.

5. Mario DeMarco, Hoot Gibson: The Photostory of "The Dean of Cowboy Stars," DeMarco Publishing, p. 21.

6. Mike Kornick, Helen Gibson, "In Very Early Days," *Films in Review*, January 1968, p. 29.

7. Edgar M. Wyatt, "The Hoxie Boys," *Wyatt Classics, Inc.*, Raleigh, N.C., 1962, p. 20.

8. Rose Gibson, unknown newspaper, May 1913, Helen Gibson Scrapbook, from the Helen Gibson collection Vancouver, Washington.

9. "Tom Mix Falls Beneath Horses," *Seattle Daily Times*, May 11, 1915, p. 12.

10. Mike Kornick, Helen Gibson, "In Very Early Days," *Films in Review*, January 1968, p. 29.

11. Shirley Freitas, "The Two Helen's: Action Women in Film," Bitterroot Mountain Publishing, June 2011, p. 4.

12. Mike Kornick, Helen Gibson, "In Very Early Days," *Films in Review*, January 1968, p. 30.

13. Gibson, Rose, unknown newspaper, 1916, Helen Gibson Scrapbook, from the Helen Gibson collection, Vancouver, Washington, p 20.

14. "A Test of Courage," unknown newspaper, October 1915, Helen Gibson Scrapbook, from the Helen Gibson collection Vancouver, Washington, p. 3.

15. "A Test of Courage," Moving Picture World, October 9, 1915, p. 318

16. "A Mile A Minute," Moving Picture World, October 16, 1915, p. 500.

17. "Gibson's in Movies," unknown newspaper, November 1915, Helen Gibson Scrapbook, from the Helen Gibson collection Vancouver, Washington, p. 3.

18. "Rescue of the Brakeman's Children," Moving Picture World, November 13, 1915, p. 1311.

19. "Rescue of the Brakeman's Children," Moving Picture World, October 23, 1915, p. 666.

20. "Danger Ahead," *Miami Herald Record*, November 7, 1915, n.p.

21. "Danger Ahead," Moving Picture World, October 30a, 1915, p. 1016.

22. "The Girl and the Special," Moving Picture World, November 20, 1915, p. 1499.

23. "The Girl and the Special," Moving Picture World, November 6, 1915, p. 1190.

24. Freddie Film, "No Headline," *Tacoma Times*, December 27, 1915, p. 6.

25. "Helen Has A Birthday," Moving Picture World, November 27, 1915, p. 1638.

26. "The Girl on the Bridge," Moving Picture World, November 27, 1915, p. 1663.

27. "The Girl on the Bridge," Moving Picture World, November 6, 1915, p. 1190.

28. "Helen Gibson Could Run a Railroad Train, She Declares," Home Edition, December 1, 1915, p. 13.

29. *New Orleans Item*, November 21, 1915, n.p.

30. "The Dynamite Train," Moving Picture World, November 13, 1915, p. 1363.

31. "Bruised Quite Often," *Riverside Independent Enterprise*, December 9, 1915, p. 2.

32. "The Tramp Telegrapher," Moving Picture World, November 27, 1915, p. 1715.

33. "Bruised Quite Often," *Riverside Independent Enterprise*, December 9, 1915, p. 2.

34. "Crossed Wires," Moving Picture World, November 27, 1915, p. 1716.

35. "Crossed Wires," *Miami Herald Record*, December 9, 1915, n.p.

36. "Too Much Care Bad," *Frederick Post*, December 13, 1915, n.p.

37. "Refuse Insurance to Kalem's Helen," Moving Picture World, December 25, 1915, p. 2344.

38. "The Wrong Train Order," Moving Picture World, December 25, 1915, p. 2388.

39. "The Wrong Train Order," Moving Picture World, December 4, 1915, p. 1890.

40. "Scene From 'A Boy at the Throttle," *Fort Wayne Journal Gazette*, December 26, 1915, n.p.

41. "A Boy at the Throttle," Moving Picture World, December 11, 1915, p. 2063.

42. *New Orleans Item*, December 26, 1915, n.p.

Chapter Four: The Hazards of Helen January – April 1916
1. "At the Risk of her Life" Moving Picture World, January 1, 1916, p. 2239.

2. "When Seconds Count" Moving Picture World, January 15, 1916, p. 441.

3. "Refuse Insurance to Kalem's Helen," Moving Picture World, December 25, 1915, p. 2344.

4. "The Haunted Station" Moving Picture World, January 15, 1916, p. 470.

5. New Orleans Item, January 18, 1916, n.p.

6. "Open Challenge," Riverside Independent Enterprise, January 19, 1916, p. 2.

7. "Open Track," Moving Picture World, January 22, 1916, p. 657.

8. "One Costly Scene," Riverside Independent Enterprise, January 20, 1916, p. 2.

9. "Daring Death Daily to Give Photoplay Fans a Thrill," Ogden Standard, January 29, 1916, n.p.

10. The Washington Times, February 19, 1916, p. 12.

11. Chicago Day Book, January 27, 1916, n.p.

12. The Tacoma Times, February 11, 1916, p. 5.

13. "Hazards in Two Reels," Moving Picture World, February 5, 1916, p. 763.

14. "Tapped Wires," Moving Picture World, January 22, 1916, p. 657.

15. Saginaw Daily News, February 19, 1916, p. 4.

16. "The Broken Wire," Moving Picture World, February 12, 1916, p. 1006.

17. "This Thrill Laid Actress Up in Bed for 3 Days," New Orleans Item, February 1, 1916, n.p.

18. "The Peril of the Rails," Moving Picture World, February 12, 1916, p. 1007.

19. "The Perilous Swing," Moving Picture World, March 4, 1916, p. 1493.

20. "The Perilous Swing," Moving Picture World, February 26, 1916, p. 1346.

21. "Rope Relayed," Anaconda Standard, March 7, 1916, p. 11.

22. "Railroad Heroine in Danger in Floods in California," February 1916, Helen Gibson Scrapbook, from the Helen Gibson collection, Vancouver, Washington, p. 28.

23. "The Girl Telegrapher's Nerve," Moving Picture World, March 11, 1916, p. 1698.

24. John J. McGowan, McFarland & Co., J.P. McGowan, 2005, p. 73.

25. "A Race for a Life," Moving Picture World, March 11, 1916, p. 2030.

26. "A Race for a Life," Moving Picture World, March 11, 1916, p. 1698.

27. "Helen Receives a Present," Moving Picture World, February 26, 1916, p. 1288.

28. Mike Kornick, Helen Gibson, "In Very Early Days," Films in Review, January 1968, p. 31.

29. "The Girl Who Dared," Moving Picture World, March 25, 1916, p. 2063.

30. "The Girl Who Dared," Moving Picture World, March 11, 1916, p. 1668.

31. "No Headline," March 1916, Helen Gibson Scrapbook, from the Helen Gibson collection, Vancouver, Washington, p. 19.

32. "Movie Gossip," The Day Book, March 13, 1916, p. 20.

33. "Screen Writer Would Have Helen Leap Over Train," March 1916, Helen Gibson Scrapbook, from the Helen Gibson collection, Vancouver, Washington, p. 15.

34. "The Detective's Peril," Moving Picture World, April 8, 1916, p. 284.

35. "The Detective's Peril," Moving Picture World, April 1, 1916, p. 134.

36. New Orleans States, February 27, 1916, n.p.

37. The Washington Times, April 4, 1916, p. 14.

38. "The Colonial," Lexington Herald, April 19, 1916, p. 6.

39. "The Trapping of "Peeler" White," Moving Picture World, April 8, 1916, p. 315.

40. "Kalem Forces Busy," April 1916, Helen Gibson Scrapbook, from the Helen Gibson collection, Vancouver, Washington, p. 12.

41. "The Record Run," Moving Picture World, April 15, 1916, p. 494.

42. "Kalem Forces Busy," April 1916, Helen Gibson Scrapbook, from the Helen Gibson collection, Vancouver, Washington, p. 12.

43. "Camera Smashed in Making New Film Thrill," n.d. Helen Gibson Scrapbook, from the Helen Gibson collection, Vancouver, Washington, p. 11.

44. "Helen Gets Grim Warning," Moving Picture World, March 25, 1916, p. 2035.

45. "Hazards of Helen," Fort Wayne News, April 17, 1916, n.p.

46. "The Race for a Siding," Moving Picture World, April 29, 1816, p. 651.

47. "Hazards of Helen," *Fort Wayne News*, April 24, 1916, n.p.

48. "The Governor's Special," Moving Picture World, May 6, 1916, p. 1020.

49. "Hazards of Helen at the Rex Tomorrow," Ogden Standard, May 20, 1916, p. 14.

50. "The Trail of Danger," Moving Picture World, May 13, 1916, p. 1213.

Chapter Five: The Hazards of Helen   May – August 1916

1. "Agents Pester Helen," *Anaconda Standard*, May 21, 1916, p. 7.

2. "The Human Telegraph," Moving Picture World, May 20, 1916, p. 1355.

3. "The Human Telegraph," Moving Picture World, May 27, 1916, p. 1565.

4. "The Bridge of Danger," Moving Picture World, May 27, 1916, p. 1536.

5. "The Bridge of Danger," Moving Picture World, June 3, 1916, p. 1742.

6. "One Chance in a Hundred," n.d. Helen Gibson Scrapbook, from the Helen Gibson collection, Vancouver, Washington, p. 4.

7. "One Chance in a Hundred," Moving Picture World, June 3, 1916, p. 1712.

8. "One Chance in a Hundred," Moving Picture World, June 10, 1916, p. 1932.

9. "The Capture of Red Stanley," n.d. Helen Gibson Scrapbook, from the Helen Gibson collection, Vancouver, Washington, p. 8.

10. "The Capture of Red Stanley," Moving Picture World, June 10, 1916, p. 1933.

11. *Anaconda Standard*, August 3, 1916, n.p.

12. "The Spiked Switch," Moving Picture World, June 17, 1916, p. 2061.

13. "The Spiked Switch," Moving Picture World, June 24, 1916, p. 2288.

14. "The Treasure Train," Moving Picture World, June 24, 1916, p. 2261.

15. "The Treasure Train," Moving Picture World, July 1, 1916, p. 134.

16. "Aero Flight Latest of Helen's Exploits," n.d. Helen Gibson Scrapbook, from the Helen Gibson collection, Vancouver, Washington, p. 16.

17. "The Mysterious Cipher," Moving Picture World, July 8, 1916, p. 264.

18. "The Mysterious Cipher," Moving Picture World, July 1, 1916, p. 134.

19. "Motion Picture Studio Directory 'Stampede Contest' Arouses Interest in the Industry," n.d. Helen Gibson Scrapbook, from the Helen Gibson collection, Vancouver, Washington, p. 11.

20. "The Engineer's Honor," Moving Picture World, July 8, 1916, p. 264.

21 ."The Engineer's Honor," Moving Picture World, July 22, 1916, p. 681.

22. "Kalem Will Produce Western Subjects," n.d. Helen Gibson Scrapbook, from the Helen Gibson collection, Vancouver, Washington, p. 6.

23. "Notch Number Nine," Moving Picture World, July 22, 1916, p. 654.

24. "Some Great Horsemanship," *Riverside Daily Press*, July 8, 1916, p. 3.

25. "To Save the Road," Moving Picture World, July 29, 1916, p. 832.

26. *New Orleans Item*, July 30, 1916, p. 21.

27. "The Broken Brake," n.d. Helen Gibson Scrapbook, from the Helen Gibson collection Vancouver, Washington, p. 16.

28. "The Broken Brake," Moving Picture World, July 29, 1916, p. 832.

29. "In Death's Pathway," Moving Picture World, August 5, 1916, p. 945.

30. "In Death's Pathway," Moving Picture World, August 5, 1916, p. 988.

31. *New Orleans States*, July 30, 1916, n.p.

32. "Kalem Girls Smash Two Automobiles in a Week," *New Orleans States*, August 13, 1916, n.p.

33. "A Plunge From The Sky," Moving Picture World, August 12, 1916, p. 1103.

34. "A Plunge From The Sky," Moving Picture World, August 12, 1916, p. 1147.

35. "No Headline," n.d. Helen Gibson Scrapbook, from the Helen Gibson collection Vancouver, Washington, p. 14.

36. "A Mystery of the Rails," Moving Picture World, August 12, 1916, p. 1101.

37. "A Mystery of the Rails," Moving Picture World, August 12, 1916, p. 1147.

38. *Daily Register Gazette*, August 18, 1916, p. 5.

39. "Hurled Through The Drawbridge," Moving Picture World, August 26, 1916, p. 1438.

Chapter Six: The Hazards of Helen September – December 1916

1. *The Frederick Post*, September 8, 1916, n.p..

2. "With The Aid of the Wrecker," Moving Picture World, September 2, 1916, p. 1557.

3. "With The Aid of the Wrecker," Moving Picture World, September 9, 1916, p. 1741.

4. "At Danger's Call," Moving Picture World, September 9, 1916, p. 1688.

5. "At Danger's Call," Moving Picture World, September 9, 1916, p. 1741.

6. "The Secret of the Box Car," Moving Picture World, September 2, 1916, p. 1531.

7. "The Secret of the Box Car," Moving Picture World, September 16, 1916, p. 1876.

8. "Ablaze on the Rails," Moving Picture World, September 9, 1916, p. 1686.

9. "Ablaze on the Rails," Moving Picture World, September 16, 1916, p. 1876.

10. "The Hoodoo of Division B," Moving Picture World, September 16, 1916, p. 1821.

11. "The Hoodoo of Division B," Moving Picture World, September 30, 1916, p. 2158.

12. "The Hoodoo of Division B," Moving Picture World, September 16, 1916, p. 1821

13. "Defying Death," Moving Picture World, September 23, 1916, p. 1960.

14. "Defying Death," Moving Picture World, September 30, 1916, p. 2158.

15. "The Death Swing," Moving Picture World, September 30, 1916, p. 2100.

16. "The Death Swing," Moving Picture World, October 14, 1916, p. 290.

17. "Helen Gibson Defending Title," *Trenton Evening Times*, September 24, 1916, n.p.

18. "Helen Winds Again," *Anaconda Standard*, October 22, 1916, n.p.

19. "The Blocked Track," Moving Picture World, October 21, 1916, p. 416.

20. "The Blocked Track," Moving Picture World, October 14, 1916, p. 290.

21. "The Blocked Track," Moving Picture World, October 7, 1916, p. 64.

22. "Film Flashes," *Anaconda Standard*, November 5, 1916, n.p.

23. "To Save the Special," Moving Picture World, October 14, 1916, p. 224.

24. *The Daily Courier*, September 30, 1916, n.p..

25. "Billy Boy Back Again," *Riverside Independent Enterprise*, September 21, 1916, p. 7.

26. "A Daring Chance," Moving Picture World, October 21, 1916, p. 379.

27. "The Lost Messenger," Moving Picture World, October 28, 1916, p. 536.

28. "The Lost Messenger," Moving Picture World, November 4, 1916, p. 747.

29. "The Gate of Death," Moving Picture World, November 11, 1916, p. 843.

30. "The Gate of Death," Moving Picture World, November 25, 1916, p. 1218.

31. "Kalem Still Turning Out 'Helen' Pictures," *Seattle Daily Times*, November 19, 1916, n.p.

32. "The Lone Point Mystery," Moving Picture World, November 25, 1916, p. 1187.

33. "The Lone Point Mystery," Moving Picture World, November 25, 1916, p. 1218.

34. "The Lone Point Mystery," Moving Picture World, November 18, 1916, p. 999.

35. "The Runaway Sleeper," Moving Picture World, December 2, 1916, p. 1348.

36. "The Runaway Sleeper," Moving Picture World, December 9, 1916, p. 1542.

37. "The Forgotten Train Order," Moving Picture World, December 9, 1916, p. 1511.

38. "The Forgotten Train Order," Moving Picture World, December 9, 1916, p. 1543.

39. "The Forgotten Train Order," Moving Picture World, December 9, 1916, p. 1511.

40. "Girl Drives Up Lookout Mountain on High," *Omaha World Herald*, November 26, 1916, p. 39.

41."Los Angeles Woman in Sensational Auto Feat," *San Jose Mercury News*, November 26, 1916, p. 28.

42. "No Headline," November 26, 1916, Helen Gibson Scrapbook, from the Helen Gibson collection, Vancouver, Washington, p. 25.

43. "The Trial Run," Moving Picture World, December 2, 1916, p. 1353.

44. "The Trial Run," Moving Picture World, December 23, 1916, p. 1851.

45. "The Lineman's Peril," Moving Picture World, December 23, 1916, p. 1852.

46. "Photo Caption," December, 1916, Helen Gibson Scrapbook, from the Helen Gibson collection, Vancouver, Washington, p. 2.

47. "The Midnight Express," Moving Picture World," December 23, 1916, p. 1852.

48. "The Vanishing Box Car," Moving Picture World, December 23, 1916, p. 1819.

49. "The Vanishing Box Car," Moving Picture World, December 23, 1916, p. 2003.

50. "The Race With Death," Moving Picture World, December 30, 1916, p. 1977.

51. "The Race With Death," Moving Picture World, December 23, 1916, p. 2003.

Chapter Seven: The Hazards of Helen Series Ends - 1917

1. "No Headline," Fall 1916, Helen Gibson Scrapbook, from the Helen Gibson collection, Vancouver, Washington, p. 20.

2. "Mario DeMarco, Hoot Gibson: The Photostory of "The Dean of Cowboy Stars," DeMarco Publishing, p. 23.

3. "The Mongol Mountain Mystery," Moving Picture World, January 6, 1917, p. 101.

4. "The Mongol Mountain Mystery," Moving Picture World, January 20, 1917, p. 414.

5. "The Firemen's Nemesis," Moving Picture World, January 13, 1917, p. 245.

6. "The Firemen's Nemesis," Moving Picture World, January 27, 1917, p. 581.

7. "The Wrecked Station," Moving Picture World, January 27, 1917, p. 546.

8. "The Wrecked Station," Moving Picture World, January 27, 1917, p. 582.

9. "Kalems for January 15," Moving Picture World, January 20, 1917, p. 359.

10. "The Railroad Claim Intrigue," Moving Picture World, January 27, 1917, p. 546.

11. "The Railroad Claim Intrigue," Moving Picture World, February 3, 1917, p. 738.

12. "Film Folks Paint and Skate at Los Angeles," *Seattle Daily Times*, February 25, 1917, n.p.

13. "No Headline," February 1917, Helen Gibson Scrapbook, from the Helen Gibson collection, Vancouver, Washington, p. 22.

14. "Local Movie Firm May Take Over Southern Studio," *Wilkes-Barre Times*, February 20, 1917, p. 16.

15. "The Death Siding," Moving Picture World, February 3, 1917, p. 706.

16. "The Death Siding," Moving Picture World, February 17, 1917, p. 1074.

17. "The Prima Donna's Special," Moving Picture World, February 17, 1917, p. 1039.

18. "The Prima Donna's Special," Moving Picture World, February 17, 1917, p. 1074.

19. "The Side-Tracked Sleeper," Moving Picture World, February 17, 1917, p. 1212.

20. "Lyceum," *Ogden Standard*, March 10, 1917, p. 8.

21. "The Side-Tracked Sleeper," Moving Picture World, February 17, 1917, p. 1244.

22. "Real Railroaders in Hazards," Moving Picture World, January 27, 1917, p. 555.

23. "Two New Kalems Under Way," Moving Picture World, February 10, 1917, p. 830.

24. "Kalem's New Series Ready March 1," Moving Picture World, February 24, 1917, p. 1216.

25. "New Kalem Studio Near Completion," Moving Picture World, February 24, 1917, p. 1197.

26. "New General Film Subjects," Moving Picture World, March 3, 1917, p. 1377.

Chapter Eight: A New Direction

1. "In the Path of Peril," Moving Picture World, March 10, 1917, p. 1592.

2. "In the Path of Peril," Moving Picture World, March 10, 1917, p. 1660.

3. "The Registered Pouch," Moving Picture World, March 10, 1917, p. 1592.

4. "The Registered Pouch," Moving Picture World, March 24, 1917, p. 1980.

5. "The Borrowed Engine," Moving Picture World, March 24, 1917, p. 1981.

6. "No Headline," Moving Picture World, March 3, 1917, p. 1365.

7. "Kalem Infuses New Blood," Moving Picture World, March 10, 1917, p. 1598.

8. "Burglars Invade Kalem Studio," Moving Picture World, March 24, 1917, p. 1928

9. "The College Boys' Special," Moving Picture World, March 24, 1917, p. 1947.
10. "A Busy Week for Kalem," Moving Picture World, April 7, 1917, p. 118.
11. "The Mystery of the Burning Freight," Moving Picture World, April 14, 1917, p. 319.
12. "Great Railroad Stunts," *Louisiana Times – Picayune*, April 8, 1917, n.p.
13. "The Lone Point Feud," Moving Picture World, April 14, 1917, p. 287.
14. "The Lone Point Feud," Moving Picture World, April 21, 1917, p. 486.
15. "The Railroad Smugglers," Moving Picture World, April 14, 1917, p. 287.
16. "The Railroad Smugglers," Moving Picture World, April 28, 1917, p. 673.
17. "Los Angeles Film Brevities," Moving Picture World, March 31, 1917, p. 2088.
18. "Helen's Motorcycle," *The Logan Republican*, March 27, 1917, p. 8.
19. "The Munitions Plot," Moving Picture World, April 28, 1917, p. 673.
20. "The Detective's Danger," Moving Picture World, May 5, 1917, p. 812.
21. "Writing for Helen," Moving Picture World, May 12, 1917, p. 965.
22. "A Race to the Drawbridge," Moving Picture World, May 19, 1917, p. 1144.
23. "A Race to the Drawbridge," Moving Picture World, May 26, 1917, p. 1333.
24. "The Deserted Engine," Moving Picture World, May 19, 1917, p. 1144.
25. "At The Kalem Studios," Moving Picture World, May 26, 1917, p. 1293.
26. "Helen's Challenge," June 1917, Helen Gibson Scrapbook, from the Helen Gibson collection, Vancouver, Washington, p. 28.

Chapter Nine: Riding With Universal - 1917

1. "Plays and Players," Photoplay, August 1917, p. 109.
2. "Millions in Moving Pictures," *Colorado Gazette Telegram*, March 4, 1917, p. 26.
3. Mike Kornick, Helen Gibson, "In Very Early Days," *Films in Review*, January 1968, p. 31.
4. Frank R. Shattuck, "List of Films, Reels and Views Explained," *Pennsylvania State Board of Censors of Moving Pictures*, 1918, p. 93.
5. *Oregonian*, June 10, 1917, p. 56.
6. *Cleveland Plain Dealer*, June 15, 1917, p. 6.
7. "The Girl That Tames Trains," July 1917, Helen Gibson Scrapbook, from the Helen Gibson collection, Vancouver, Washington, p. 27.
8. "Universal Film Mfg Company," Moving Picture World, July 7, 1917, p. 82.
9. "Universal Bison Western Features," Moving Picture World, August 11, 1917, p. 968.
10. "Lyric Today," *Tulsa World*, September 10, 1917, p. 8.
11. "The Perilous Leap," Moving Picture World, September 15, 1917, p. 1742.
12. Mario DeMarco, Hoot Gibson: The Photostory of "The Dean of Cowboy Stars," DeMarco Publishing, p. 24.
13. "Hoot Would Drive for a General," *Winston-Salem Journal* (NC), November 4, 1917, p. 15.
14. "The Dynamite Special," Moving Picture World, September 29, 1917, p. 2044.
15. "Saving the Fast Mail," Moving Picture World, October 13, 1917, p. 253.
16. "Saving the Fast Mail," Moving Picture World, October 13, 1917, p. 290.
17. "The End of the Run," Moving Picture World, October 27, 1917, p. 576.
18. "Helen Gibson Films - Daughter of Daring," November 1917, Helen Gibson Scrapbook, from the Helen Gibson collection, Vancouver, Washington, p. 17.
19. "Laemmle Explains Policy," Moving Picture World, November 10, 1917, p. 863.
20. "Butterfly Program," Moving Picture World, November 17, 1917, p. 1050.
21. "Fighting Mad," Moving Picture World, December 15, 1917, p. 1642.
22. "No Headline," December 1917, Helen Gibson Scrapbook, from the Helen Gibson collection, Vancouver, Washington, p. 38.
23. "Kalem Suspends Production," *Cleveland Plain Dealer*, December 31, 1917, p. 4.
24. Mario DeMarco, Hoot Gibson: The Photostory of "The Dean of Cowboy Stars," DeMarco Publishing, p. 24.

Chapter Ten: Helen's Ride at Universal Continues - 1918

1. "Screen Gossip," *Oregonian*, January 11, 1916, n.p.
2. "200 Cowpunchers Ready for Rodeo," January 18, 1918, Helen Gibson Scrapbook, from the Helen Gibson collection, Vancouver, Washington, p. 26.
3. "Marines Aid Red Cross Rodeo," *Coconino Sun* (AZ), January 25, 1918, p. 5.
4. "The Strand," *Lima Daily News (OH)*, July 21, 1918, n.p.
5. "Play Straight of Fight," Moving Picture World, June 29, 1918, p. 1892.
6. "Quick Triggers," Moving Picture World, June 29, 1918, p.1919.
7. "Princess Theater," *Aberdeen American* (SD), August 30, 1918, p. 8.
8. "The Midnight Flyer," July, 1918, Helen Gibson Scrapbook, from the Helen Gibson collection, Vancouver, Washington, p. 17.
9. "The Branded Man," July, 1918, Helen Gibson Scrapbook, from the Helen Gibson collection, Vancouver, Washington, p. 6.
10. "A Shooting Party," *Jonesboro Evening Sun*, September 23, 1918, p. 1.
11. "The Payroll Express," Moving Picture World, August 3, 1918, p. 721.
12. "Bawled Out" (Universal), Moving Picture World, August 17, 1918, p. 1002.
13. "Lion Theater," *Muskegon Chronicle*, December 13. 1918, p. 18.
14. "Beating the Limited," Moving Picture World, August 31, 1918, p. 1310.
15. "Danger Ahead," September, 1918, Helen Gibson Scrapbook, from the Helen Gibson collection, Vancouver, Washington, p. 10.
16. "Under False Pretences," September, 1918, Helen Gibson Scrapbook, from the Helen Gibson collection, Vancouver, Washington, p. 10.
17. "Under False Pretences," Moving Picture World, September 28, 1918, p. 1921.
18. "The Fast Mail," October, 1918, Helen Gibson Scrapbook, from the Helen Gibson collection, Vancouver, Washington, p. 9.
19. "The Fast Mail," Moving Picture World, October 5, 1918, p. 122.
20. "Film Shortage is not Critical," *Cleveland Plain Dealer*, October 19, 1918, p. 7.
21. "The Dead Shot," Moving Picture World, October 12, 1918, p. 276.
22. "The Dead Shot," November, 1918, Helen Gibson Scrapbook, from the Helen Gibson collection, Vancouver, Washington, p. 21.
23. "The Silent Sentinel," Moving Picture World, October 19, 1918, p. 447.
24. "The Silent Sentinel," December, 1918, Helen Gibson Scrapbook, from the Helen Gibson collection, Vancouver, Washington, p. 21.
25. "Captured Alive," December, 1918, Helen Gibson Scrapbook, from the Helen Gibson collection, Vancouver, Washington, p. 20.
26. "Mae Murray Hit in St. Regis Film," *Trenton Evening News*, January 9, 1919, p. 7.
27. "Hoot Comes Back," December, 1918, Helen Gibson Scrapbook, from the Helen Gibson collection, Vancouver, Washington, p. 29.
28. Mario DeMarco, Hoot Gibson: The Photostory of "The Dean of Cowboy Stars," DeMarco Publishing, p. 24.
29. "Wolves of the Range," Moving Picture World, December 28, 1918, p. 1556.

Chapter Eleven: Helen Departs Universal at Year's End

1. "Current Film Release Dates," Moving Picture World, January 4, 1919, p. 124.
2. "In Title Role," *Ohio Repository*, January 28, 1919, p. 10.
3. "The Canyon Mystery," Frederick Post (MD), February 12, 1919, n.p.
4. "Second Influenza Wave Hits Coast," Moving Picture World, February 1, 1919, p. 601.
5. "Current Film Release Dates," Moving Picture World, February 22, 1919, p. 1116.
6. "Riding Wild," Moving Picture World, June 7, 1919, p. 1543
7. "Studio Shots," Moving Picture World, March 29, 1919, p. 1794.

8. "The Black Horse Bandit," March, 1919, Helen Gibson Scrapbook, from the Helen Gibson collection, Vancouver, Washington, p. 21.

9. "Gibson in Cast of Fighting Brothers," Moving Picture World, March 22, 1919, p. 1684.

10. "Worked as Extras," July 22, 1953, Helen Gibson Scrapbook, from the Helen Gibson collection, Vancouver, Washington, p. 45.

11. "Mike Kornick, Helen Gibson, "In Very Early Days," Films in Review, January 1968, p. 32.

12. "Universal Call for New Writers," Louisiana Times Picayune, June 8, 1919, n.p.

13. "Two Reel Westerns," June, 1919, Helen Gibson Scrapbook, from the Helen Gibson collection, Vancouver, Washington, p. 21.

14. "For Eddie Polo," Ohio Repository, May 19, 1919, n.p.

15. "No Title," July, 1919, Helen Gibson Scrapbook, from the Helen Gibson collection, Vancouver, Washington, p. 22.

16. "Horseshoe Tires," The Literary Digest, July 12, 1919, p.59.

17. "Horseshoe Tires," The Saturday Evening Post, February 7, 1920, p. 74.

18. "Universal Finishes Loot," Moving Picture World, September 13, 1919, p. 1645.

19. "Loot," Moving Picture World, September 27, 1919, p. 2022.

20. "Ted French," interviewed by Robert S. Birchard, 1971.

21. Mario DeMarco, Hoot Gibson: The Photostory of "The Dean of Cowboy Stars," DeMarco Publishing, p. 24.

Chapter Twelve: Helen Signs with Capital Film Company - 1919

1."Full page ad," September, 1919, Helen Gibson Scrapbook, from the Helen Gibson collection, Vancouver, Washington, p. 23.

2. Mike Kornick, Helen Gibson, "In Very Early Days," Films in Review, January 1968, p. 32.

3. "Capital Film Taking Pains In Presentations of Short Subjects," Moving Picture World, October 4, 1919, p. 87.

4. "Helen Gibson Will Star in Twenty-four Capital Films," Moving Picture World, October 4, 1919, p. 98.

5. "Screen Gossip," The Oregonian, November 25, 1919, n.p.

6. "Capital Film Enlarges Its West Coast Studios," Moving Picture World, December 20, 1919, p. 995.

7. "The Opium Runners," Muskegon Chronicle (IL), November 13, 1919, p. 9.

8. "The Trail of the Rails," Muskegon Chronicle (IL), November 15, 1919, p. 2.

9. "Daring Danger," Muskegon Chronicle (IL), December 12, 1919, p. 8.

10. "At The Grand," Riverside Independent Enterprise (CA), April 3, 1920, p. 6.

11."Flirting with Terror," Muskegon Chronicle (IL), December 24, 1919, p. 11.

12. "The Clutch of the Law," Muskegon Chronicle (IL), January 23, 1920, p. 22.

13. "Capital Film Planning to Increase Production," Moving Picture World, December 27, 1919, p. 1174.

14. "The Broken Trestle," Lexington Herald (KY), February 9, 1920, p.5.

15. "The Golden Star Bandits," Muskegon Chronicle (IL), February 14, 1920, p. 10.

16. "The Border Watch Dogs," State (SC), February 22, 1920, p. 44.

17. "Lion Theater," Muskegon Chronicle (IL), March 20, 1920, p. 4

18. Ghost of the Canyon. DVD. Directed by Robert Myles 1920; The Library of Congress, 2012.

19. "Lyric," Kansas City Star (MO), March 31, 1920, p. 18.

20. "Variety Program," Richmond Times Dispatch (VA), April 30, 1920, p. 10.

21. Mike Kornick, Helen Gibson, "In Very Early Days," Films in Review, January 1968, p. 32.

22. "Capital-Super Short Features," Moving Picture World, February 28, 1920, n.p.

23. "At the Grand," Lexington Herald (KY), May 3, 1920, p. 34.

24. Winning the Franchise. DVD. Directed by Robert Myles 1920; The Library of Congress, 2012.

25. "Bluebird Variety," Richmond Times Dispatch (VA), May 15, 1929, p. 5.

26. "On The Program," Trenton Evening Times (NJ), May 23, 1920, p. 39.

27. "Fame Cuts Knot," June 4, 1920, Helen Gibson Scrapbook, from the Helen Gibson collection, Vancouver, Washington, p. 30.

28. "Bluebird," *Richmond Times Dispatch* (VA), June 12, 1920, p. 7.

29. "The Broken Brake," *Richmond Times Dispatch* (VA), June 26, 1920, p. 6.

30. "Running Wild," *Lexington Herald* (KY), August 8, 1920, p 7.

31. "Boy's Cinema," November 13, 1920, Helen Gibson Scrapbook, from the Helen Gibson collection, Vancouver, Washington, p. 36.

32. "Racine, Belle City of the Lakes, and Racine County, Wisconsin," S. J. Clarke Publisher, 1916, p.1216.

Chapter Thirteen: Hard Times Ahead - 1920

1. Mike Kornick, Helen Gibson, "In Very Early Days," *Films in Review*, January 1968, p. 32.

2. "Helen Gibson Productions Organized," October 1920, Helen Gibson Scrapbook, from the Helen Gibson collection, Vancouver, Washington, p. 33.

3. "Picture Star Heroine Does Real Rescue Act," November 28, 1920, Helen Gibson Scrapbook, from the Helen Gibson collection, Vancouver, Washington, p. 35.

4. Mahar, Karen Ward. "Women Filmmakers in Hollywood," Johns Hopkins University Press, 2006, p. 120.

5. Mike Kornick, Helen Gibson, "In Very Early Days," *Films in Review*, January 1968, p. 32.

6. Acker, Ally. "Reel Women," Continuum Publishing Co., New York. 1991, p. 254.

7. "Helen Gibson Finishing Six-Reel Thriller for Release Thru Associated Photo Plays," December 1920, Helen Gibson Scrapbook, from the Helen Gibson collection, Vancouver, Washington, p. 35.

8. Langman, Larry. "A Guide to Silent Westerns," Greenwood Press. Westport, CT. 1992, p. 303.

9. Mike Kornick, Helen Gibson, "In Very Early Days," *Films in Review*, January 1968, p. 33.

10. "Three Daredevils Seen in Great Outdoor Picture," *Bridgeton Evening News* (NJ), June 25, 1921, p.1.

11. "At The Bijou," *Bridgeton Evening News* (NJ), June 25, 1921, p. 8.

12. Langman, Larry. "A Guide to Silent Westerns," Greenwood Press. Westport, CT. 1992, p. 520.

13. "Best Horses in the Land Seen in Wolverine," *Wyoming Star Tribune*, December 16, 1921, p. 5.

14. "Victor Fischer Leaves for Conference," Moving Picture World, April 23, 1921, p. 865.

15. Mike Kornick, Helen Gibson, "In Very Early Days," *Films in Review*, January 1968, p. 33.

16. Rix Sells Story to Film Producers," *Riverside Independent Enterprise* (CA), March 13, 1921, p. 4.

17. Mike Kornick, Helen Gibson, "In Very Early Days," *Films in Review*, January 1968, p. 33.

18. Shirley Freitas, Helen Holmes Great-Granddaughter, Interviewed by author by telephone. Coeur d'Alene, ID July 25, 2012.

19. "Actress Files $10,000 Action," *San Francisco Examiner* (CA), August 14, 1921, p. 3.

20. "New Movie Outfit Permanently at Topango Beach," August 1922, Helen Gibson Scrapbook, from the Helen Gibson collection, Vancouver, Washington, p. 35.

21. Mike Kornick, Helen Gibson, "In Very Early Days," *Films in Review*, January 1968, p. 33.

22. "Settle Two Suits Against Film Co," March 15, 1922, Helen Gibson Scrapbook, from the Helen Gibson collection, Vancouver, Washington, p. 34.

23. "Hoot Gibson Marries," *Oregonian* (OR), April 1, 1922, p. 1.

24. Acker, Ally. "Reel Women," Continuum Publishing Co., New York. 1991, p. 254.

25. Mike Kornick, Helen Gibson, "In Very Early Days," *Films in Review*, January 1968, p. 33.

26. "Western Film Actress Tells of Thrillers," *Duluth News-Tribune* (MN), April 29, 1922, p. 10.

27. "From the Studios," *Kansas City Star*, May 7, 1922, .np.

28. "Asks Justice to Hollywood," *Eau Claire Leader* (WS), May 7, 1922, n.p.

29. "City Briefs," Grand Forks Herald, May 30, 1922, p. 2.

30. "Roping Title and Big Stake Round-up Prize," *Tulsa World*, August 22, 1922, p. 4.

31. "Helen Gibson, Movie Star, to be in Rodeo," *San Antonio Evening News*, September 2, 1922, n.p.

32. "New Movie Outfit Permanently at Topango Beach," August 1922, Helen Gibson Scrapbook, from the Helen Gibson collection, Vancouver, Washington, p. 35.

33. "The Thoroughbred," Moving Picture World, November 4, 1922, p. 82.

34. "Helen Gibson," 1923, Helen Gibson Scrapbook, from the Helen Gibson collection, Vancouver, Washington, p. 39.

Chapter Fourteen: Lure of the Circus Then Vaudeville - 1924

1. Mike Kornick, Helen Gibson, "In Very Early Days," *Films in Review*, January 1968, p. 33.
2. Fred Dahlinger Jr., Curator of Circus History, John and Mable Ringling Museum of Art, Sarasota, FL., October 10, 2011.
3. "Still Wearing 'Em in 2-Gallon Sizes," *San Diego Evening News*, May 1, 1924, p.28.
4. "Motion Picture Actress, Here," *Evening World Herald* (NE), November 28, 1924, p.28.
5. "John Polacek," Ringling Bros. and Barnum & Bailey Circus, 1954 Route Book.
6. ."The Billboard," May 3, 1926, Helen Gibson Scrapbook, from the Helen Gibson collection, Vancouver, Washington, p. 40.
7. "Family Re-United at Circus," August, 1926, Helen Gibson Scrapbook, from the Helen Gibson collection, Vancouver, Washington, p. 40.
8. Mike Kornick, Helen Gibson, "In Very Early Days," *Films in Review*, January 1968, p. 33.
9. "Pleasant Novelty by Indians in Cohen's," *Newburgh News* (PA), October 11, 1926, p. 10.
10. "Hopi Indians on Bill at Broadway Next Week," *Springfield Daily Republican* (IL), November 19, 1926 , p. 9.
11. "Hopis to Appear at Keith's St. James," *Boston Herald* (MA), November 25, 1926, p. 24.
12. "Helen Gibson – No. 1," August, 1926, Helen Gibson Scrapbook, from the Helen Gibson collection, Vancouver, Washington, p. 34.

Chapter Fifteen: Hollywood, Serials, Stunt Work, and Romance -1927

1. "Seattle Stampede," *Seattle Daily Times*, July 3, 1927, p. 4.
2. "Thousands Have Seen the Seattle Stampede," *Seattle Daily Times*, July 9, 1927, p. 2.
3. Mike Kornick, Helen Gibson, "In Very Early Days," *Films in Review*, January 1968, p. 34.
4. "Free Victory Carnival," *San Diego Evening Tribune*, September 23, 1927, p. 17.
5. Jon Tuska. "The Vanishing Legion," McFarland Publishing Co., Jefferson, NC. 1982, p. 16.
6. Kalton Lahue. *Bound and Gagged: The Story of the Silent Serial*. A.S. Barnes and Company, 1968. p. 257.
7. Jon Tuska. "The Vanishing Legion," McFarland Publishing Co., Jefferson, NC. 1982, p. 18.
8. Kalton Lahue. *Bound and Gagged: The Story of the Silent Serial*. A.S. Barnes and Company, 1968. p. 94.
9. "Divorce is Sought from Hoot Gibson," *Trenton Evening Times* (NJ), January 15, 1929, p. 3.
10. "Noted Woman Rider is Dead," *Ogden Standard Examiner* (UT), October 1, 1929, n.p.
11. Mary Lou LeCompte, "Cowgirls of the Rodeo," University of Illinois, Chicago, 1993, p. 95.
12. "Hoot, Sally Ride Out on Life as One," *Seattle Daily Times*, June 28, 1930, p. 1.
13. "Art Acord, Cowboy Actor, Ends Life," *Canton Repository* (OH), January 5, 1931, p. 6.
14. Kalton Lahue *Continued Next Week*. University of Oklahoma, Norman, 1964. p. 86
15. Mario DeMarco, Hoot Gibson: The Photostory of "The Dean of Cowboy Stars," DeMarco Publishing, p. 33.
16. Internet Movie Data Base "The Lightning Warrior," July 31, 2012, http://www.imdb.com/title/tt0022078/
17. *Jon Tuska. "The Vanishing Legion," McFarland Publishing Co., Jefferson, NC. 1982, p. 50.*
18. ***"Many Film Stars of Yesterday Glad for Occasional Small Roles," Boston Herald (MA)***, December 26, 1931, p. 4.
19. *Internet Movie Data Base. The Cheyenne Cyclone, http://www.imdb.com/name/nm0189076/bio*
20. Internet Movie Data Base "Human Targets," July 31, 2012, http://www.imdb.com/title/tt0023035/
21. "One of 600 Extra's," April, 1932, Helen Gibson Scrapbook, from the Helen Gibson collection, Vancouver, Washington, p. 43.
22. "600 Extras Used by Producers in Silver Lining," *Seattle Daily Times*, June 16, 1932, p. 10.
23. Jack Backstreet. "Alan Crosland," http://www.imdb.com/name/nm0189076/bio

24. "Ellers-Gibson Split Blamed on Success," *Canton Repository* (OH), May 9, 1932, p. 11.

25. "Rodeo Winners to be Decided," *San Diego Union*, July 31, 1932, p. 5.

26. "Big Horse Show," *Riverside Daily Press*, November 18, 1932, p. 13.

27. "In Benefit Show," November 10, 1932, Helen Gibson Scrapbook, from the Helen Gibson collection, Vancouver, Washington, p. 39.

28. "Glorilla Ship," *Augusta Chronicle*, January 8, 1933, p. 16.

29. "Helen Gibson," December 8, 1932, Helen Gibson Scrapbook, from the Helen Gibson collection, Vancouver, Washington, p. 39.

30. "People and Events," *Riverside Daily Press*, May 10, 1933, p. 10.

31. Internet Movie Data Base "King of the Arena," July 31, 2012, http://www.imdb.com/title/tt0024218/

32. "Does Fine Bit," June 1933, Helen Gibson Scrapbook, from the Helen Gibson collection, Vancouver, Washington, p. 37.

33. "Hoot Gibson Hurt in Air Race Crash," *Cleveland Plain Dealer*, July 4, 1933, p. 12.

34. "Hoot Gibson, Crash Victim, Out of Danger," *Times Picayune* (LA), July 5, 1933, p. 16.

35. Divorce of Hoot Gibson and Sally Ellers Near," *Springfield Republican* (MA), July 10, 1933, p. 4.

36. Internet Movie Data Base "Wheels of Destiny," August 5, 2012, http://www.imdb.com/title/tt0025978/

37. Internet Movie Data Base "Mini Biography," August 5, 2012, http://www.imdb.com/name/nm0562770/bio

38. Internet Movie Data Base "Rocky Rhodes," July 31, 2012, http://www.imdb.com/title/tt0025729/

39. "Helen Gibson's Mother Dead," September 1934, Helen Gibson Scrapbook, from the Helen Gibson collection, Vancouver, Washington, p. 37.

40. Internet Movie Data Base "The Way of the West," August 5, 2012, http://www.imdb.com/title/tt0025962/

41. Internet Movie Data Base "365 Nights in Hollywood," August 5, 2012, http://www.imdb.com/title/tt0024808/

42. "Former Stars are Flocking into the Ranks of Extras," *San Antonio Express*, March 3, 1935, n.p.

43. Internet Movie Data Base "Cyclone of the Saddle," August 5, 2012, http://www.imdb.com/title/tt0026254/

44. Internet Movie Data Base "Fighting Caballero," August 5, 2012, http://www.imdb.com/title/tt0026349/

45. "Former Western Star," *Hollywood Filmography*, July 20, 1935, n.p.

46. Michael R. Pitts. "Poverty Row Studios, 1929-1940," McFarland Publishing Co., Jefferson, NC. 1997, p. 371.

Chapter Sixteen: A Bride, Stunt Work, And More Bit Parts - 1935

1. "Actress in Western Films Married in Home Ceremony," August 21, 1935, Helen Gibson Scrapbook, from the Helen Gibson collection, Vancouver, Washington, p. 37.

2. "Some Belated Details," August 1935, Helen Gibson Scrapbook, from the Helen Gibson collection, Vancouver, Washington, p. 37.

3. "No Headline," October 25, 1935, Helen Gibson Scrapbook, from the Helen Gibson collection, Vancouver, Washington, p. 37.

4. "Out of the Shadows," November 5, 1957, Helen Gibson Scrapbook, from the Helen Gibson collection, Vancouver, Washington, p. 37.

5. Internet Movie Data Base "Custer's Last Stand," August 8, 2012, http://www.imdb.com/title/tt0027488/

6. Internet Movie Data Base "The Lawless Nineties," August 8, 2012, http://www.imdb.com/title/tt0027876/

7. Internet Movie Data Base "Lady of Secrets," August 8, 2012, http://www.imdb.com/title/tt0027865/

8. "Pioneer Stars Accorded Tribute," May 28, 1936, Helen Gibson Scrapbook, from the Helen Gibson collection, Vancouver, Washington, p. 37.

9. Michael R. Pitts. "Poverty Row Studios, 1929-1940," McFarland Publishing Co., Jefferson, NC. 1997, p. 385.

10. Internet Movie Data Base "Last of the Warrens," August 8, 2012, http://www.imdb.com/title/tt0027870/

11. Michael R. Pitts. "Poverty Row Studios, 1929-1940," McFarland Publishing Co., Jefferson, NC. 1997, p. 336.

12. Internet Movie Data Base "Winds of the Wasteland," August 8, 2012, http://www.imdb.com/title/tt0028510/

13. Internet Movie Data Base "Jungle Jim," August 8, 2012, http://www.imdb.com/title/tt0027829/

14. "Hollywood," *Frederick Post* (MD), October 11, 1937, n.p.

15. Internet Movie Data Base "High, Wide, and Handsome," August 8, 2012, http://www.imdb.com/title/tt0029000/

16. Internet Movie Data Base "Danger Valley," August 8, 2012, http://www.imdb.com/title/tt0028760/

16. "Screen Thriller Star Finishes New Picture," January 31, 1938, Helen Gibson Scrapbook, from the Helen Gibson collection, Vancouver, Washington, p. 37.

17. Internet Movie Data Base "The Old Barn Dance," August 11, 2012, http://www.imdb.com/title/tt0029337/

18. "Condemned Women," January 1938, Helen Gibson Scrapbook, from the Helen Gibson collection, Vancouver, Washington, p. 37.

19. Internet Movie Data Base "Condemned Women," August 11, 2012, http://www.imdb.com/title/tt0030010/

20. "Serial Queen of Silent Era in Prison Film," *Syracuse Herald* (NY), March 21, 1938, n.p.

21. "Helen Gibson," *Indiana Evening Gazette* (PA), March 24, 1938, n.p.

22. "Former Star of Westerns Likes to 'Play' at Murder," The Cleveland News (OH), May 17, 1938, n.p.

23. Internet Movie Data Base "Flaming Frontiers," August 8, 2012, http://www.imdb.com/title/tt0030137/

24. "Star of 'Silents' Gets Unexpected Anniversary Present," August 8, 1938, Helen Gibson Scrapbook, from the Helen Gibson collection, Vancouver, Washington, p. 46.

25. "Silent Day Star Heads Riding and Stunt Girls," August 18, 1938, Helen Gibson Scrapbook, from the Helen Gibson collection, Vancouver, Washington, p. 46.

26. "Film Stunt Girls Accomplish Aims, Disband," August 19, 1938, Helen Gibson Scrapbook, from the Helen Gibson collection, Vancouver, Washington, p. 46.

27. Internet Movie Data Base "Stagecoach," August 8, 2012, http://www.imdb.com/title/tt0031971/

28. J. McGowan. "J.P. McGowan," McFarland Publishing Co., Jefferson, NC. 2005, p. 111.

29. Internet Movie Data Base "Southward Ho," August 11, 2012, http://www.imdb.com/title/tt0031958/

30. Internet Movie Data Base "The Oregon Trail," August 8, 2012, http://www.imdb.com/title/tt0031764/

31. Internet Movie Data Base "New Frontier," August 11, 2012, http://www.imdb.com/title/tt0031718/

32. Internet Movie Data Base "The Marshall of Mesa City," August 11, 2012, http://www.imdb.com/title/tt0031630/

33. Internet Movie Data Base "Saga of Death Valley," August 10, 2012, http://www.imdb.com/title/tt0031889/

34. Internet Movie Data Base "Cowboys From Texas," August 8, 2012, http://www.imdb.com/title/tt0031189/

35. Internet Movie Data Base "Covered Wagon Trails," August 8, 2012, http://www.imdb.com/title/tt0032363/

36. Internet Movie Data Base "Deadwood Dick," August 8, 2012. http://www.imdb.com/title/tt0032386/

37. Internet Movie Data Base "Young Bill Hickok," August 15, 2012, http://www.imdb.com/title/tt0033286/

38. Internet Movie Data Base "The Trail Blazers," August 15, 2012, http://www.imdb.com/title/tt0033179/

Chapter Seventeen: World War II, Stunt Doubling and More Bit Parts - 1941

1. Internet Movie Data Base "The Singing Hill," August 8, 2012, http://www.imdb.com/title/tt0034192/

2. Internet Movie Data Base "Sheriff of Tombstone," August 8, 2012, http://www.imdb.com/title/tt0034183/

3. Mike Kornick, Helen Gibson, "In Very Early Days," *Films in Review*, January 1968, p. 34.

4. Internet Movie Data Base "The Sombrero Kid," August 8, 2012, http://www.imdb.com/title/tt0035355/

5. Internet Movie Data Base "The Valley of Vanishing Men," August 18, 2012, http://www.imdb.com/title/tt0035501/

6. Internet Movie Data Base "The Blocked Trail," August 18, 2012, http://www.imdb.com/title/tt0035683/

7. Internet Movie Data Base "The Climax," August 18, 2012, http://www.imdb.com/title/tt0036715/

8. Johnson, Gayla. Interviewed by author. Digital recording. Vancouver, WA August 29, 2009.

9. Internet Movie Data Base "The Scarlet Horseman," August 25, 2012, http://www.imdb.com/title/tt0038909/fullcredits#cast

10. Internet Movie Data Base "The Scarlet Horseman," August 25, 2012, http://www.imdb.com/title/tt0038909/

11. Internet Movie Data Base "The Scarlet Horseman," August 25, 2012, http://www.imdb.com/title/tt0038909/trivia

12. Internet Movie Data Base "Cheyenne Cowboy," August 26, 2012, http://www.imdb.com/title/tt0228129/

13. "Ex-Star Gallops Again," *Cleveland Plains Dealer* (OH), October 31, 1948, p. 99.

14. Internet Movie Data Base "Outcasts of the Trail," August 18, 2012, http://www.imdb.com/title/tt0041722/

Chapter Eighteen: Helen in the 1950s – A Decade of Change

1. Internet Movie Data Base "Caged," August 28, 2012, http://www.imdb.com/title/tt0042296/

2. "Prison Drama," *Dallas Morning News* (TX), July 18, 1950, p. 7.

3. Internet Movie Data Base "Crocked River," August 26, 2012, http://www.imdb.com/title/tt0042356/

4. Internet Movie Data Base "Fast on the Draw," August 26, 2012, http://www.imdb.com/title/tt0042448/

5. "Helen Holmes Dies at 58," July 10, 1950, Helen Gibson Scrapbook, from the Helen Gibson collection, Vancouver, Washington, p. 1.

6. "This Pair Long in Movies," *Portland Press Herald* (ME), July 9, 1950, n.p.

7. Internet Movie Data Base "Kansas Raiders," August 26, 2012, http://www.imdb.com/title/tt0042629/

8. "Helen Gibson," *Dixon Evening Telegraph* (IL), February 1, 1951, n.p.

9. "Silent Day Film Folk Paid Honor," May 9, 1951, Helen Gibson Scrapbook, from the Helen Gibson collection, Vancouver, Washington, p. 40.

10. Mike Kornick, Helen Gibson, "In Very Early Days," *Films in Review*, January 1968, p. 34.

11. Internet Movie Data Base "The Hollywood Story," August 26, 2012, http://www.imdb.com/title/tt0043646/

12. Internet Movie Data Base "The Dakota Kid," August 26, 2012, http://www.imdb.com/title/tt0043445/

13. "Hollywood," *Yuma Daily Sun* (AZ), July 14, 1951, n.p.

14. Internet Movie Data Base "The Treasure of Lost Canyon," August 26, 2012, http://www.imdb.com/title/tt0044144/

15. Internet Movie Data Base "Ma and Pa Kettle at the Fair," August 26, 2012, http://www.imdb.com/title/tt0044862/

16. Internet Movie Data Base "Horizons West," August 26, 2012, http://www.imdb.com/title/tt0044722/

17. "Silent Star," *State Times Advocate* (LA), March 2, 1953, p. 36.

18. Internet Movie Data Base "City That Never Sleeps," August 26, 2012, http://www.imdb.com/title/tt0045631/

19. Internet Movie Data Base "The Man from the Alamo," August 26, 2012, http://www.imdb.com/title/tt0046035/

20. "A Double Milestone," *State Times Advocate* (LA), May 7, 1953, p. 41.

21. "Life Story," *Walla Walla Union Bulletin* (WA), September 23, 1953, n.p.

22. Internet Movie Data Base "Ma and Pa Kettle at Home," August 26, 2012, http://www.imdb.com/title/tt0047197/

23. Mike Kornick, Helen Gibson, "In Very Early Days," *Films in Review*, January 1968, p. 34.

24. "Actress Makes Home in Diamond Springs," August 23, 1956, Helen Gibson Scrapbook, from the Helen Gibson collection, Vancouver, Washington, p. 43

25. "A Twenty-First Anniversary," August 1956, Helen Gibson Scrapbook, from the Helen Gibson collection, Vancouver, Washington, p. 43.

26. "Former Diamond Springs Resident Returns to Career of Movie Life," October 1957, Helen Gibson Scrapbook, from the Helen Gibson collection, Vancouver, Washington, p. 41

27. "Out of the Shadows," November 5, 1957, Helen Gibson Scrapbook, from the Helen Gibson collection, Vancouver, Washington, p. 37.

28. "El Dorado Woman Recalls days When Villains of Movies Pursued Her," August 14, 1957, Helen Gibson Scrapbook, from the Helen Gibson collection, Vancouver, Washington, p. 43.

29. Internet Movie Data Base "The Last Town Car," August 25, 2012, http://www.imdb.com/title/tt0821393/

30. "Former Diamond Springs Resident Returns to Career of Movie Life," October 1957, Helen Gibson Scrapbook, from the Helen Gibson collection, Vancouver, Washington, p. 41.

31. "Former Residents Inspect Property near Diamond Springs," July 1959, Helen Gibson Scrapbook, from the Helen Gibson collection, Vancouver, Washington, p. 46

Chapter Nineteen: Helen's Second Retirement Begins - 1962

1. "Helen Gibson's 50th," February 17, 1961, Helen Gibson Scrapbook, from the Helen Gibson collection, Vancouver, Washington, p. 43.
2. Internet Movie Data Base "The Man Who Shot Liberty Valance," August 26, 2012, http://www.imdb.com/title/t0056217/
3. "Silent Film 'Stock Troupe' Plays in John Ford Movie," *Omaha World Herald* (NE), December 22, 1961, p.26.
4. Internet Movie Data Base "The Man Who Shot Liberty Valance," August 26, 2012, http://www.imdb.com/title/t0056217/
5. "Cowboy Actor Hoot Gibson Succumbs to Cancer at 70," *Augusta Chronicle* (GA), August 24, 1962, p. 6a.
6. "Hoot Gibson Rites Held," *Baton Rogue Advocate* (LA), August 28, 1962, p. 6.
7. "Hazards of Helen Those Were Days!," September 9, 1962, Helen Gibson Scrapbook, from the Helen Gibson collection, Vancouver, Washington, p. 41.
8. Johnson, Gayla. Interviewed by author. Digital recording. Vancouver, WA August 29, 2009.
9. "Star of Silent Screen Now Living in Roseburg," July 1963, Helen Gibson Scrapbook, from the Helen Gibson collection, Vancouver, Washington, p. 45.
10. Kalton Lahue *Continued Next Week*. University of Oklahoma, Norman, 1964. p. 25
11. Mike Kornick, Helen Gibson, "In Very Early Days," *Films in Review*, January 1968, p. 34.
12. Arthur Wise, Derek Ware. "Stunting in the Cinema," St. Martins Press, New York 1973, p. 81.

Chapter Twenty: Life Far From the Silver Screen

1. Johnson, Gayla. Interviewed by author. Digital recording. Vancouver, WA August 29, 2009.
2. Peterson, Robert. Interviewed by author. Digital recording. Post Falls, ID June 9, 2012.
3. "From Hollywood to Roseburg – A Long Journey," *The News Review* (OR), May 15, 1975, p.7-8.
4. Johnson, Gayla. Interviewed by author. Digital recording. Vancouver, WA August 29, 2009.

Bibliography

Acker, Ally (1991). *Reel Women: Pioneers of the Cinema 1896 to the Present*. London: Batsford. ISBN 0-7134-6960-9.

Baxter, John O. (1974). *Stunt: The Story of the Great Movie Stunt Men*. Garden City, N.Y: Doubleday. ISBN 0-385-06520-5.

Balio, Tino. (1985). The American Film Industry. Madison, Wisconsin: University of Wisconsin Press. ISBN 0-299-09870-2.

Cline, William C. (1984) *In the Nick of Time*. Jefferson, North Carolina. McFarland. ISBN 0-89950-101-X

Cline, William C. (1994) *Serials-ly Speaking: Essays on Cliffhangers*. Jefferson, North Carolina. McFarland. ISBN 0-89950-909-6

Compiled (1933) *The Picturegoer's Who's Who and Encyclopedia of the Screen Today*, Long Acre, London: Greycaine Book Manufacturing Company.

DeMarco, Mario. (2010). *Hoot Gibson: The Photostory of the Dean of Cowboy Stars*. DeMarco Publishing.

Flood, Elizabeth Claire. (2000) *Cowgirls: Women of the West*. Santa Fe, New Mexico: Zon International Publishing. ISBN:0-939549-18-2.

Foster, Charles. (2000) *Stardust and Shadows*. Toronto, Ontario, Canada, Dundurn Press. ISBN 1-55002-348-9.

Gibson, Helen; Mike Kornick (1968-01). "In Very Early Days, Screen Acting Was Often a Matter of Guts". *Films in Review - January 1968*.

"Horse Show Promising". *L.A.Times*. July 22, 1931.

"In Very Early Days" *Films in Review*. January, 1968

Langman, Larry. (1992) *A Guide to Silent Westerns*. Westport, Connecticut. Greenwood Press. ISBN 0-313-27858-X

Lahue, Kalton C. (1968*). Bound and Gagged: The Story of the Silent Serial*. A.S. Barnes and Company.

Lahue, Kalton C. (1964). *Continued Next Week : A History of the Moving Picture Serial*. Norman: University of Oklahoma Press.

Lowe, Denise (2005). *An Encyclopedic Dictionary of Women in Early American Films, 1895-1930*. New York: Haworth Press. ISBN 0-7890-1843-8.

Mahar, Karen Ward (2006) *Women Filmmakers in Hollywood*. Baltimore, MD. The Johns Hopkins University Press. ISBN 978-0-8018-9084-0.

Maturi Richard J and Mary Buckingham Maturi. (1998). *Francis X. Bushman: A Biography and Filmography*. Jefferson, North Carolina. McFarland. 0-7864-0485-X

McKinney, Grange B. (2000) *Art Acord and the Movies*. Raleigh, North Carolina. Wyatt Classics, Inc.

Miller, Lee O. (1979) *The Great Cowboy Stars of Movies & Television*. New Rochelle, New York. Arlington House. ISBN 0-87000-429-8

Pitts, Michael R. (1997). *Poverty Row Studios, 1929-1940*. Jefferson, North Carolina. McFarland & Company, Inc. ISBN 0-7864-0168-0

Roach, Joyce Gibson (1990). *The Cowgirls*. Denton, Tex: University of North Texas Press. ISBN 0-929398-15-7.

Singer, Ben (2001). *Melodrama and Modernity: Early Sensational Cinema and its Contexts*. New York: Columbia University Press. ISBN 0-231-11329-3.

Slide, Anthony (1994) *Early American Cinema*. Metuchen, N.J. The Scarecrow Press. ISBN 0-8108-2722-0.

Slide, Anthony (1987) *The Big V: History of the Vitagraph Company*. Metuchen, N.J. The Scarecrow Press. ISBN 0-8108-2030-7.

Terry, Cleo Tom, Osie Wilson (1957*) The Rawhide Tree: The Story of Florence Reynolds in Rodeo*. Clarendon, Texas: Clarendon Press

Truitt, Evelyn Mack (1984). *Who Was Who on Screen*. New York: Bowker. ISBN 0-8352-1906-2.

Tuska, Jon. (1982). *The Vanishing Legion: A History of Mascot Pictures 1927-1935*. Jefferson, North Carolina. McFarland. ISBN 0-89950-030-7

Vardac, A. Nicholas (1949). *Stage to Screen - Theatrical Origins of Early Film: David Garrick to D.W. Griffith*. Cambridge, Massachusetts: Da Capo Press, Inc. ISBN 0-306-80308-9

Vazzana, Eugine Michael.(1995) *Silent Film Necrology*. Jefferson, North Carolina. McFarland. ISBN 0-7864-132-X

Wallis, Michael. (1999) *The Real Wild West: The 101 Ranch and the Creation of the American West*. New York: St. Martin's Griffin. ISBN 0-312-26381-3

Ware, Derek; Wise, Arthur (1973). *Stunting in the Cinema*. London: Constable. ISBN 0-09-459090-7.

Wyatt. Edgar M. (1992). *The Hoxie Boys: The Lives and Films of Jack and Al Hoxie*. Raleigh, North Carolina. Wyatt Classics, Inc.

INDEX

ABOUT THE AUTHOR

Photo by John Hollar Jr.

LARRY TELLES became interested in silent films at age fifteen in 1952. Television in those early day used silent films to fill part of the evening hours before leaving the air at 9 p.m. His grandmother saw his interest in silent movies, and gave him Blum's book, *A Pictorial History of the Silent Screen*. Larry was hooked from that day on. Since those many years ago he has branched out by collecting all types of memorabilia from cliffhanger serial to "B" Westerns.

Larry is one of the founding members of the Niles Essanay Silent Film Museum in Niles, California. His position on the board is webmaster and film historian. He participates in the museum's Broncho Billy Silent Film Festival every June. This is one of the many film festival's across the U.S. that continues to bring attention to the silent film era for those who are not aware of its existence.

Larry's first book, *A Brief History of the Silent Screen and the World at that Time*, is built around the film world. How did silent film affect the film world and how did the world affect silent film. Larry has also produced a Helen Gibson companion DVD for this book. The DVD contains six of Helen Gibson's surviving silent films. It is a look into the role that one woman played in the history of film.

www.hazards-of-helen.com
www.essanayfilmmfgco.com
www.BitterrootMountainLLC.com